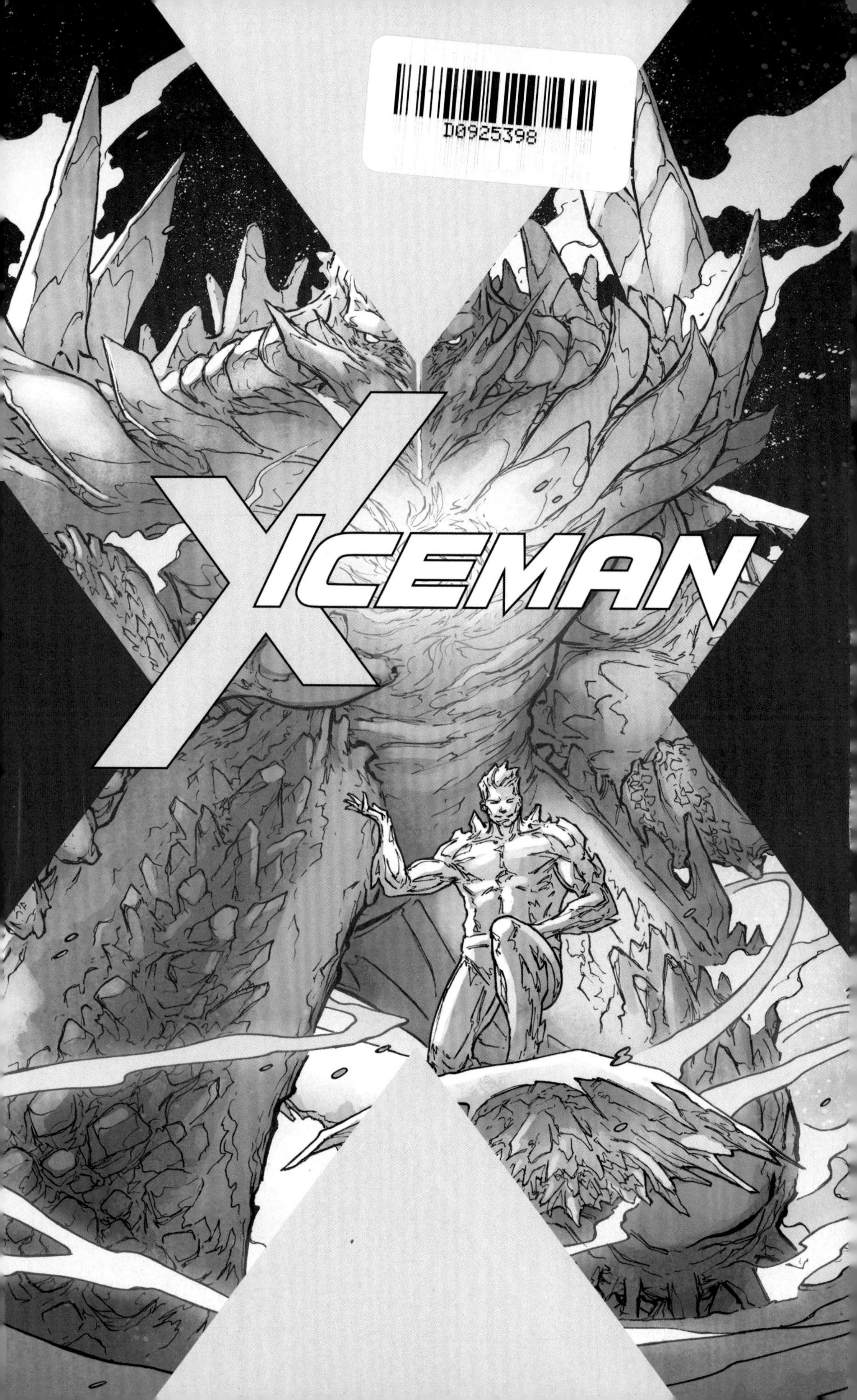
X ICEMAN

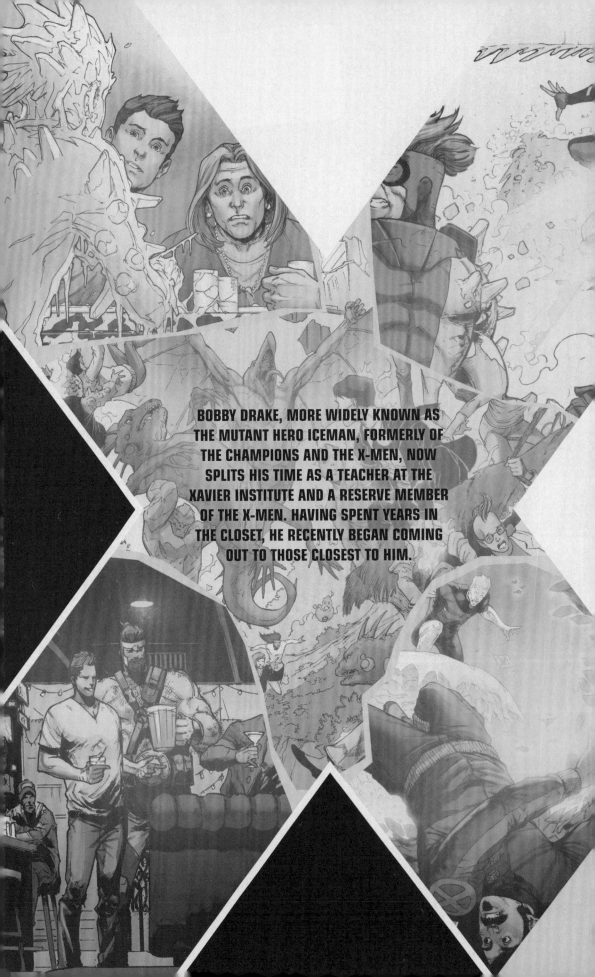

BOBBY DRAKE, MORE WIDELY KNOWN AS THE MUTANT HERO ICEMAN, FORMERLY OF THE CHAMPIONS AND THE X-MEN, NOW SPLITS HIS TIME AS A TEACHER AT THE XAVIER INSTITUTE AND A RESERVE MEMBER OF THE X-MEN. HAVING SPENT YEARS IN THE CLOSET, HE RECENTLY BEGAN COMING OUT TO THOSE CLOSEST TO HIM.

ICEMAN

ABSOLUTE ZERO

Writer/**SINA GRACE**

Pencilers/**ROBERT GILL** with **SINA GRACE** (#11)

Inkers/**ROBERT GILL** with **ED TADEO** (#9-10)

Color Artist/**RACHELLE ROSENBERG**

Letterer/**VC's JOE SABINO**

Cover Art/**KEVIN WADA**

Editors/**DARREN SHAN** & **CHRIS ROBINSON**
X-Men Group Editor/**MARK PANICCIA**

ICEMAN CREATED BY **STAN LEE** & **JACK KIRBY**

Collection Editor/**JENNIFER GRÜNWALD** • Assistant Editor/**CAITLIN O'CONNELL**
Associate Managing Editor/**KATERI WOODY** • Editor, Special Projects/**MARK D. BEAZLEY**
VP Production & Special Projects/**JEFF YOUNGQUIST** • SVP Print, Sales & Marketing/**DAVID GABRIEL**
Book Designer/**JAY BOWEN**

Editor in Chief/**C.B. CEBULSKI** • Chief Creative Officer/**JOE QUESADA**
President/**DAN BUCKLEY** • Executive Producer/**ALAN FINE**

ICEMAN VOL. 2: ABSOLUTE ZERO. Contains material originally published in magazine form as ICEMAN #6-11. First printing 2018. ISBN 978-1-302-90880-5. Published by MARVEL WORLDWIDE, INC., a subsidiary of MARVEL ENTERTAINMENT, LLC. OFFICE OF PUBLICATION: 135 West 50th Street, New York, NY 10020. **Printed in Canada.** DAN BUCKLEY, President, Marvel Entertainment; JOHN NEE, Publisher; JOE QUESADA, Chief Creative Officer; TOM BREVOORT, SVP of Publishing; DAVID BOGART, SVP of Business Affairs & Operations, Publishing & Partnership; DAVID GABRIEL, SVP of Sales & Marketing, Publishing; JEFF YOUNGQUIST, VP of Production & Special Projects; DAN CARR, Executive Director of Publishing Technology; ALEX MORALES, Director of Publishing Operations; SUSAN CRESPI, Production Manager; STAN LEE, Chairman Emeritus. For information regarding advertising in Marvel Comics or on Marvel.com, please contact Vit DeBellis, Custom Solutions & Integrated Advertising Manager, at vdebellis@marvel.com. For Marvel subscription inquiries, please call 888-511-5480. **Manufactured between 3/2/2018 and 4/3/2018 by SOLISCO PRINTERS, SCOTT, QC, CANADA.**

10 9 8 7 6 5 4 3 2 1

6

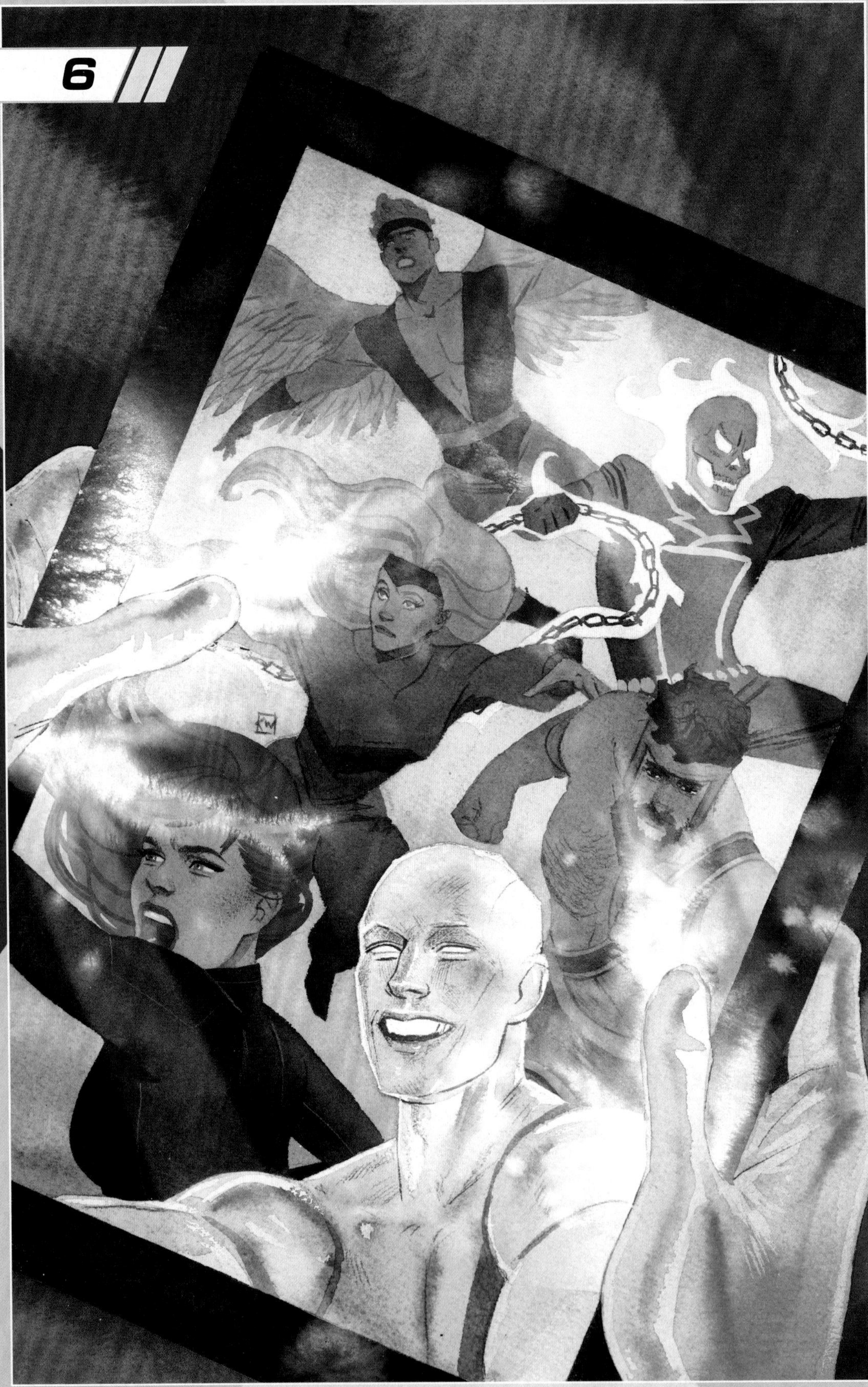

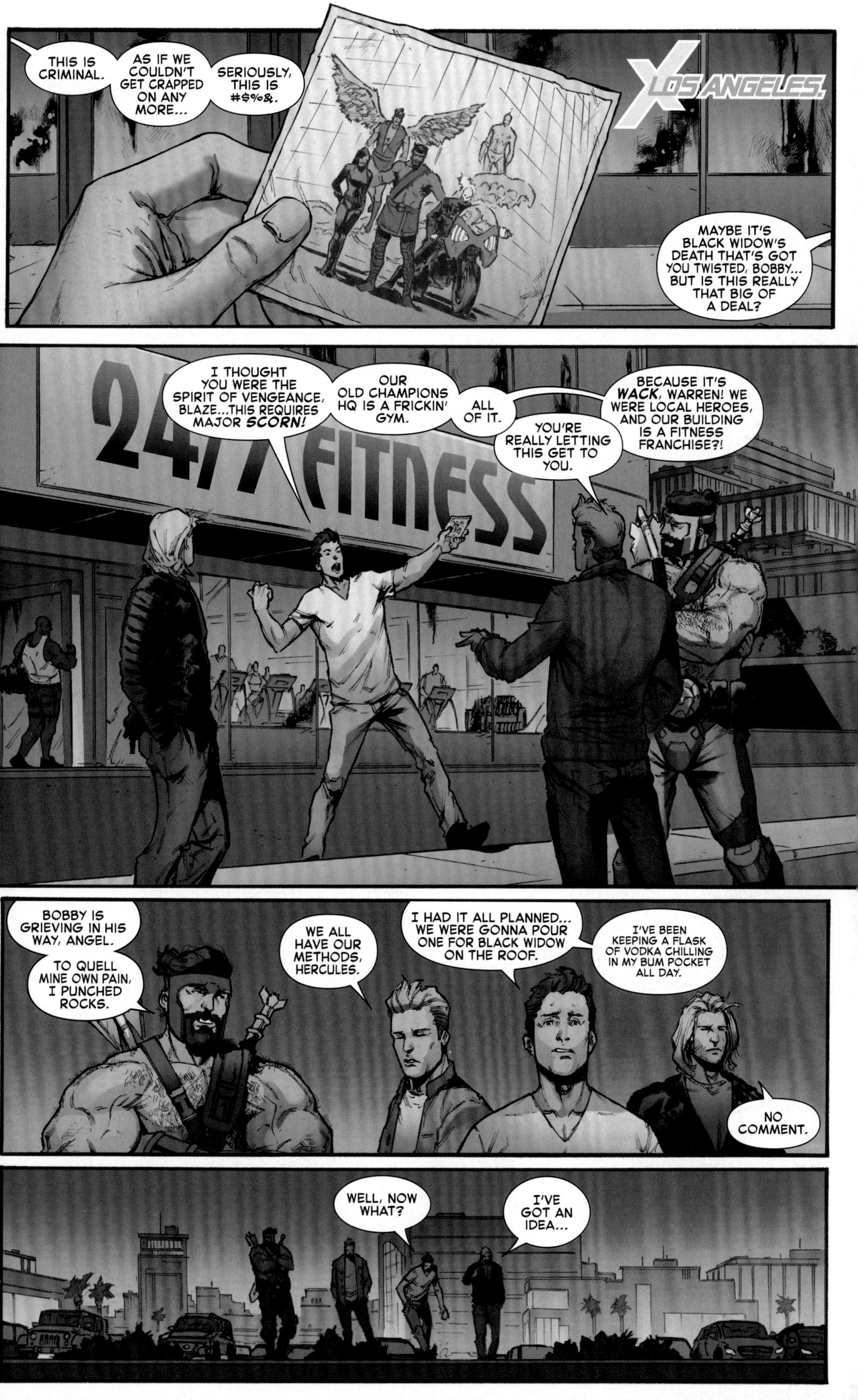
THIS IS CRIMINAL.
AS IF WE COULDN'T GET CRAPPED ON ANY MORE...
SERIOUSLY, THIS IS #$%&.
X LOS ANGELES.
MAYBE IT'S BLACK WIDOW'S DEATH THAT'S GOT YOU TWISTED, BOBBY... BUT IS THIS REALLY THAT BIG OF A DEAL?
24/7 FITNESS
I THOUGHT YOU WERE THE SPIRIT OF VENGEANCE, BLAZE...THIS REQUIRES MAJOR SCORN!
OUR OLD CHAMPIONS HQ IS A FRICKIN' GYM.
ALL OF IT.
YOU'RE REALLY LETTING THIS GET TO YOU.
BECAUSE IT'S WACK, WARREN! WE WERE LOCAL HEROES, AND OUR BUILDING IS A FITNESS FRANCHISE?!
BOBBY IS GRIEVING IN HIS WAY, ANGEL.
TO QUELL MINE OWN PAIN, I PUNCHED ROCKS.
WE ALL HAVE OUR METHODS, HERCULES.
I HAD IT ALL PLANNED... WE WERE GONNA POUR ONE FOR BLACK WIDOW ON THE ROOF.
I'VE BEEN KEEPING A FLASK OF VODKA CHILLING IN MY BUM POCKET ALL DAY.
NO COMMENT.
WELL, NOW WHAT?
I'VE GOT AN IDEA...

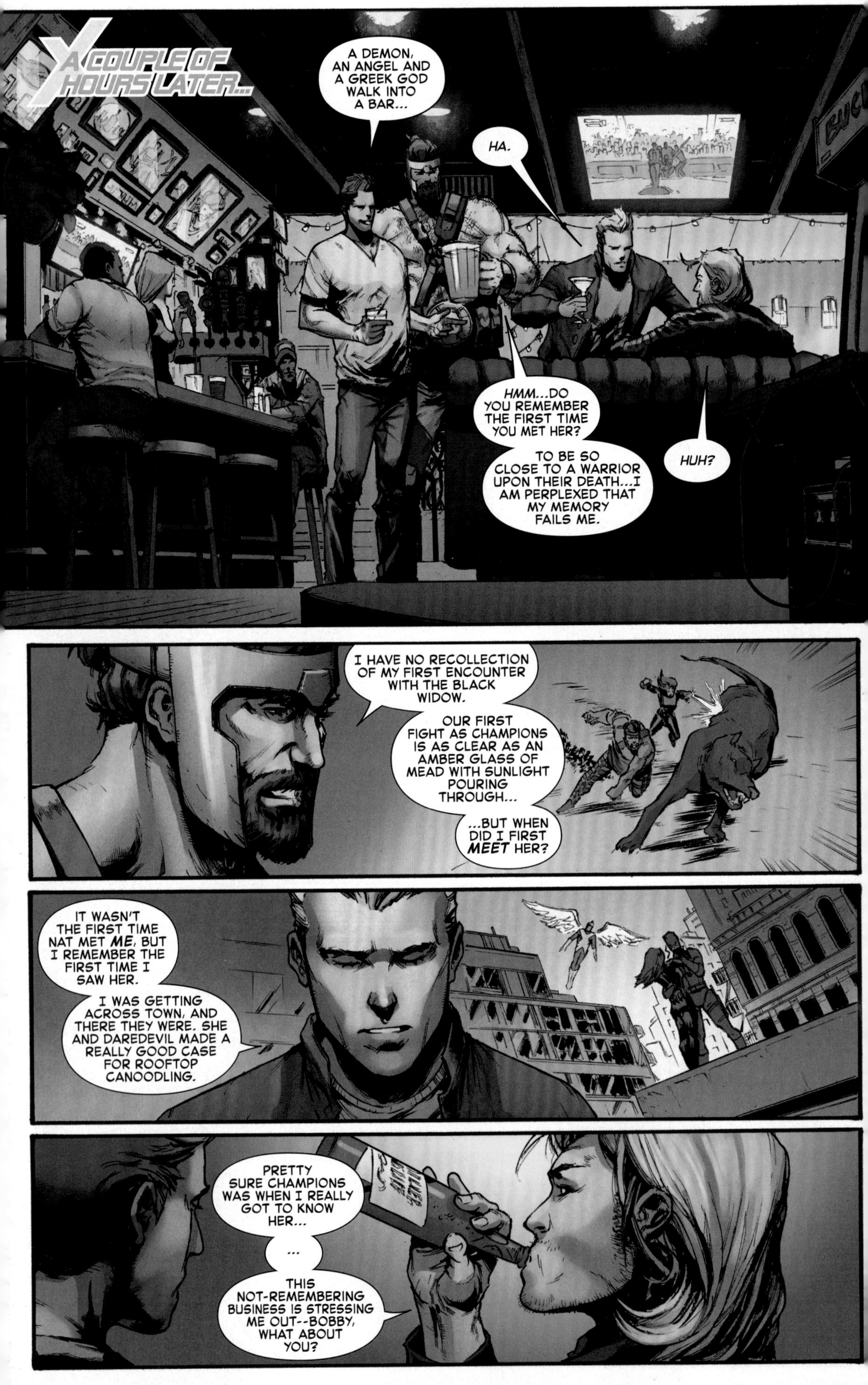
A COUPLE OF HOURS LATER...
A DEMON, AN ANGEL AND A GREEK GOD WALK INTO A BAR...
HA.
HMM...DO YOU REMEMBER THE FIRST TIME YOU MET HER?
TO BE SO CLOSE TO A WARRIOR UPON THEIR DEATH...I AM PERPLEXED THAT MY MEMORY FAILS ME.
HUH?
I HAVE NO RECOLLECTION OF MY FIRST ENCOUNTER WITH THE BLACK WIDOW.
OUR FIRST FIGHT AS CHAMPIONS IS AS CLEAR AS AN AMBER GLASS OF MEAD WITH SUNLIGHT POURING THROUGH...
...BUT WHEN DID I FIRST MEET HER?
IT WASN'T THE FIRST TIME NAT MET ME, BUT I REMEMBER THE FIRST TIME I SAW HER.
I WAS GETTING ACROSS TOWN, AND THERE THEY WERE. SHE AND DAREDEVIL MADE A REALLY GOOD CASE FOR ROOFTOP CANOODLING.
PRETTY SURE CHAMPIONS WAS WHEN I REALLY GOT TO KNOW HER...
...
THIS NOT-REMEMBERING BUSINESS IS STRESSING ME OUT--BOBBY, WHAT ABOUT YOU?

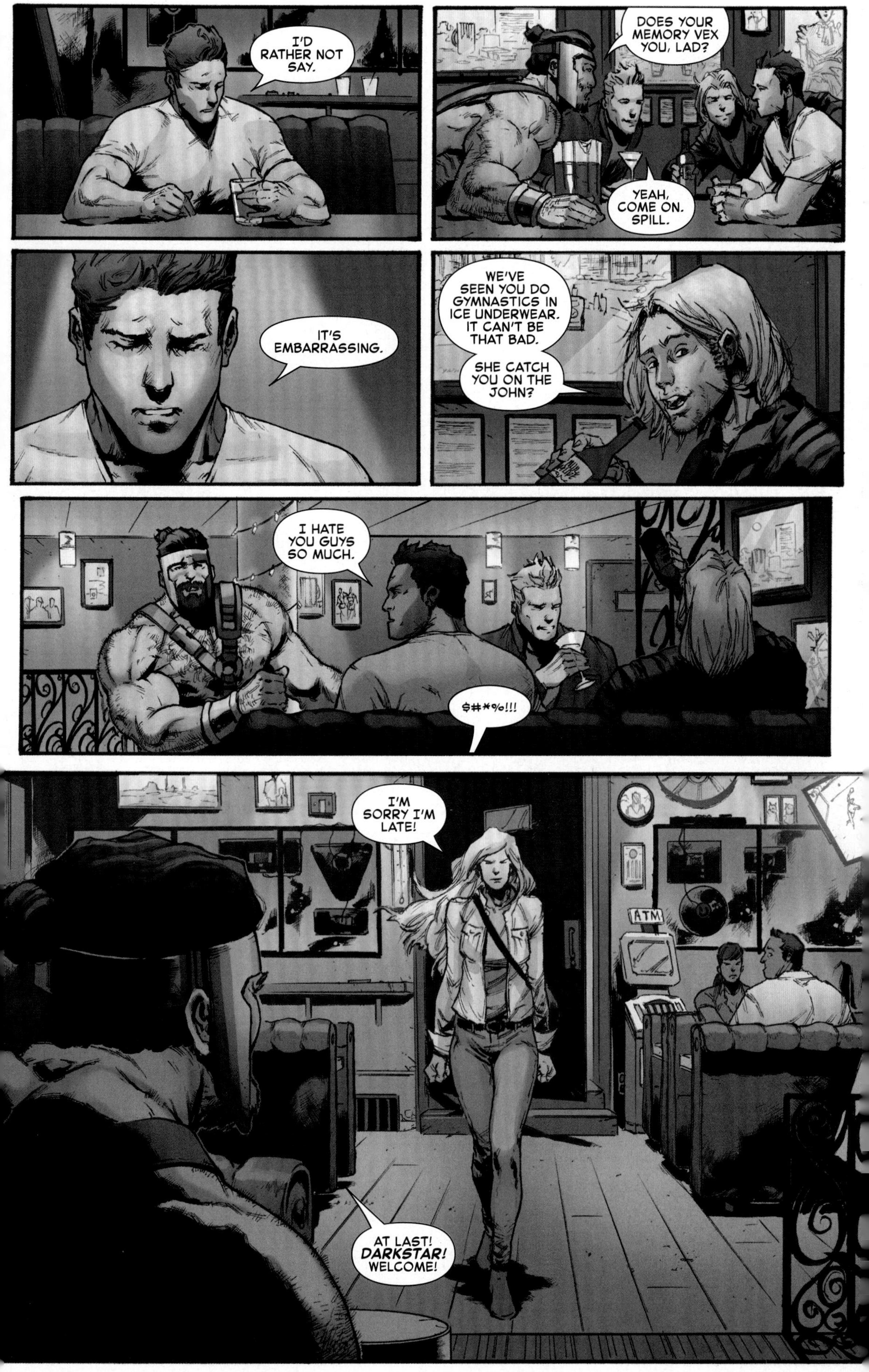
I'D RATHER NOT SAY.
DOES YOUR MEMORY VEX YOU, LAD?
YEAH, COME ON. SPILL.
IT'S EMBARRASSING.
WE'VE SEEN YOU DO GYMNASTICS IN ICE UNDERWEAR. IT CAN'T BE THAT BAD.
SHE CATCH YOU ON THE JOHN?
I HATE YOU GUYS SO MUCH.
$#*%!!!
I'M SORRY I'M LATE!
AT LAST! DARKSTAR! WELCOME!

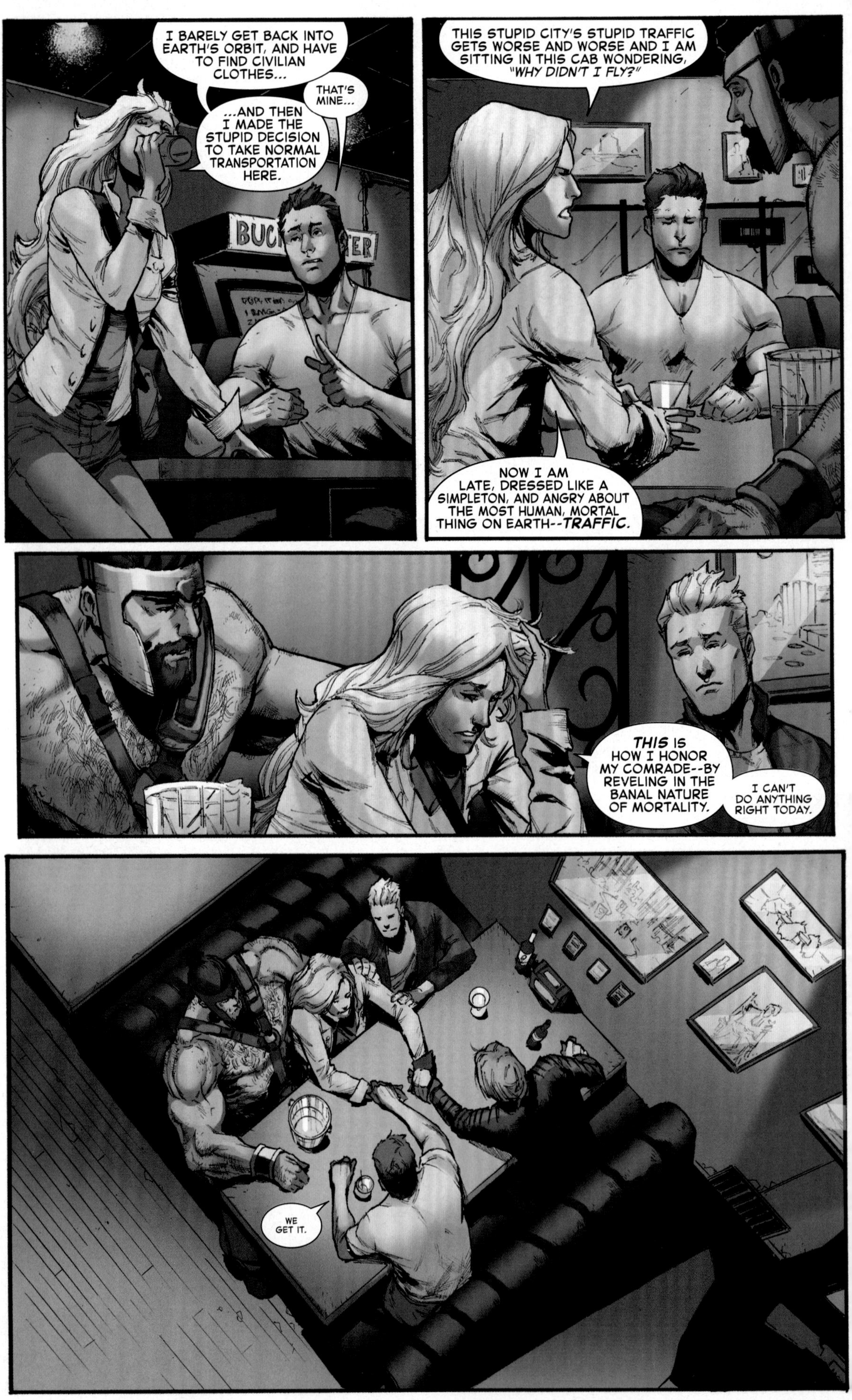
I BARELY GET BACK INTO EARTH'S ORBIT, AND HAVE TO FIND CIVILIAN CLOTHES...
...AND THEN I MADE THE STUPID DECISION TO TAKE NORMAL TRANSPORTATION HERE.
THAT'S MINE...
BUCK
TER
THIS STUPID CITY'S STUPID TRAFFIC GETS WORSE AND WORSE AND I AM SITTING IN THIS CAB WONDERING, "WHY DIDN'T I FLY?"
NOW I AM LATE, DRESSED LIKE A SIMPLETON, AND ANGRY ABOUT THE MOST HUMAN, MORTAL THING ON EARTH--TRAFFIC.
THIS IS HOW I HONOR MY COMRADE--BY REVELING IN THE BANAL NATURE OF MORTALITY.
I CAN'T DO ANYTHING RIGHT TODAY.
WE GET IT.

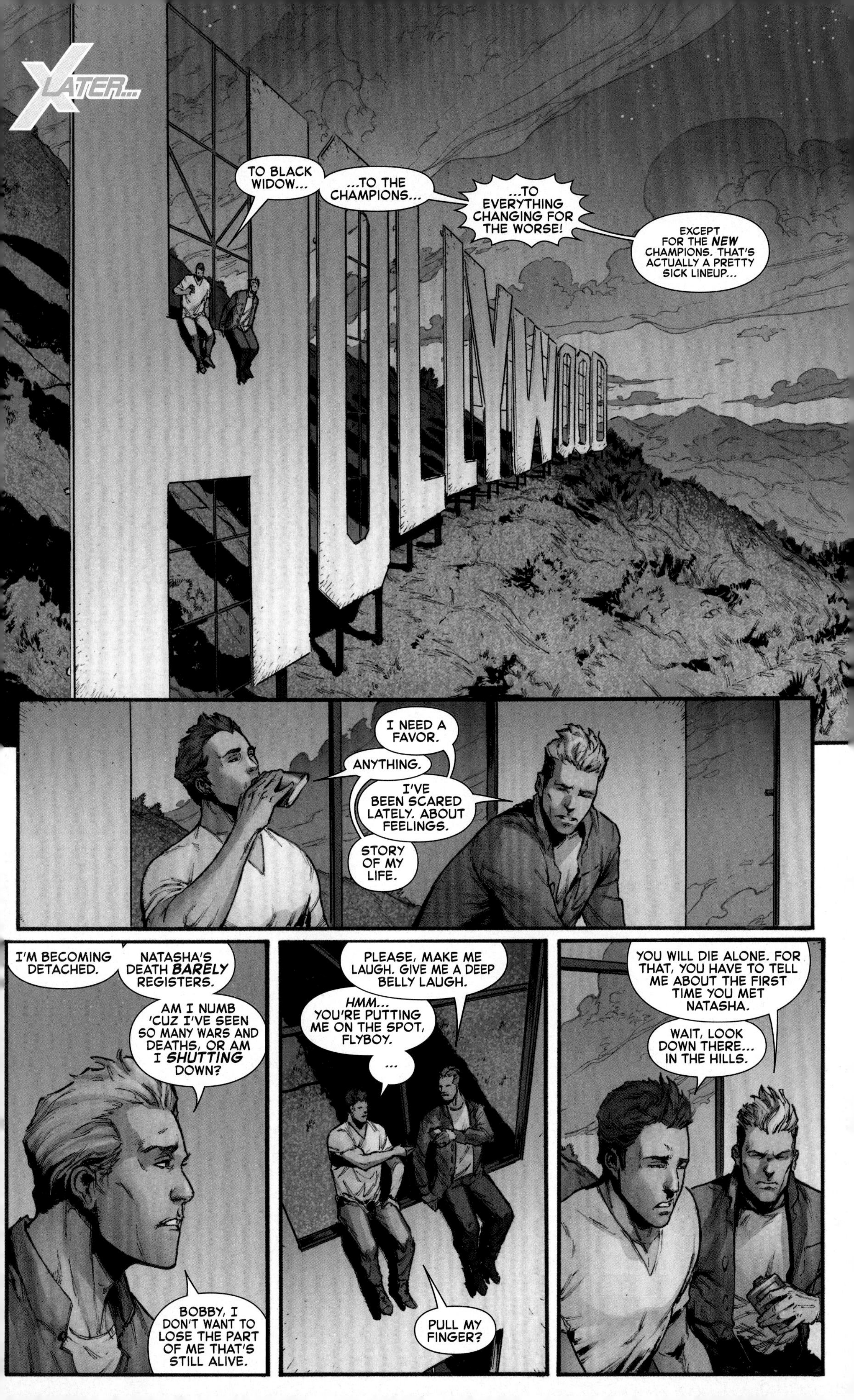
LATER...
TO BLACK WIDOW...
...TO THE CHAMPIONS...
...TO EVERYTHING CHANGING FOR THE WORSE!
EXCEPT FOR THE NEW CHAMPIONS. THAT'S ACTUALLY A PRETTY SICK LINEUP...
I NEED A FAVOR.
ANYTHING.
I'VE BEEN SCARED LATELY. ABOUT FEELINGS.
STORY OF MY LIFE.
I'M BECOMING DETACHED.
NATASHA'S DEATH BARELY REGISTERS.
AM I NUMB 'CUZ I'VE SEEN SO MANY WARS AND DEATHS, OR AM I SHUTTING DOWN?
BOBBY, I DON'T WANT TO LOSE THE PART OF ME THAT'S STILL ALIVE.
PLEASE, MAKE ME LAUGH. GIVE ME A DEEP BELLY LAUGH.
HMM... YOU'RE PUTTING ME ON THE SPOT, FLYBOY.
...
PULL MY FINGER?
YOU WILL DIE ALONE. FOR THAT, YOU HAVE TO TELL ME ABOUT THE FIRST TIME YOU MET NATASHA.
WAIT, LOOK DOWN THERE... IN THE HILLS.

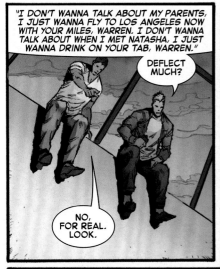

"I DON'T WANNA TALK ABOUT MY PARENTS, I JUST WANNA FLY TO LOS ANGELES NOW WITH YOUR MILES, WARREN. I DON'T WANNA TALK ABOUT WHEN I MET NATASHA, I JUST WANNA DRINK ON YOUR TAB, WARREN."

DEFLECT MUCH?

NO, FOR REAL. LOOK.

DO YOU SEE WHAT I SEE?

...

WHAT?

I'M TRYING TO FIGURE OUT IF THIS IS AN ELABORATELY LAME PLAY ON A KNOCK-KNOCK JOKE.

YOU'VE KNOWN ME FOR, LIKE, 200 YEARS, I'M BETTER AT SETUPS THAN THAT. SERIOUSLY, LOOK SOUTH AND WEST.

OH... TROUBLE.

FOUR MORE WEEKS...TUNNEL VISION, LETI.

IT'LL ALL WORK OUT IN LESS THAN 30 DAYS.

GET THESE BAD BOYS TO JUST WALK AND IT'LL ALL TURN AROUND...

NO "SMALL JOBS," OR "SIDE GIGS" EVER AGAIN... JUST FOUR WEEKS 'TIL YOU'VE GOT A FULL-FLEDGED ABOVEBOARD BUSINESS--

AHEM.

WE NEED TO HAVE A TALK ABOUT THE SENTINEL IN THE ROOM.

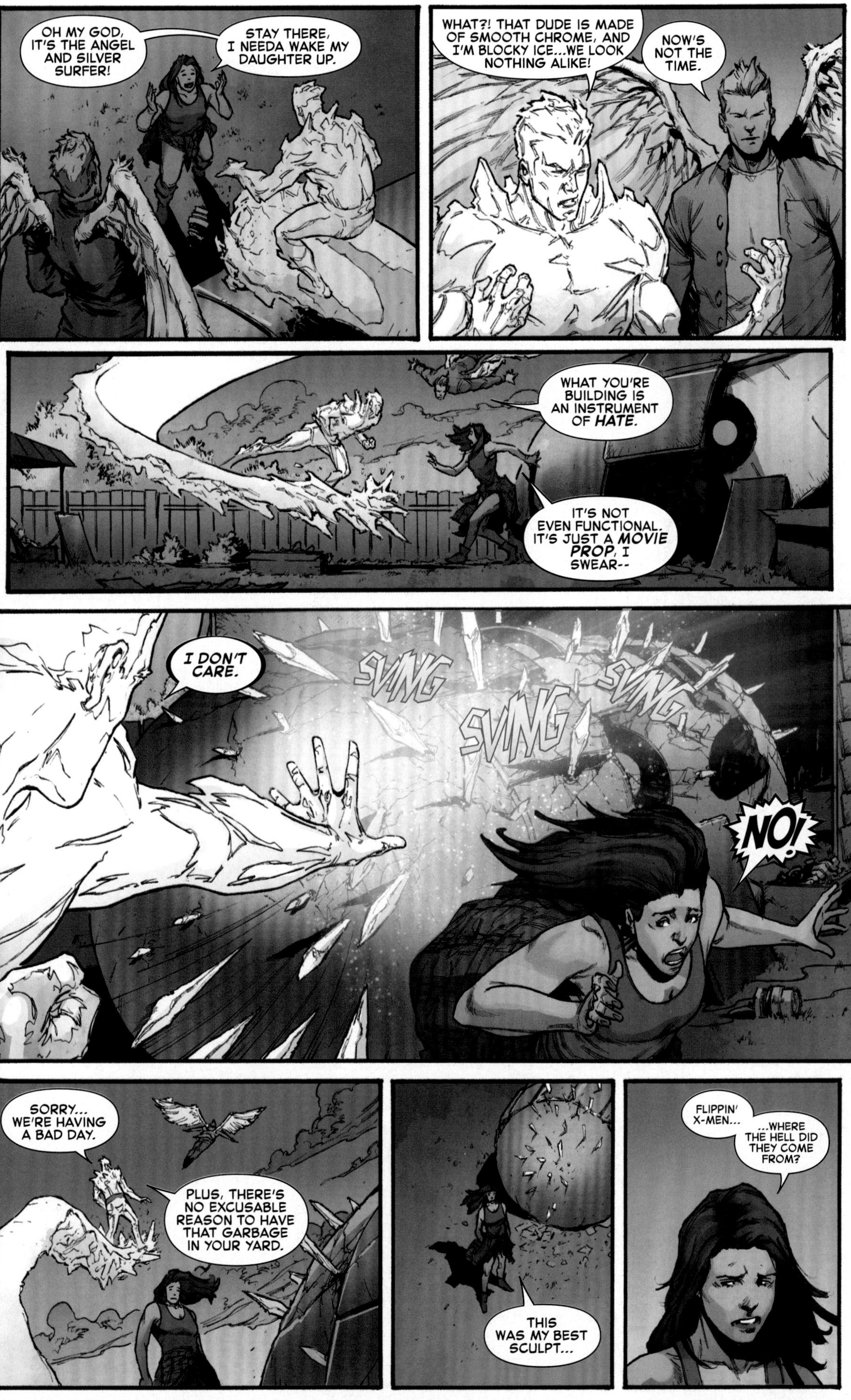

OH MY GOD, IT'S THE ANGEL AND SILVER SURFER!
STAY THERE, I NEEDA WAKE MY DAUGHTER UP.
WHAT?! THAT DUDE IS MADE OF SMOOTH CHROME, AND I'M BLOCKY ICE...WE LOOK NOTHING ALIKE!
NOW'S NOT THE TIME.
WHAT YOU'RE BUILDING IS AN INSTRUMENT OF HATE.
IT'S NOT EVEN FUNCTIONAL. IT'S JUST A MOVIE PROP, I SWEAR--
I DON'T CARE.
SVING
SVING
SVING
NO!
SORRY... WE'RE HAVING A BAD DAY.
PLUS, THERE'S NO EXCUSABLE REASON TO HAVE THAT GARBAGE IN YOUR YARD.
THIS WAS MY BEST SCULPT...
FLIPPIN' X-MEN...
...WHERE THE HELL DID THEY COME FROM?

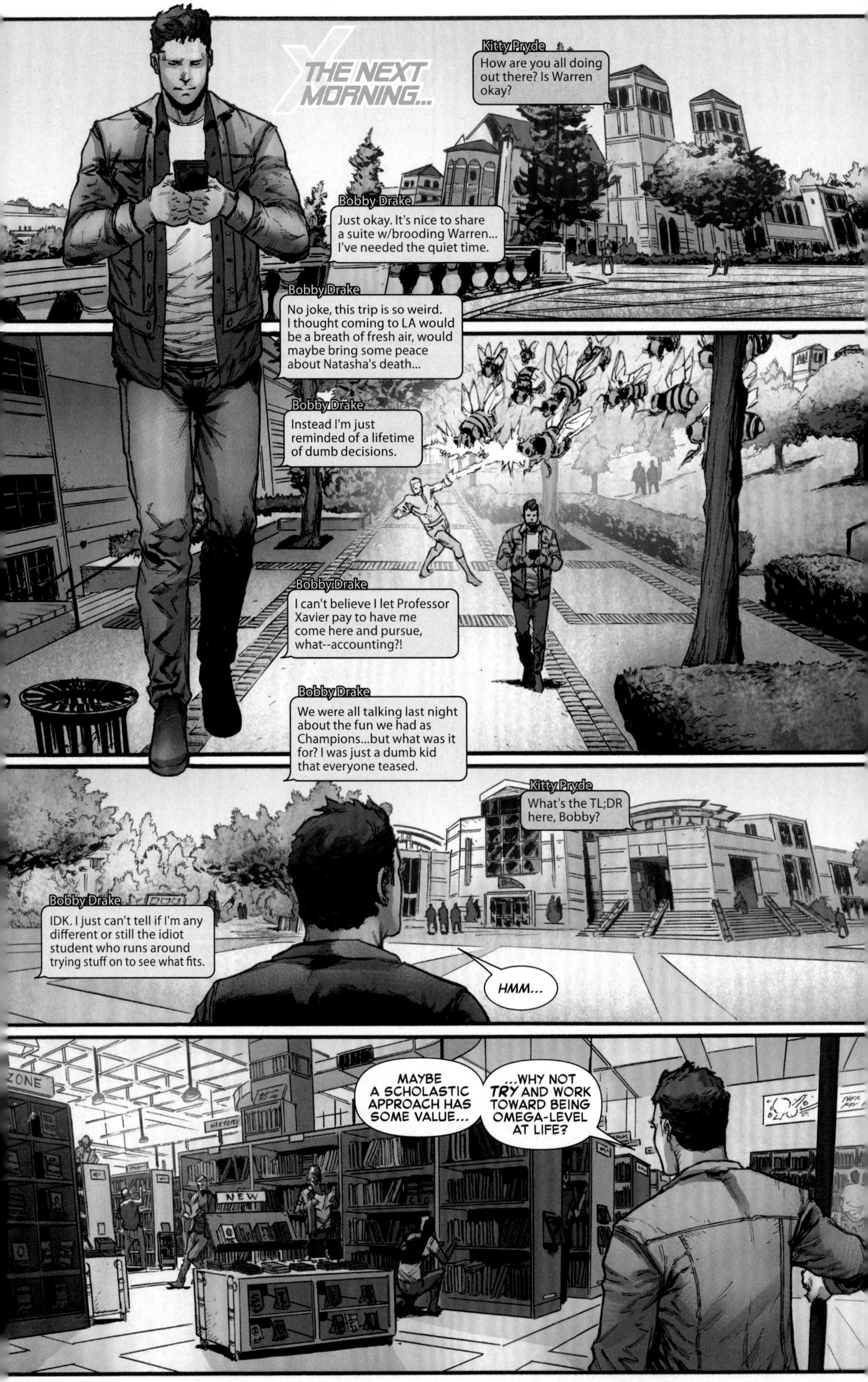
THE NEXT MORNING...
Kitty Pryde
How are you all doing out there? Is Warren okay?
Bobby Drake
Just okay. It's nice to share a suite w/brooding Warren... I've needed the quiet time.
Bobby Drake
No joke, this trip is so weird. I thought coming to LA would be a breath of fresh air, would maybe bring some peace about Natasha's death...
Bobby Drake
Instead I'm just reminded of a lifetime of dumb decisions.
Bobby Drake
I can't believe I let Professor Xavier pay to have me come here and pursue, what--accounting?!
Bobby Drake
We were all talking last night about the fun we had as Champions...but what was it for? I was just a dumb kid that everyone teased.
Kitty Pryde
What's the TL;DR here, Bobby?
Bobby Drake
IDK. I just can't tell if I'm any different or still the idiot student who runs around trying stuff on to see what fits.
HMM...
ZONE
NEW
MAYBE A SCHOLASTIC APPROACH HAS SOME VALUE...
...WHY NOT TRY AND WORK TOWARD BEING OMEGA-LEVEL AT LIFE?

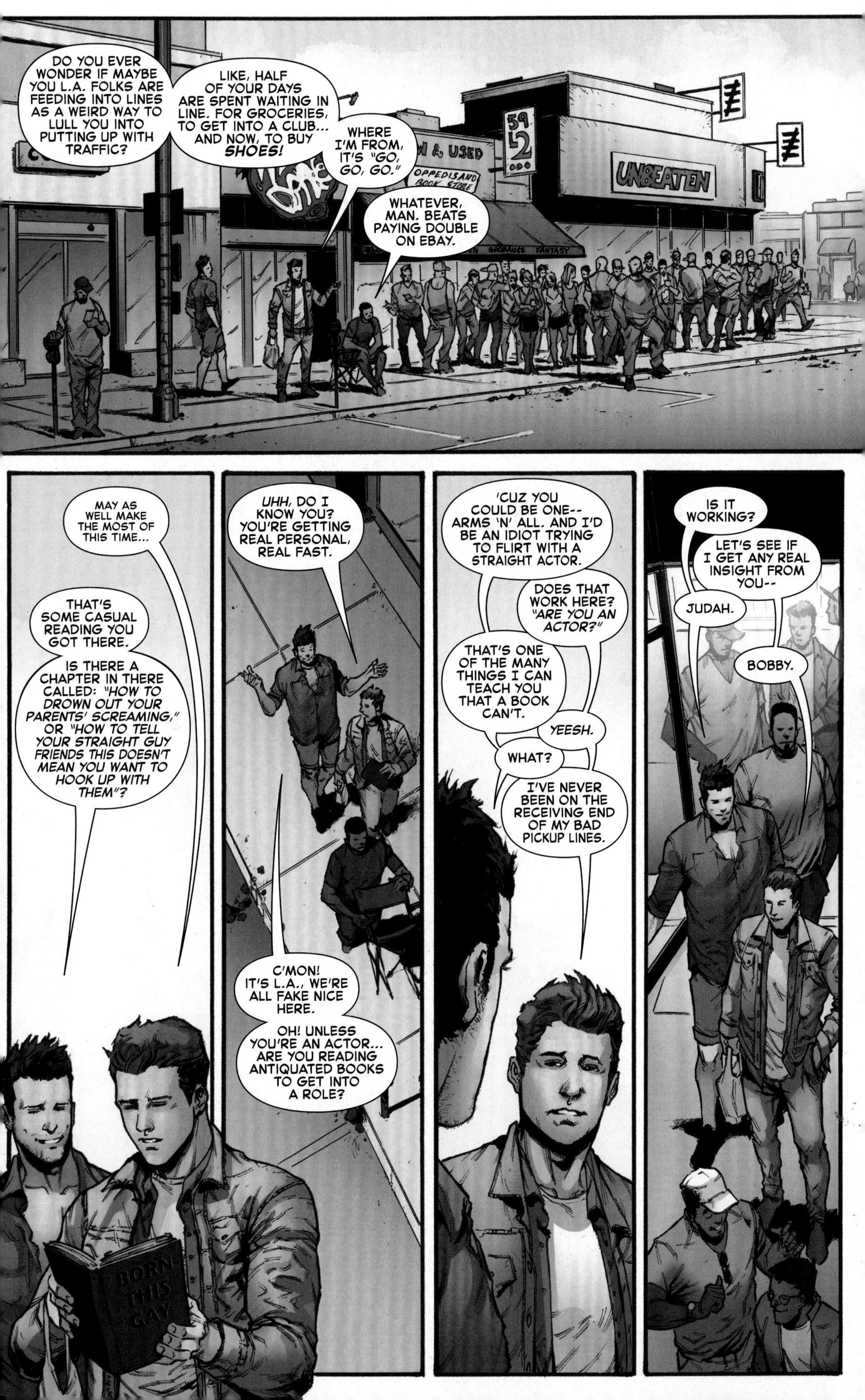
DO YOU EVER WONDER IF MAYBE YOU L.A. FOLKS ARE FEEDING INTO LINES AS A WEIRD WAY TO LULL YOU INTO PUTTING UP WITH TRAFFIC?
LIKE, HALF OF YOUR DAYS ARE SPENT WAITING IN LINE. FOR GROCERIES, TO GET INTO A CLUB... AND NOW, TO BUY ***SHOES!***
WHERE I'M FROM, IT'S *"GO, GO, GO."*
UNBEATEN
WHATEVER, MAN. BEATS PAYING DOUBLE ON EBAY.
MAY AS WELL MAKE THE MOST OF THIS TIME...
THAT'S SOME CASUAL READING YOU GOT THERE.
IS THERE A CHAPTER IN THERE CALLED: *"HOW TO DROWN OUT YOUR PARENTS' SCREAMING,"* OR *"HOW TO TELL YOUR STRAIGHT GUY FRIENDS THIS DOESN'T MEAN YOU WANT TO HOOK UP WITH THEM"*?
BORN THIS GAY
UHH, DO I KNOW YOU? YOU'RE GETTING REAL PERSONAL, REAL FAST.
C'MON! IT'S L.A., WE'RE ALL FAKE NICE HERE.
OH! UNLESS YOU'RE AN ACTOR... ARE YOU READING ANTIQUATED BOOKS TO GET INTO A ROLE?
'CUZ YOU COULD BE ONE-- ARMS 'N' ALL. AND I'D BE AN IDIOT TRYING TO FLIRT WITH A STRAIGHT ACTOR.
DOES THAT WORK HERE? *"ARE YOU AN ACTOR?"*
THAT'S ONE OF THE MANY THINGS I CAN TEACH YOU THAT A BOOK CAN'T.
YEESH.
WHAT?
I'VE NEVER BEEN ON THE RECEIVING END OF MY BAD PICKUP LINES.
IS IT WORKING?
LET'S SEE IF I GET ANY REAL INSIGHT FROM YOU--
JUDAH.
BOBBY.

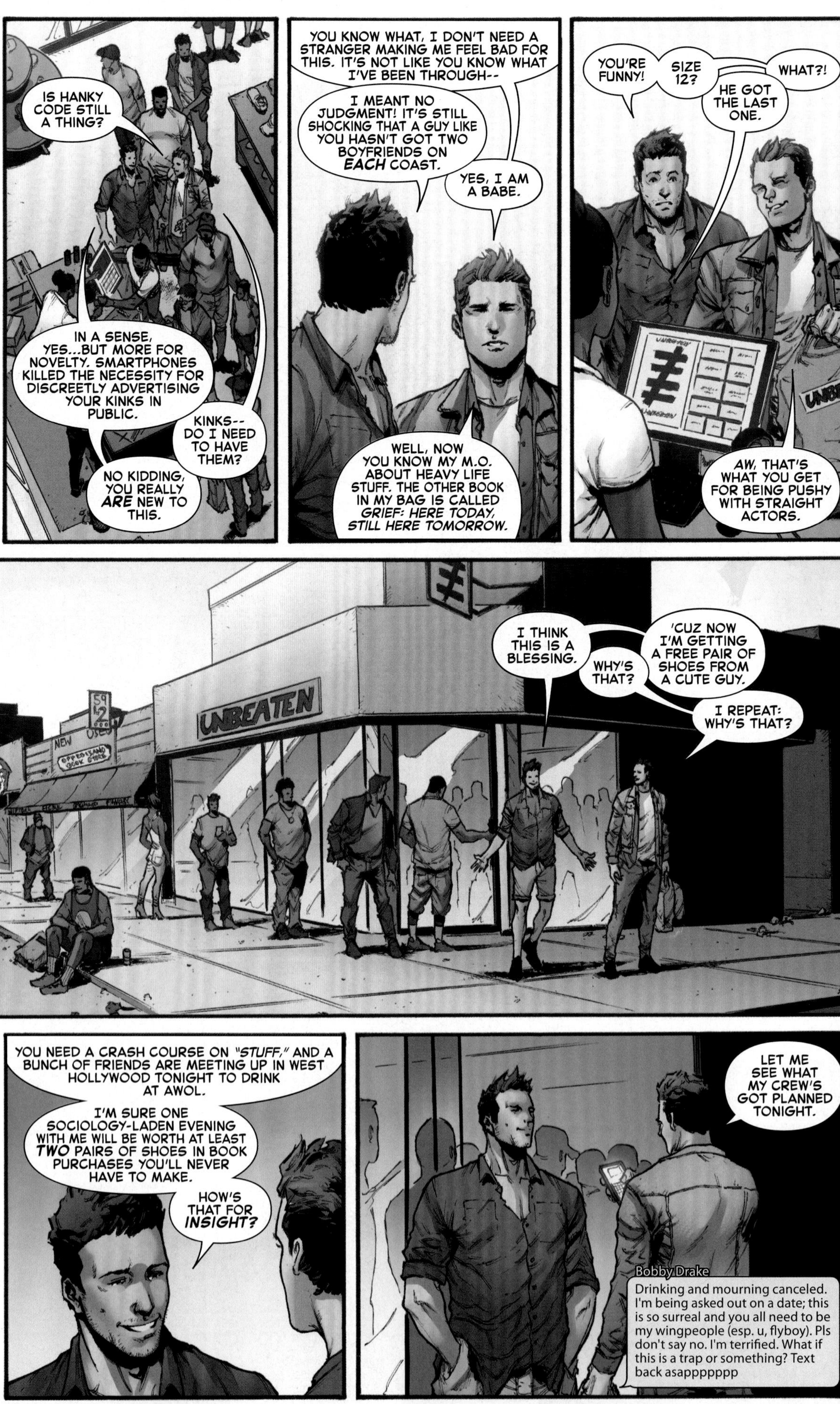
IS HANKY CODE STILL A THING?
IN A SENSE, YES...BUT MORE FOR NOVELTY. SMARTPHONES KILLED THE NECESSITY FOR DISCREETLY ADVERTISING YOUR KINKS IN PUBLIC.
KINKS-- DO I NEED TO HAVE THEM?
NO KIDDING, YOU REALLY ARE NEW TO THIS.
YOU KNOW WHAT, I DON'T NEED A STRANGER MAKING ME FEEL BAD FOR THIS. IT'S NOT LIKE YOU KNOW WHAT I'VE BEEN THROUGH--
I MEANT NO JUDGMENT! IT'S STILL SHOCKING THAT A GUY LIKE YOU HASN'T GOT TWO BOYFRIENDS ON EACH COAST.
YES, I AM A BABE.
WELL, NOW YOU KNOW MY M.O. ABOUT HEAVY LIFE STUFF. THE OTHER BOOK IN MY BAG IS CALLED GRIEF: HERE TODAY, STILL HERE TOMORROW.
YOU'RE FUNNY!
SIZE 12?
WHAT?!
HE GOT THE LAST ONE.
AW, THAT'S WHAT YOU GET FOR BEING PUSHY WITH STRAIGHT ACTORS.
UNBEATEN
I THINK THIS IS A BLESSING.
WHY'S THAT?
'CUZ NOW I'M GETTING A FREE PAIR OF SHOES FROM A CUTE GUY.
I REPEAT: WHY'S THAT?
YOU NEED A CRASH COURSE ON "STUFF," AND A BUNCH OF FRIENDS ARE MEETING UP IN WEST HOLLYWOOD TONIGHT TO DRINK AT AWOL.
I'M SURE ONE SOCIOLOGY-LADEN EVENING WITH ME WILL BE WORTH AT LEAST TWO PAIRS OF SHOES IN BOOK PURCHASES YOU'LL NEVER HAVE TO MAKE.
HOW'S THAT FOR INSIGHT?
LET ME SEE WHAT MY CREW'S GOT PLANNED TONIGHT.
Bobby Drake
Drinking and mourning canceled. I'm being asked out on a date; this is so surreal and you all need to be my wingpeople (esp. u, flyboy). Pls don't say no. I'm terrified. What if this is a trap or something? Text back asappppppp

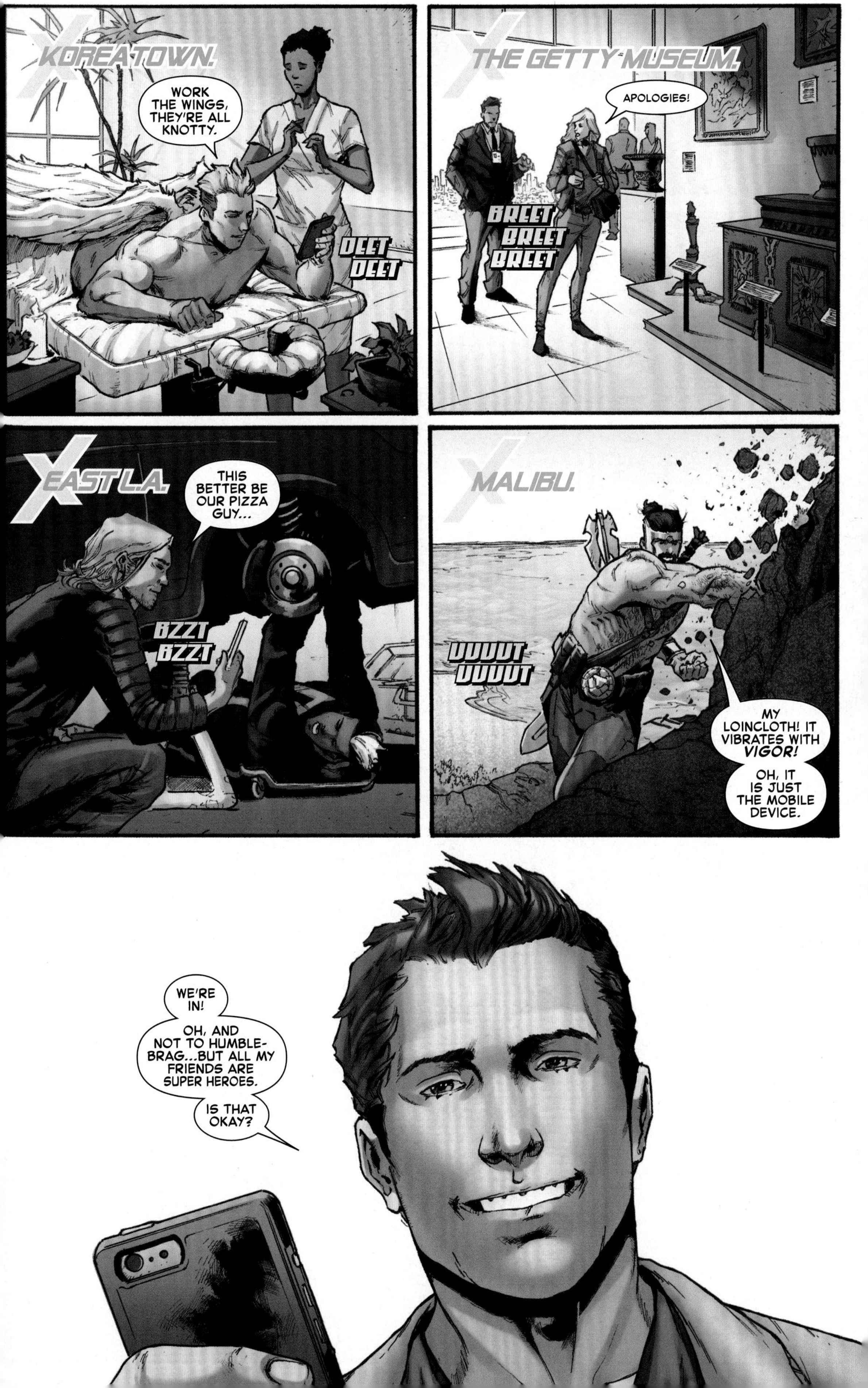
KOREATOWN.
WORK THE WINGS, THEY'RE ALL KNOTTY.
DEET DEET
THE GETTY MUSEUM.
APOLOGIES!
BREET BREET BREET
EAST L.A.
THIS BETTER BE OUR PIZZA GUY...
BZZT BZZT
MALIBU.
VVVVT VVVVT
MY LOINCLOTH! IT VIBRATES WITH VIGOR!
OH, IT IS JUST THE MOBILE DEVICE.
WE'RE IN!
OH, AND NOT TO HUMBLE-BRAG...BUT ALL MY FRIENDS ARE SUPER HEROES.
IS THAT OKAY?

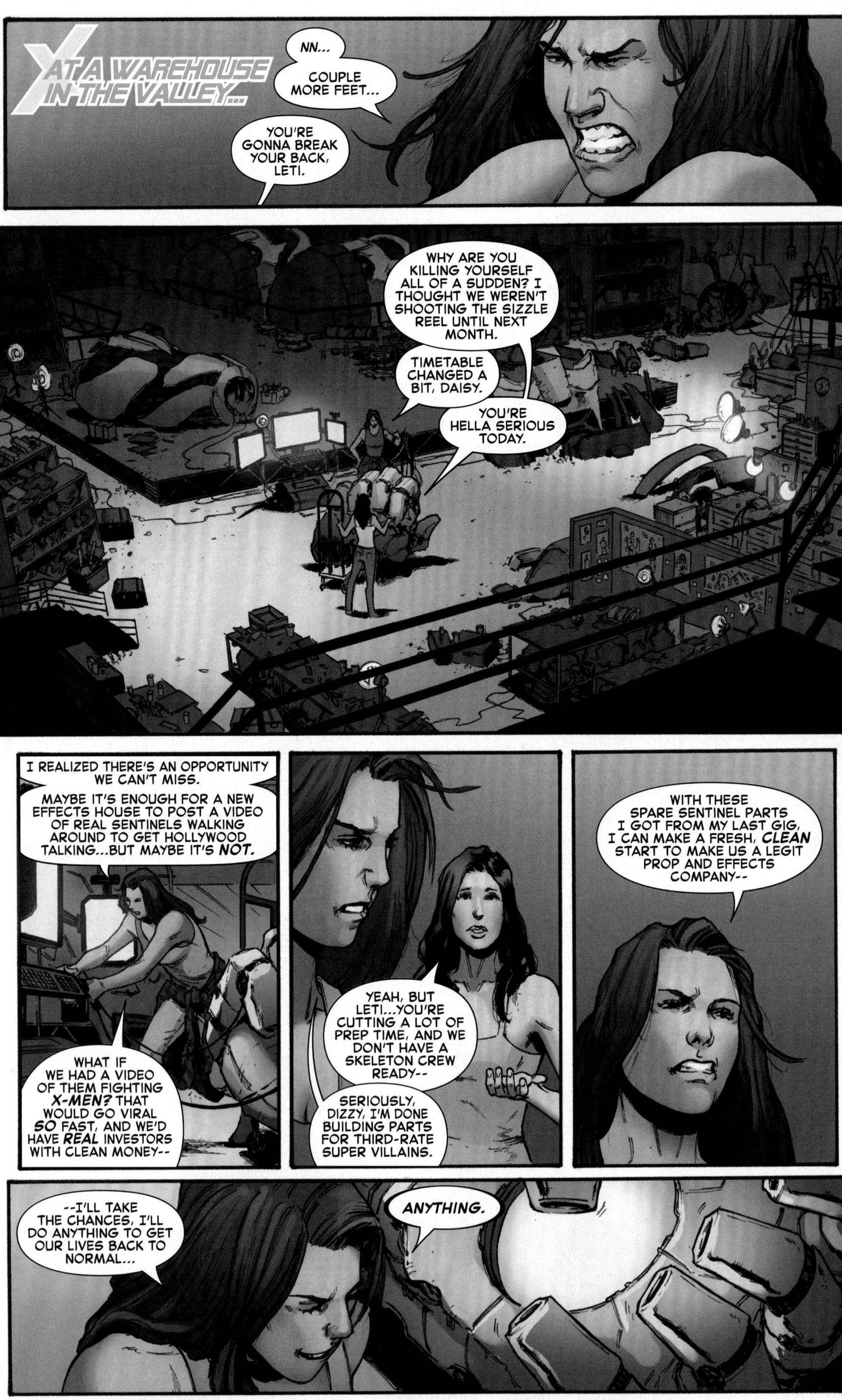
AT A WAREHOUSE IN THE VALLEY...
NN...
COUPLE MORE FEET...
YOU'RE GONNA BREAK YOUR BACK, LETI.
WHY ARE YOU KILLING YOURSELF ALL OF A SUDDEN? I THOUGHT WE WEREN'T SHOOTING THE SIZZLE REEL UNTIL NEXT MONTH.
TIMETABLE CHANGED A BIT, DAISY.
YOU'RE HELLA SERIOUS TODAY.
I REALIZED THERE'S AN OPPORTUNITY WE CAN'T MISS.
MAYBE IT'S ENOUGH FOR A NEW EFFECTS HOUSE TO POST A VIDEO OF REAL SENTINELS WALKING AROUND TO GET HOLLYWOOD TALKING...BUT MAYBE IT'S *NOT.*
WHAT IF WE HAD A VIDEO OF THEM FIGHTING *X-MEN?* THAT WOULD GO VIRAL *SO* FAST, AND WE'D HAVE *REAL* INVESTORS WITH CLEAN MONEY--
YEAH, BUT LETI...YOU'RE CUTTING A LOT OF PREP TIME, AND WE DON'T HAVE A SKELETON CREW READY--
SERIOUSLY, DIZZY, I'M DONE BUILDING PARTS FOR THIRD-RATE SUPER VILLAINS.
WITH THESE SPARE SENTINEL PARTS I GOT FROM MY LAST GIG, I CAN MAKE A FRESH, *CLEAN* START TO MAKE US A LEGIT PROP AND EFFECTS COMPANY--
--I'LL TAKE THE CHANCES, I'LL DO ANYTHING TO GET OUR LIVES BACK TO NORMAL...
ANYTHING.

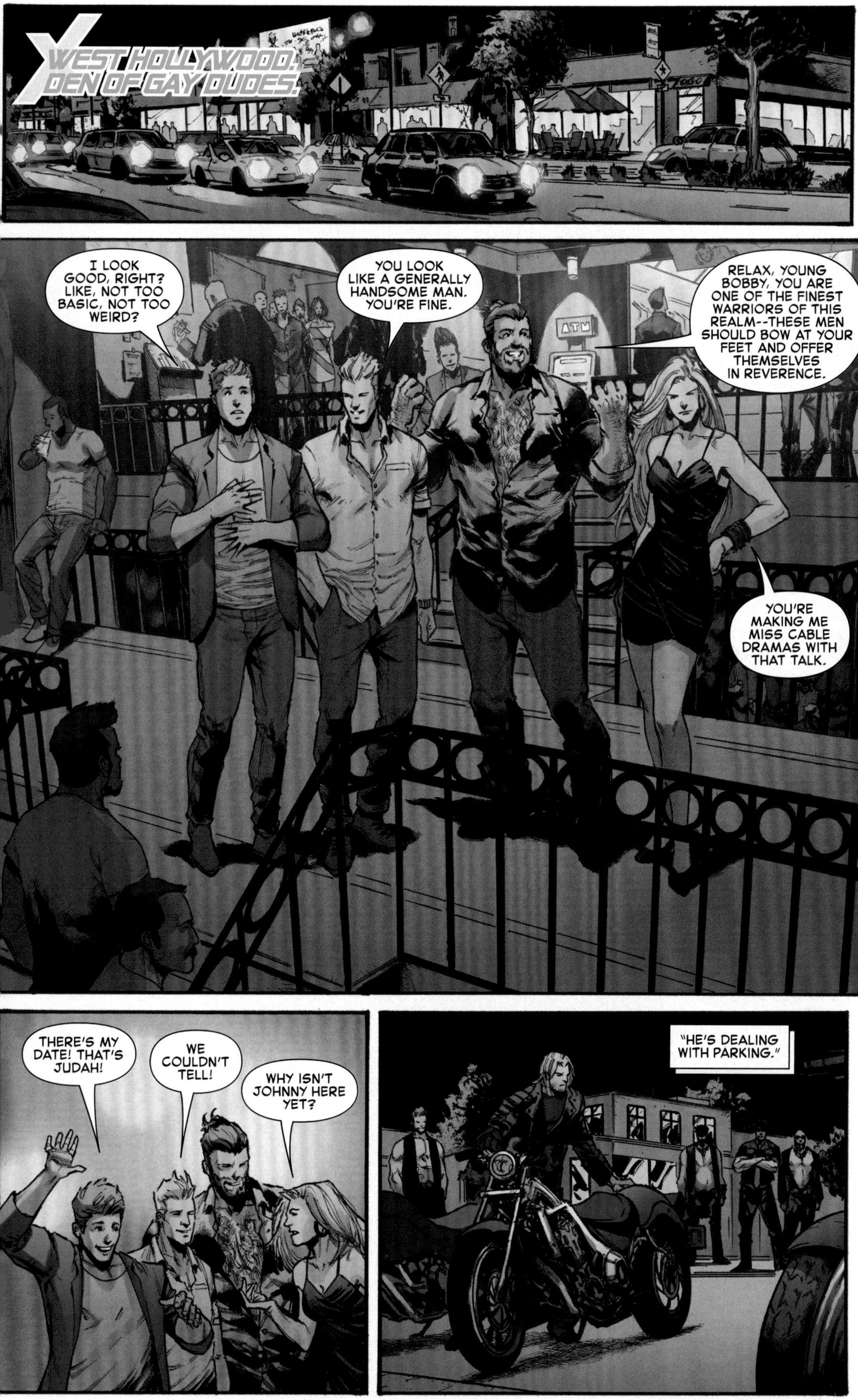
WEST HOLLYWOOD: DEN OF GAY DUDES.
I LOOK GOOD, RIGHT? LIKE, NOT TOO BASIC, NOT TOO WEIRD?
YOU LOOK LIKE A GENERALLY HANDSOME MAN. YOU'RE FINE.
RELAX, YOUNG BOBBY, YOU ARE ONE OF THE FINEST WARRIORS OF THIS REALM--THESE MEN SHOULD BOW AT YOUR FEET AND OFFER THEMSELVES IN REVERENCE.
YOU'RE MAKING ME MISS CABLE DRAMAS WITH THAT TALK.
ATM
THERE'S MY DATE! THAT'S JUDAH!
WE COULDN'T TELL!
WHY ISN'T JOHNNY HERE YET?
"HE'S DEALING WITH PARKING."

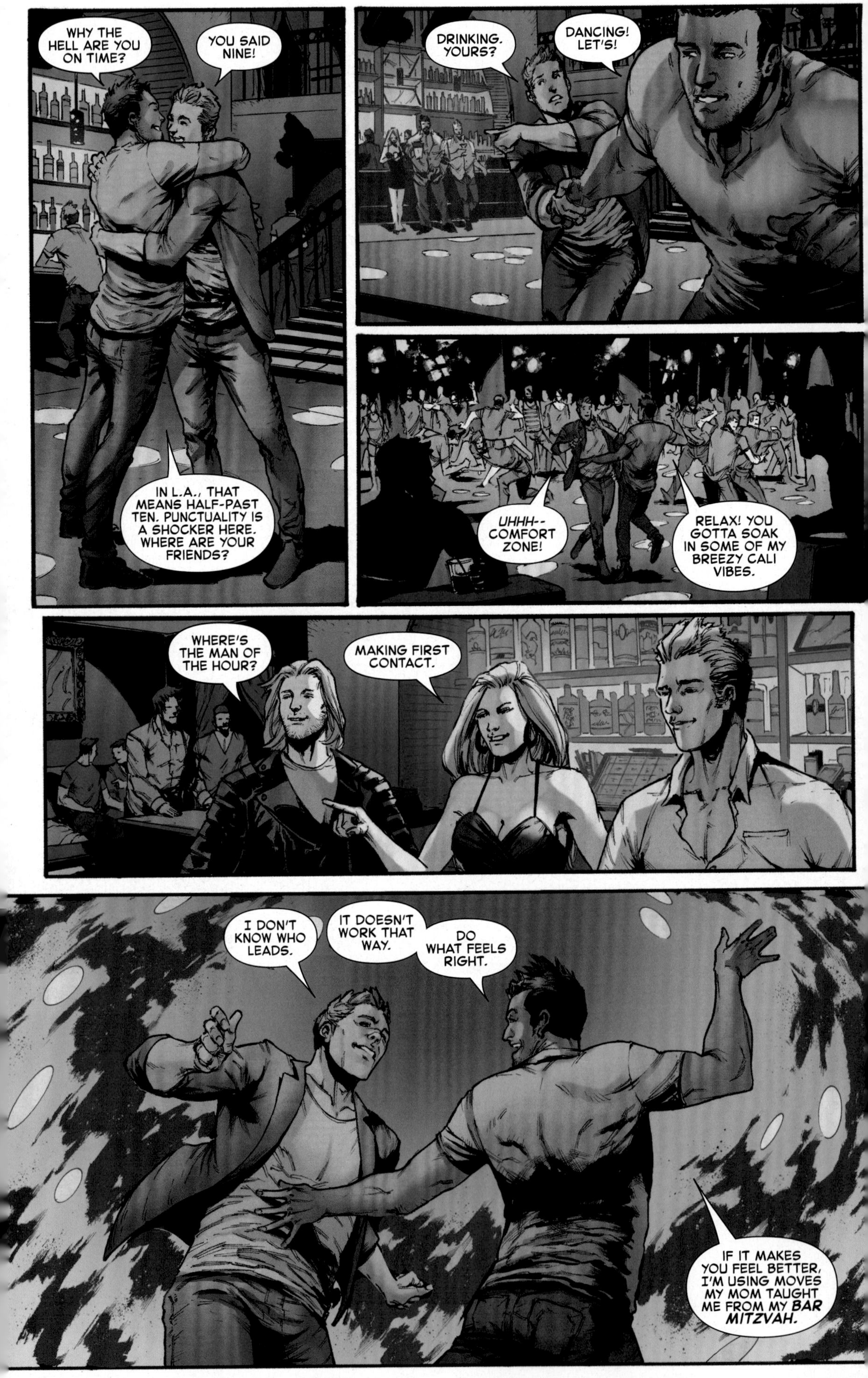
WHY THE HELL ARE YOU ON TIME?
YOU SAID NINE!
IN L.A., THAT MEANS HALF-PAST TEN. PUNCTUALITY IS A SHOCKER HERE. WHERE ARE YOUR FRIENDS?
DRINKING. YOURS?
DANCING! LET'S!
UHHH-- COMFORT ZONE!
RELAX! YOU GOTTA SOAK IN SOME OF MY BREEZY CALI VIBES.
WHERE'S THE MAN OF THE HOUR?
MAKING FIRST CONTACT.
I DON'T KNOW WHO LEADS.
IT DOESN'T WORK THAT WAY.
DO WHAT FEELS RIGHT.
IF IT MAKES YOU FEEL BETTER, I'M USING MOVES MY MOM TAUGHT ME FROM MY BAR MITZVAH.

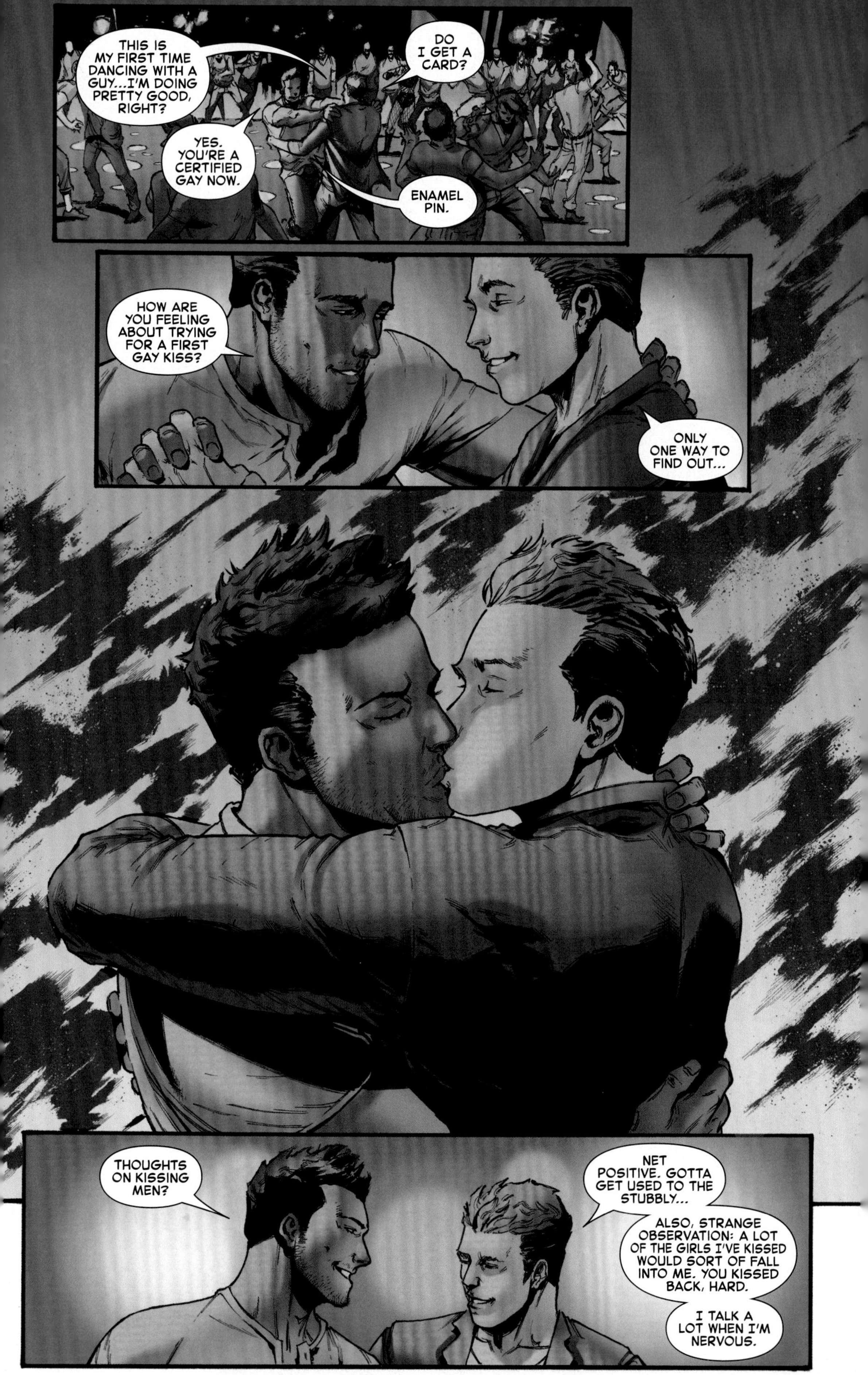
THIS IS MY FIRST TIME DANCING WITH A GUY...I'M DOING PRETTY GOOD, RIGHT?
YES. YOU'RE A CERTIFIED GAY NOW.
DO I GET A CARD?
ENAMEL PIN.
HOW ARE YOU FEELING ABOUT TRYING FOR A FIRST GAY KISS?
ONLY ONE WAY TO FIND OUT...
THOUGHTS ON KISSING MEN?
NET POSITIVE. GOTTA GET USED TO THE STUBBLY...
ALSO, STRANGE OBSERVATION: A LOT OF THE GIRLS I'VE KISSED WOULD SORT OF FALL INTO ME. YOU KISSED BACK, HARD.
I TALK A LOT WHEN I'M NERVOUS.

I GOT AN IDEA.

IS IT ONE THAT DOESN'T INCLUDE MY FRIENDS WATCHING MY EVERY MOVE?

'CUZ THAT'S NOT WEIRDING *ME* OUT IN THE SLIGHTEST.

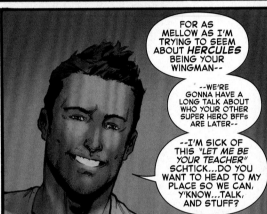

FOR AS MELLOW AS I'M TRYING TO SEEM ABOUT *HERCULES* BEING YOUR WINGMAN--

--WE'RE GONNA HAVE A LONG TALK ABOUT WHO YOUR OTHER SUPER HERO BFFs ARE LATER--

--I'M SICK OF THIS "LET ME BE YOUR TEACHER" SCHTICK...DO YOU WANT TO HEAD TO MY PLACE SO WE CAN, Y'KNOW...TALK, AND STUFF?

YOU'RE ALL RIGHT LEAVING THE PARTY LIFE?

'CUZ I'M AMENABLE TO THAT.

I ONLY AGREED TO MEET MY FRIENDS TONIGHT BECAUSE I NEEDED AN EASY WAY TO SEE YOU AGAIN.

BARS ARE LIKE DISNEYLAND-- I'VE GOT MAYBE TWO VISITS A YEAR IN ME, AT THAT.

THAT'S ABOUT AS OFTEN AS I GET OUT. IF WE'RE NOT DOING X-MEN STUFF, WE USUALLY JUST PLAY AN UNHEALTHY AMOUNT OF BASEBALL TO UNWIND.

HAH! WELL, LEMME CLOSE OUT MY TAB AND EXTRICATE MYSELF FROM THE SOCIAL GROUP...

PLAY IT COOL, PLAY IT COOL, DON'T TRY AND IMPRESS HIM WITH YOUR POWERS, JUST BE--

KABABOOOOOM

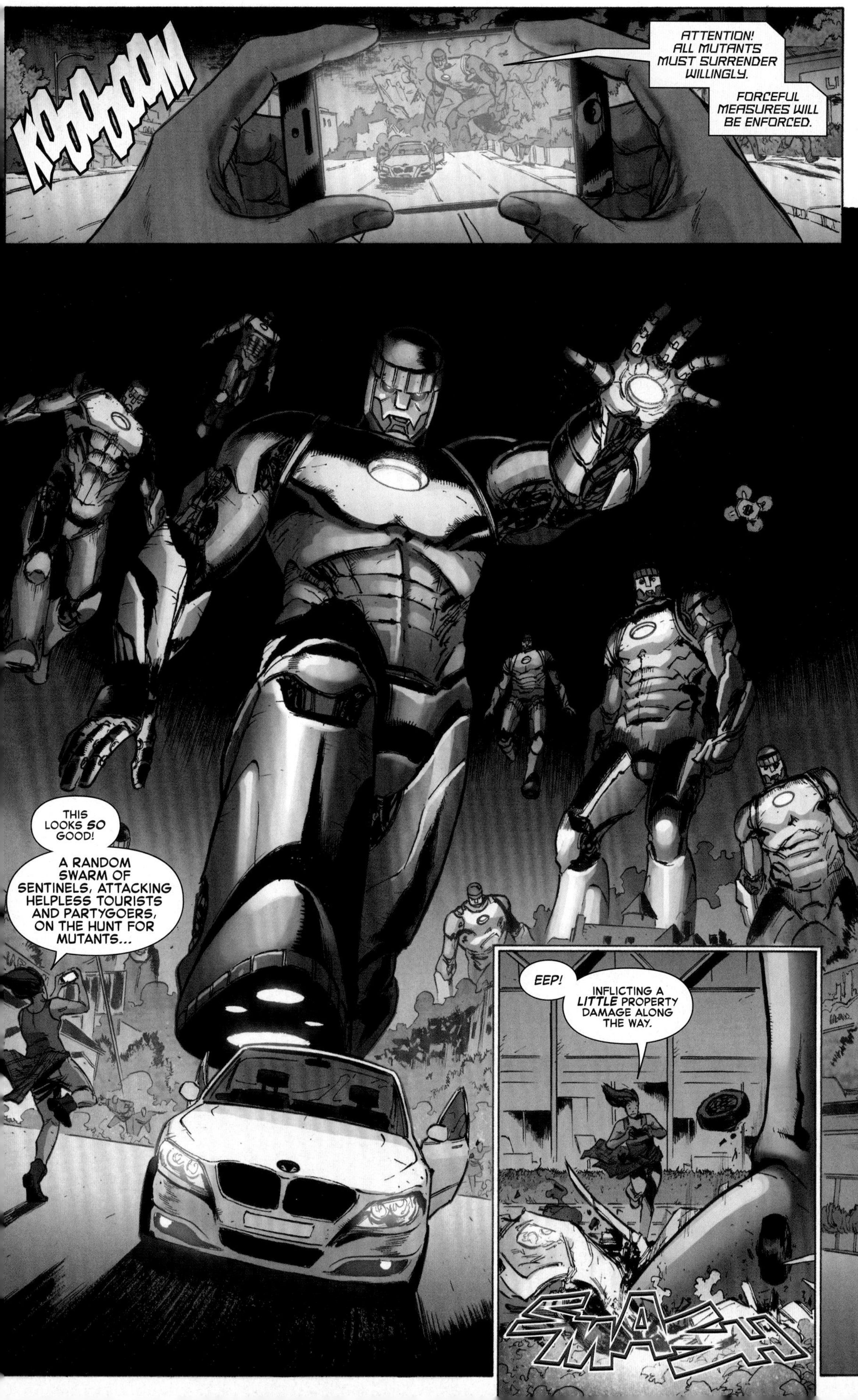
KOOOOOOM
ATTENTION! ALL MUTANTS MUST SURRENDER WILLINGLY.
FORCEFUL MEASURES WILL BE ENFORCED.
THIS LOOKS SO GOOD!
A RANDOM SWARM OF SENTINELS, ATTACKING HELPLESS TOURISTS AND PARTYGOERS, ON THE HUNT FOR MUTANTS...
EEP!
INFLICTING A LITTLE PROPERTY DAMAGE ALONG THE WAY.
SMASH

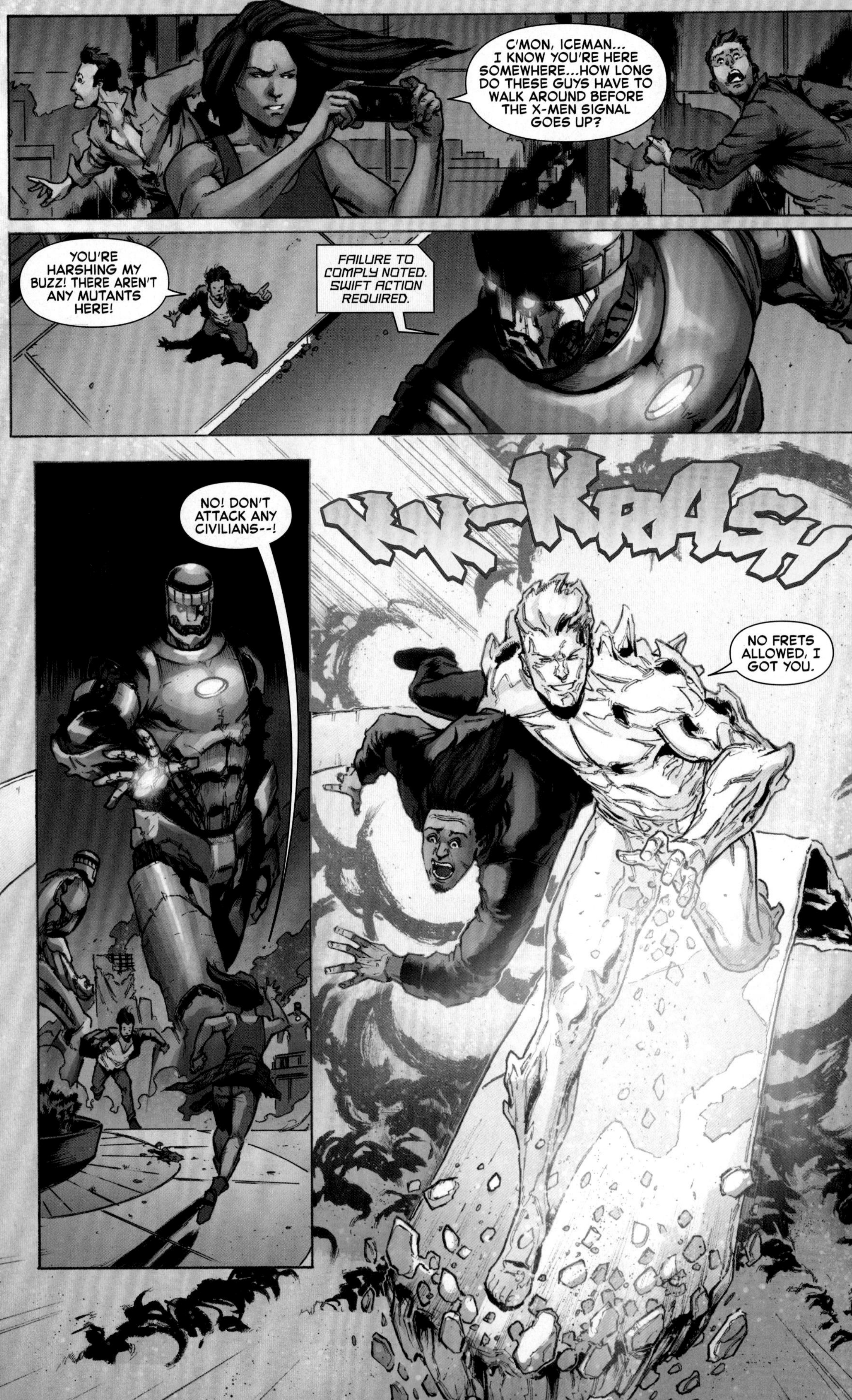
C'MON, ICEMAN... I KNOW YOU'RE HERE SOMEWHERE...HOW LONG DO THESE GUYS HAVE TO WALK AROUND BEFORE THE X-MEN SIGNAL GOES UP?
YOU'RE HARSHING MY BUZZ! THERE AREN'T ANY MUTANTS HERE!
FAILURE TO COMPLY NOTED. SWIFT ACTION REQUIRED.
NO! DON'T ATTACK ANY CIVILIANS--!
KK-KRASH
NO FRETS ALLOWED, I GOT YOU.

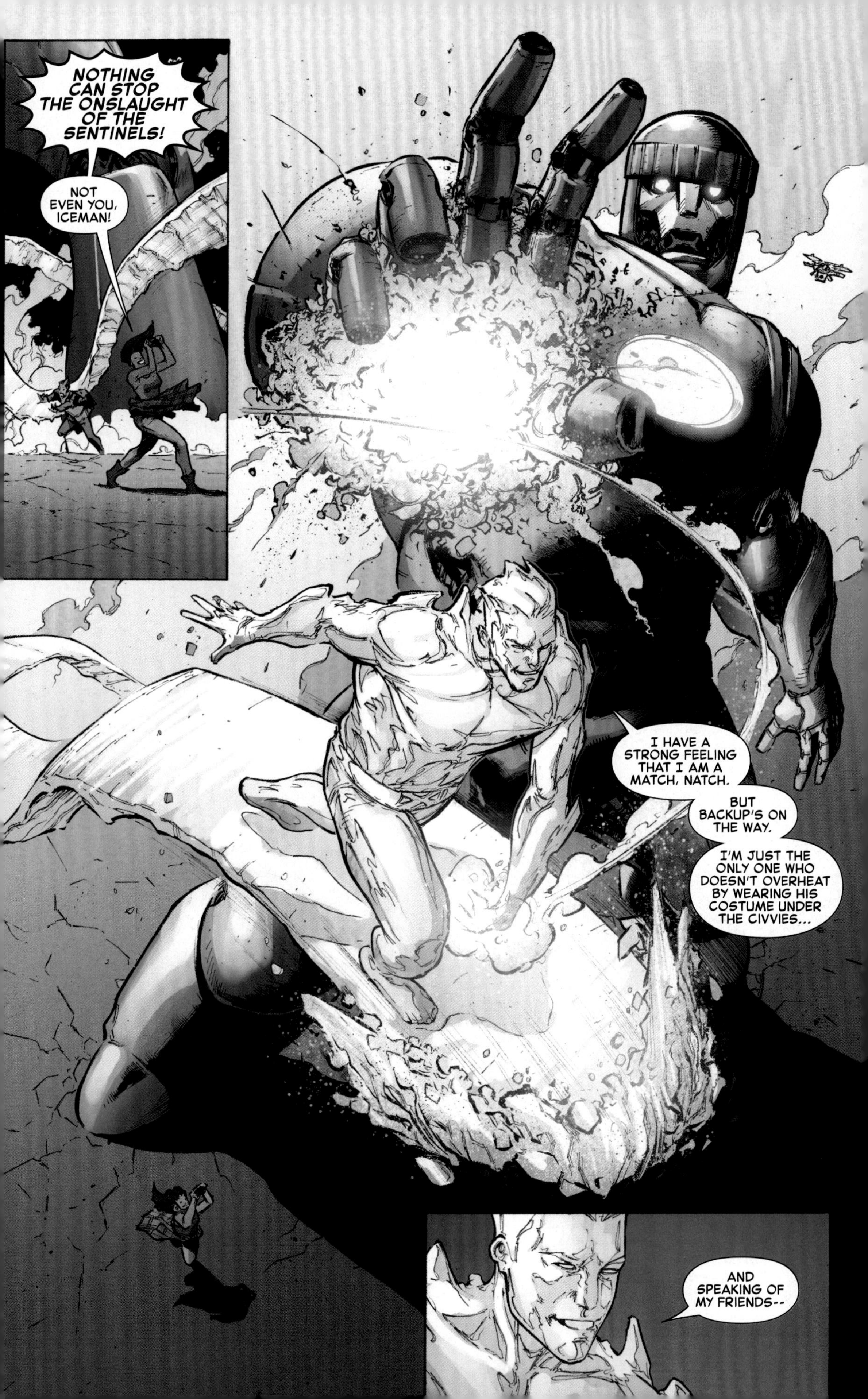

NOTHING CAN STOP THE ONSLAUGHT OF THE SENTINELS!
NOT EVEN YOU, ICEMAN!
I HAVE A STRONG FEELING THAT I AM A MATCH, NATCH.
BUT BACKUP'S ON THE WAY.
I'M JUST THE ONLY ONE WHO DOESN'T OVERHEAT BY WEARING HIS COSTUME UNDER THE CIVVIES...
AND SPEAKING OF MY FRIENDS--

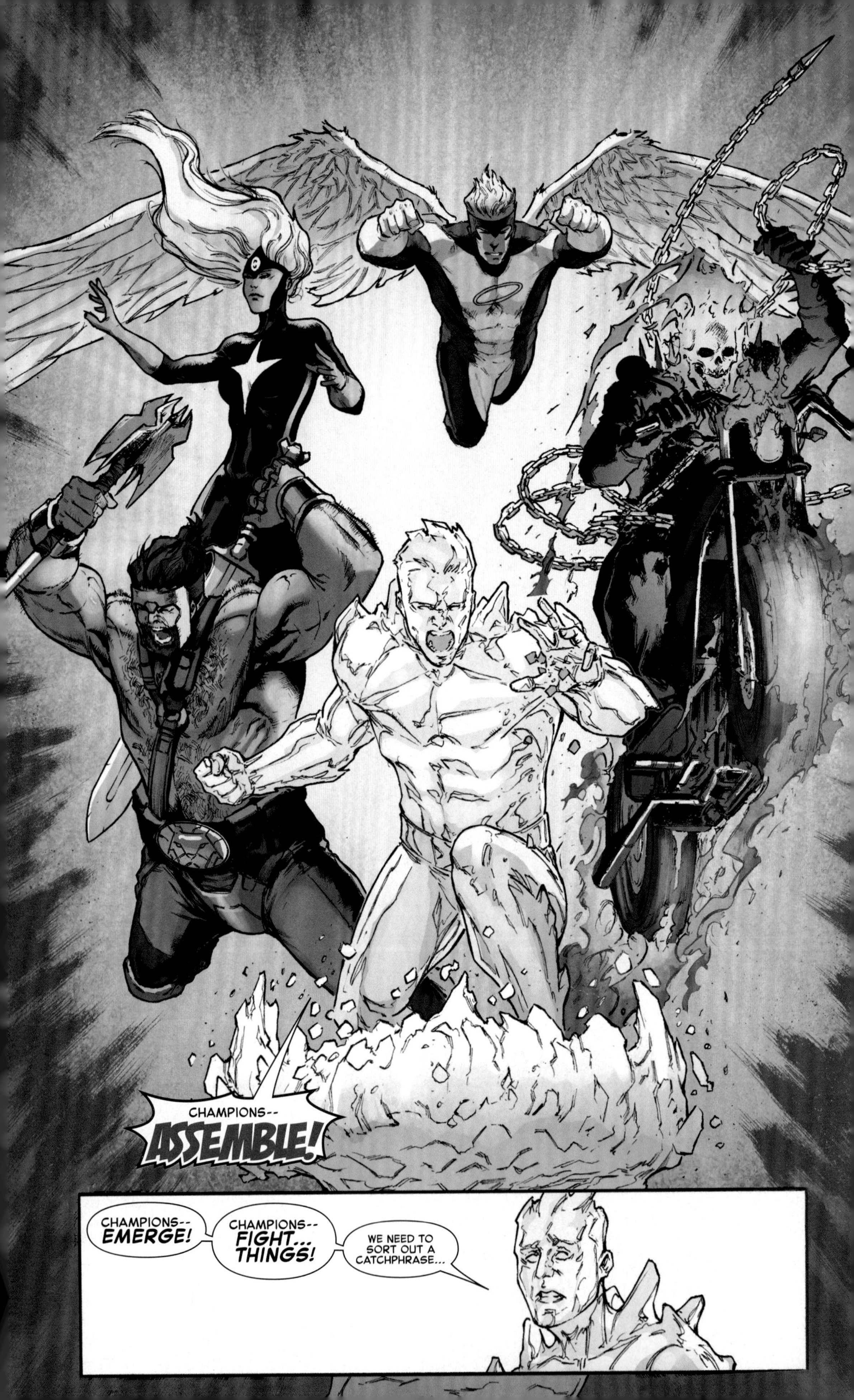
CHAMPIONS--
ASSEMBLE!
CHAMPIONS-- EMERGE!
CHAMPIONS-- FIGHT... THINGS!
WE NEED TO SORT OUT A CATCHPHRASE...

7

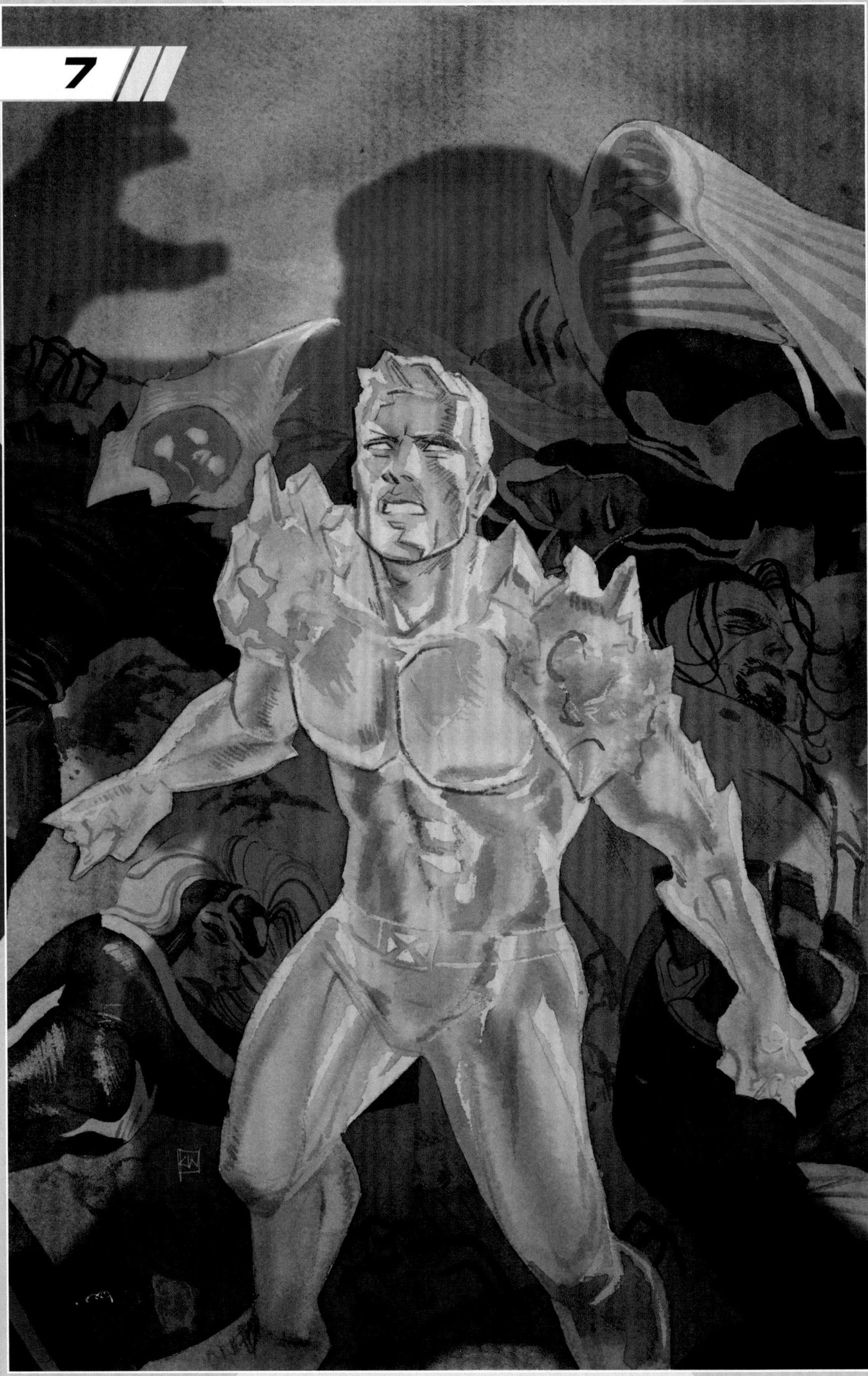

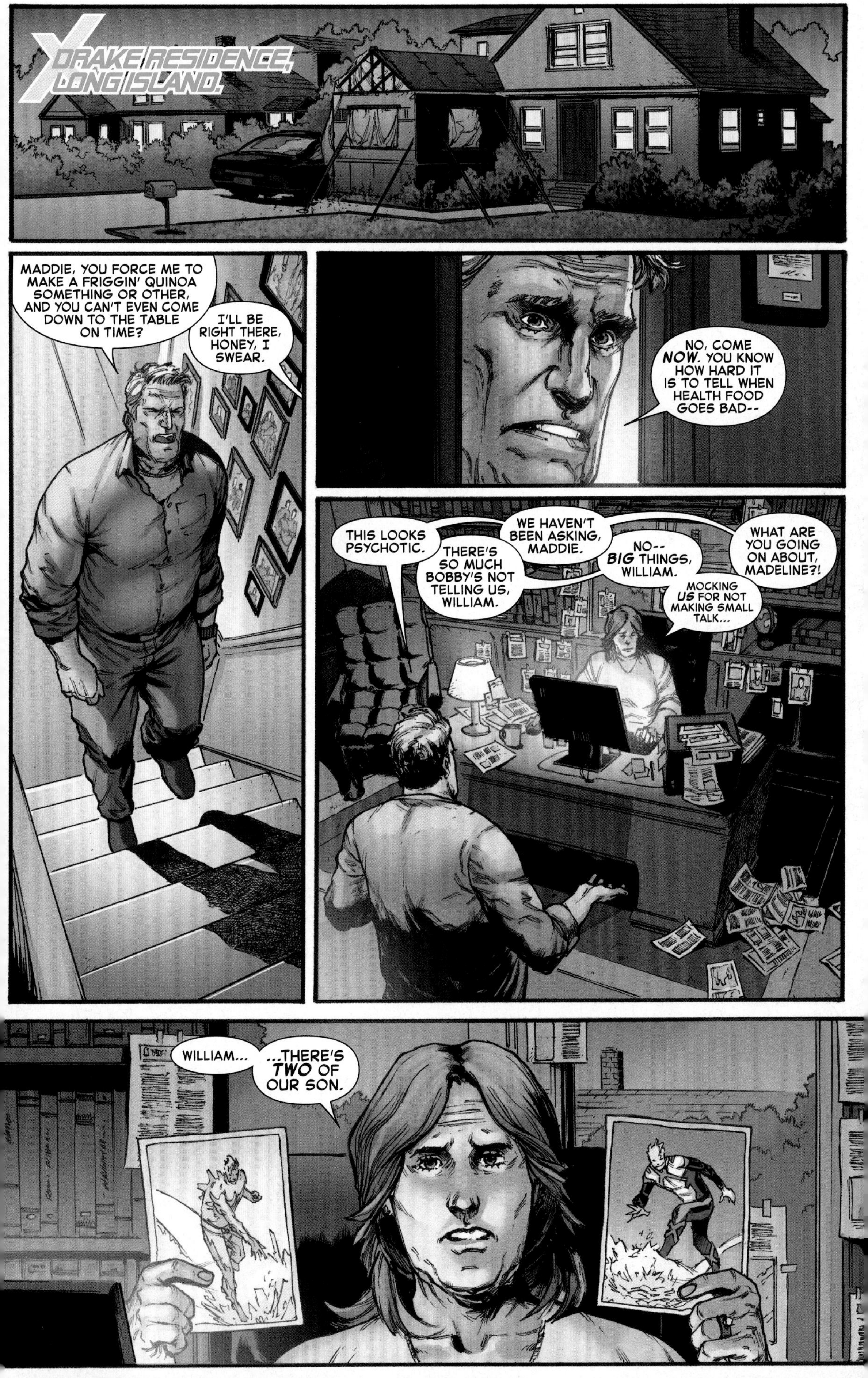
DRAKE RESIDENCE, LONG ISLAND.
MADDIE, YOU FORCE ME TO MAKE A FRIGGIN' QUINOA SOMETHING OR OTHER, AND YOU CAN'T EVEN COME DOWN TO THE TABLE ON TIME?
I'LL BE RIGHT THERE, HONEY, I SWEAR.
NO, COME NOW. YOU KNOW HOW HARD IT IS TO TELL WHEN HEALTH FOOD GOES BAD--
THIS LOOKS PSYCHOTIC.
THERE'S SO MUCH BOBBY'S NOT TELLING US, WILLIAM.
WE HAVEN'T BEEN ASKING, MADDIE.
NO-- BIG THINGS, WILLIAM.
WHAT ARE YOU GOING ON ABOUT, MADELINE?!
MOCKING US FOR NOT MAKING SMALL TALK...
WILLIAM...
...THERE'S TWO OF OUR SON.

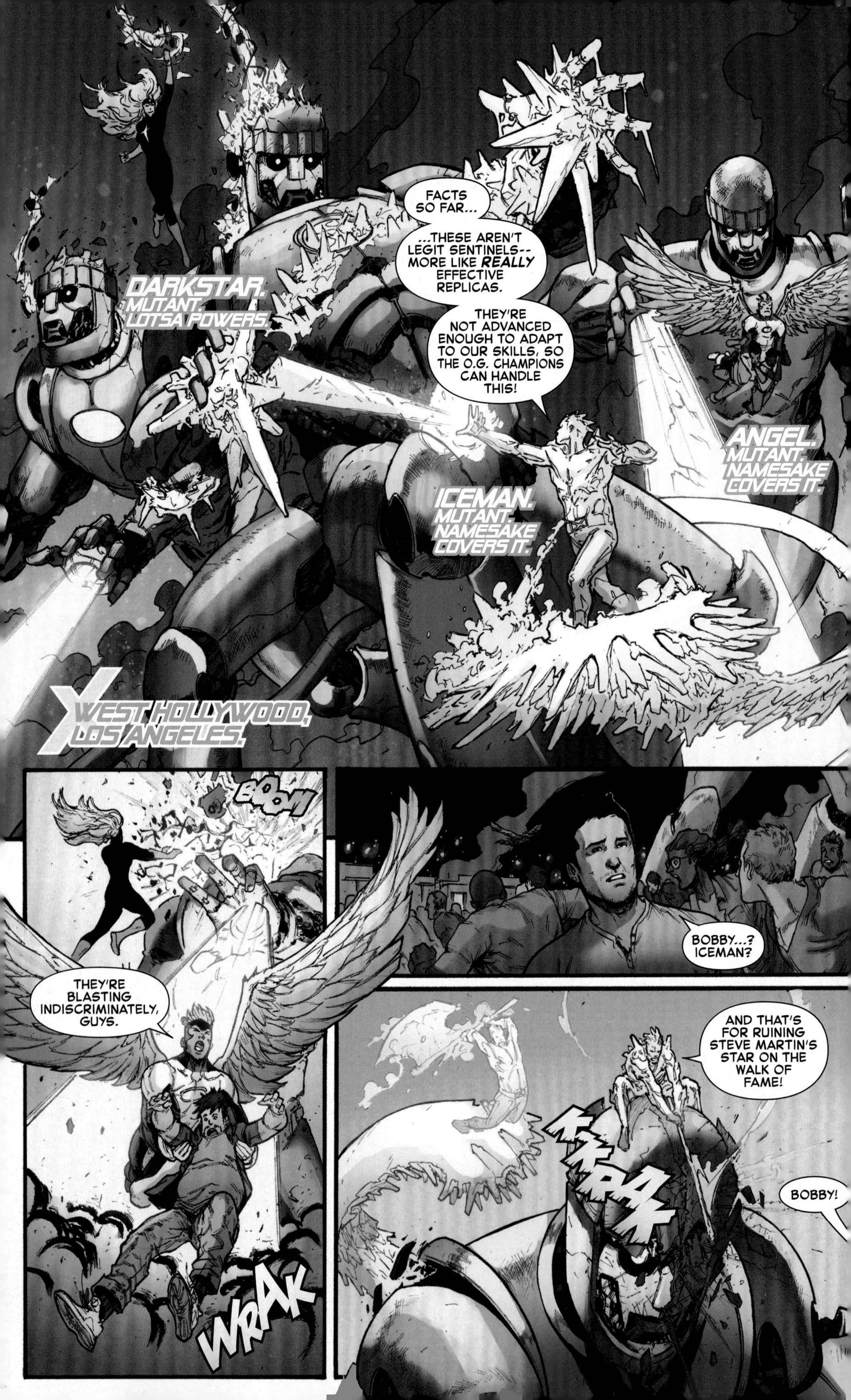
FACTS SO FAR...
...THESE AREN'T LEGIT SENTINELS--MORE LIKE REALLY EFFECTIVE REPLICAS.
THEY'RE NOT ADVANCED ENOUGH TO ADAPT TO OUR SKILLS, SO THE O.G. CHAMPIONS CAN HANDLE THIS!
DARKSTAR. MUTANT. LOTSA POWERS.
ICEMAN. MUTANT. NAMESAKE COVERS IT.
ANGEL. MUTANT. NAMESAKE COVERS IT.
WEST HOLLYWOOD, LOS ANGELES.
BOOM
THEY'RE BLASTING INDISCRIMINATELY, GUYS.
WRAK
BOBBY...? ICEMAN?
AND THAT'S FOR RUINING STEVE MARTIN'S STAR ON THE WALK OF FAME!
KRAK
BOBBY!

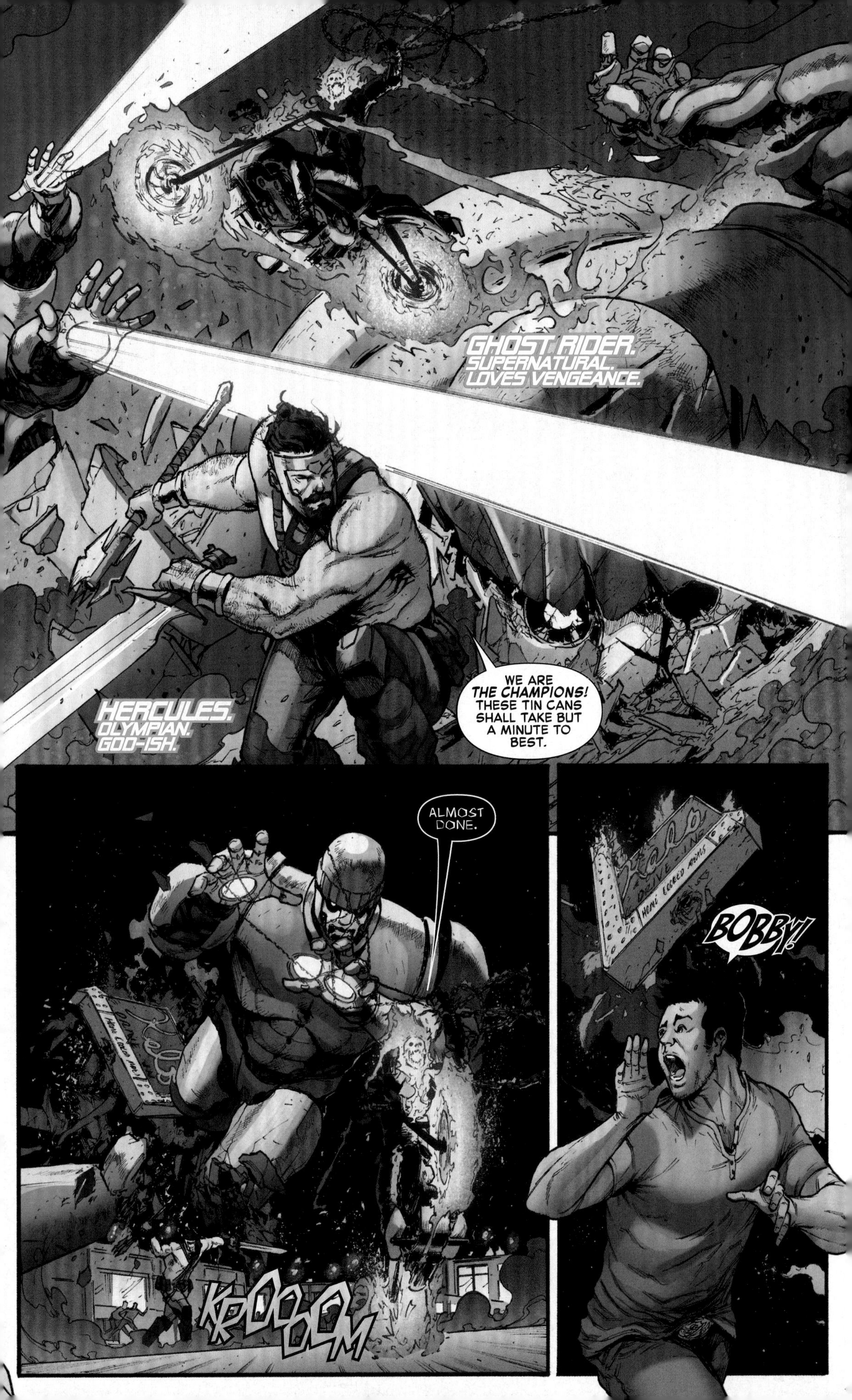
GHOST RIDER.
SUPERNATURAL.
LOVES VENGEANCE.
HERCULES.
OLYMPIAN.
GOD-ISH.
WE ARE THE CHAMPIONS! THESE TIN CANS SHALL TAKE BUT A MINUTE TO BEST.
ALMOST DONE.
KROOOOM
BOBBY!

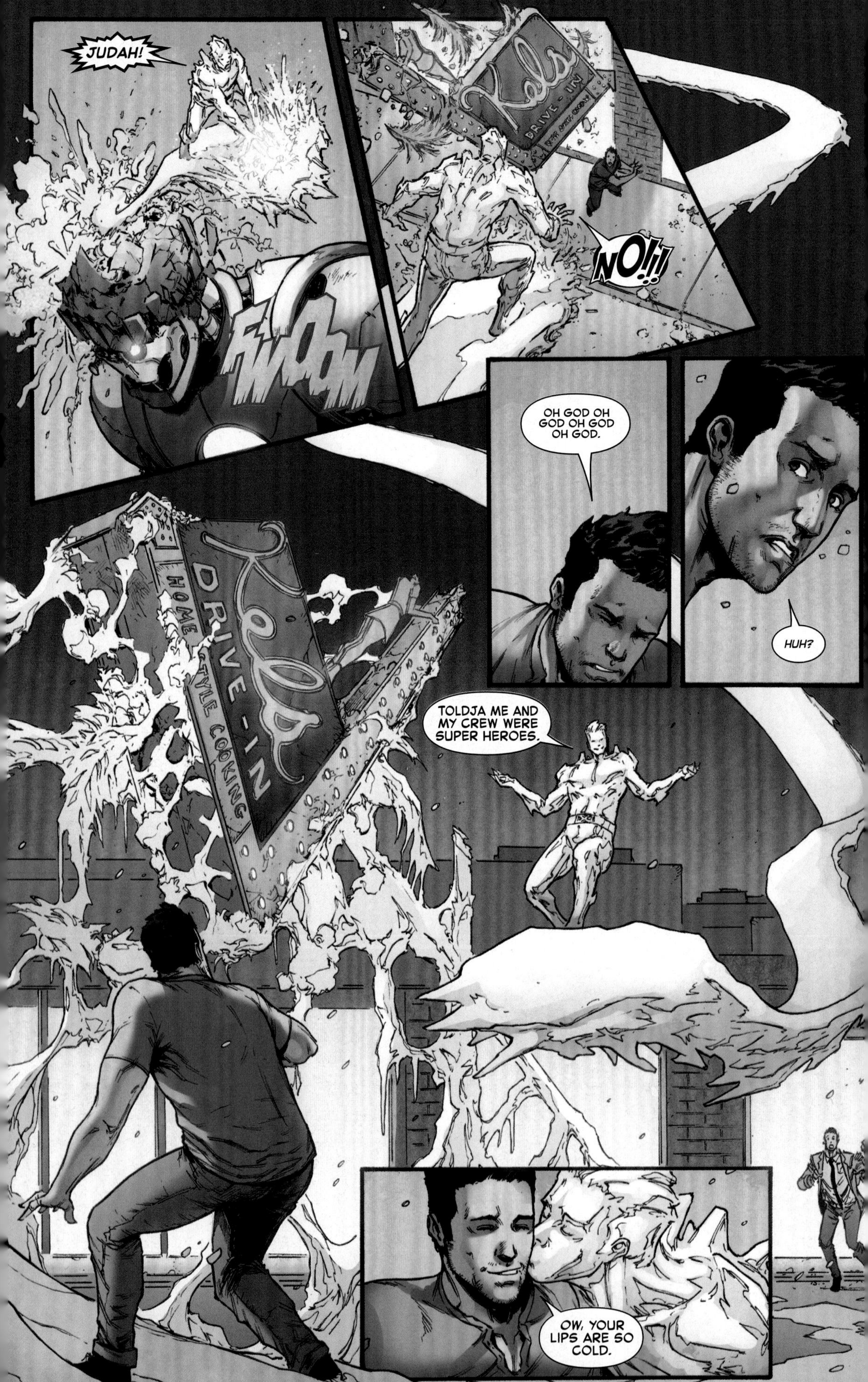
JUDAH!
FWOOM
NO!!!
OH GOD OH GOD OH GOD OH GOD.
HUH?
TOLDJA ME AND MY CREW WERE SUPER HEROES.
OW, YOUR LIPS ARE SO COLD.

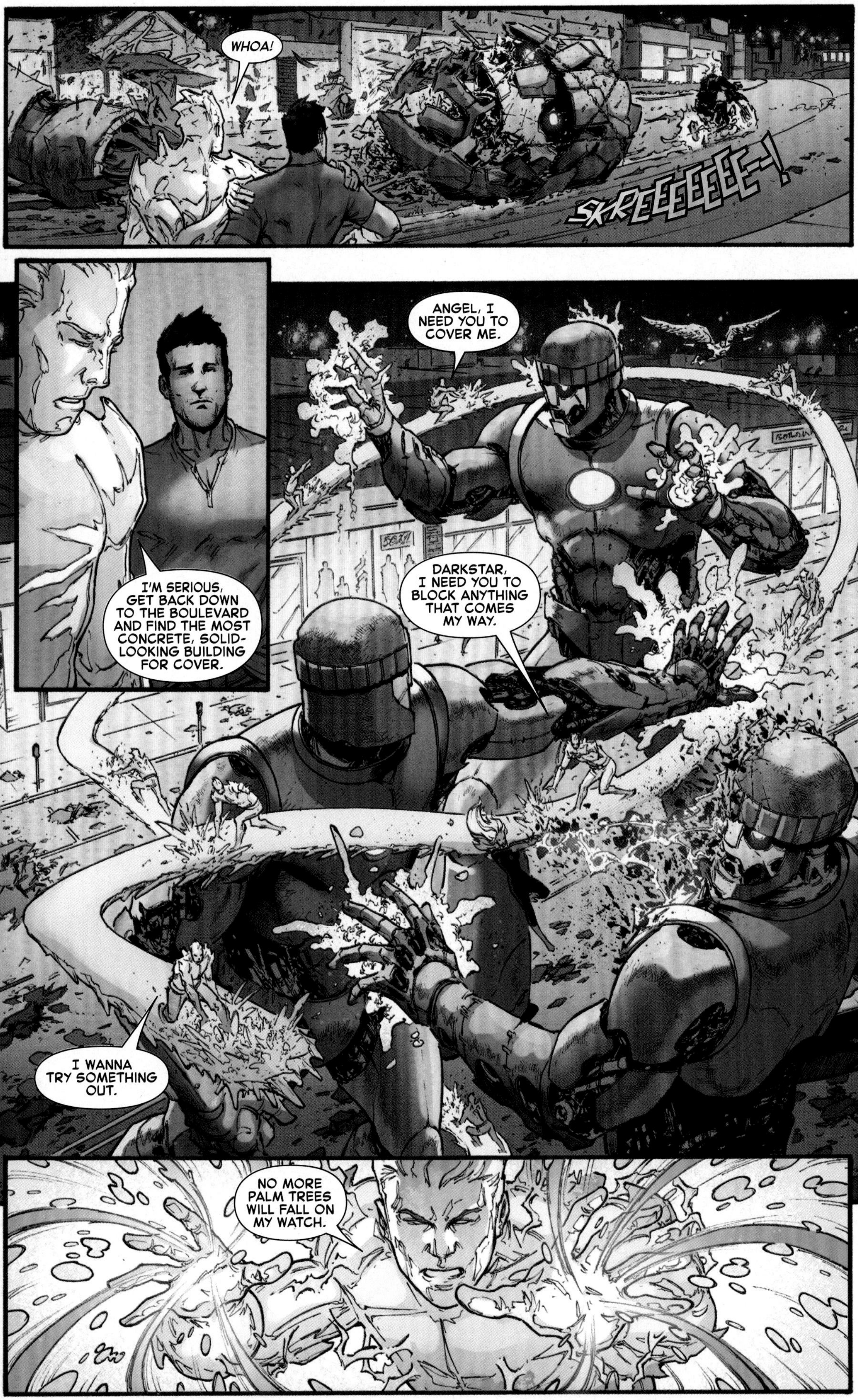
WHOA!
SKREEEEEEE--!
I'M SERIOUS, GET BACK DOWN TO THE BOULEVARD AND FIND THE MOST CONCRETE, SOLID-LOOKING BUILDING FOR COVER.
ANGEL, I NEED YOU TO COVER ME.
DARKSTAR, I NEED YOU TO BLOCK ANYTHING THAT COMES MY WAY.
I WANNA TRY SOMETHING OUT.
NO MORE PALM TREES WILL FALL ON MY WATCH.

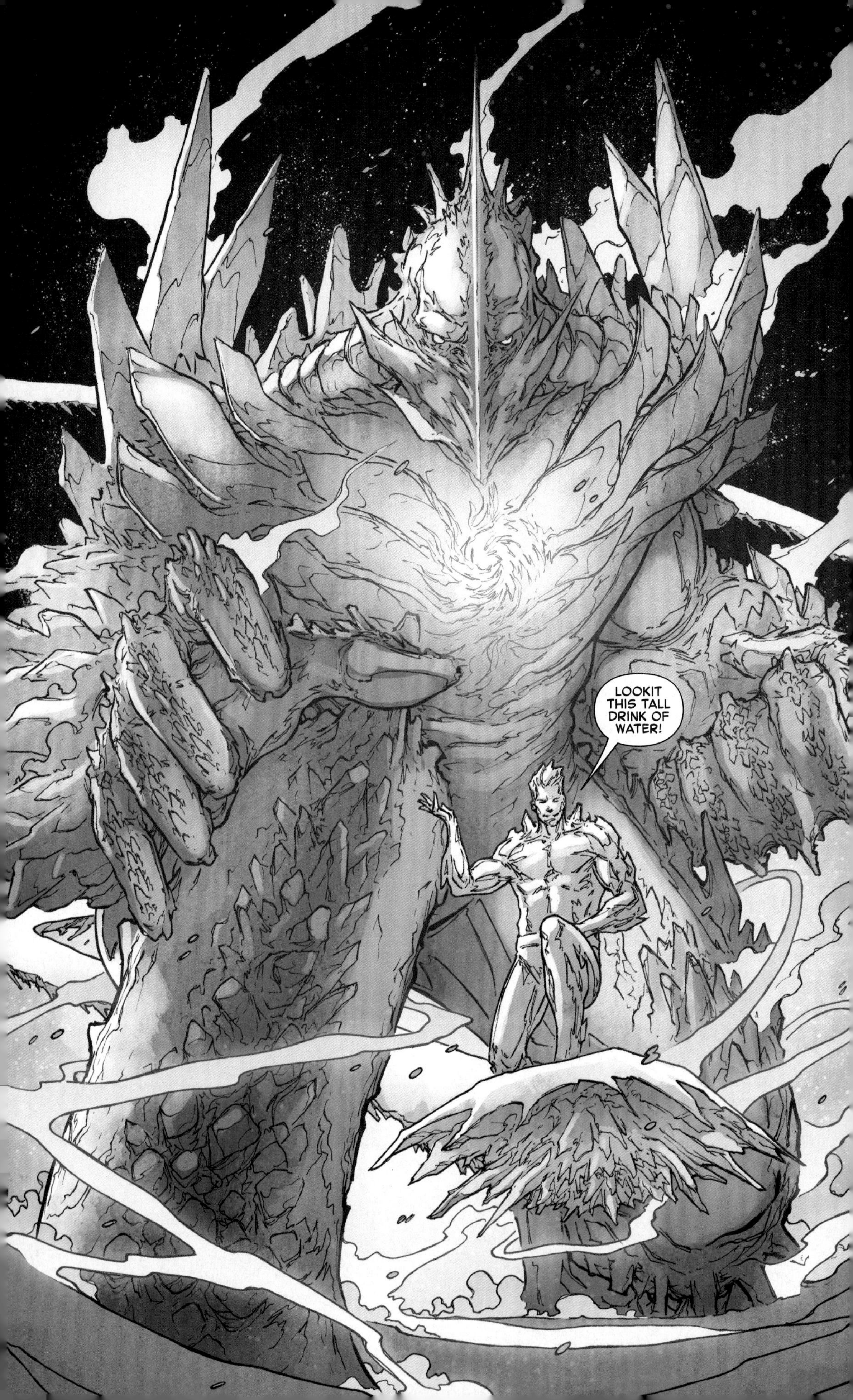
LOOKIT THIS TALL DRINK OF WATER!

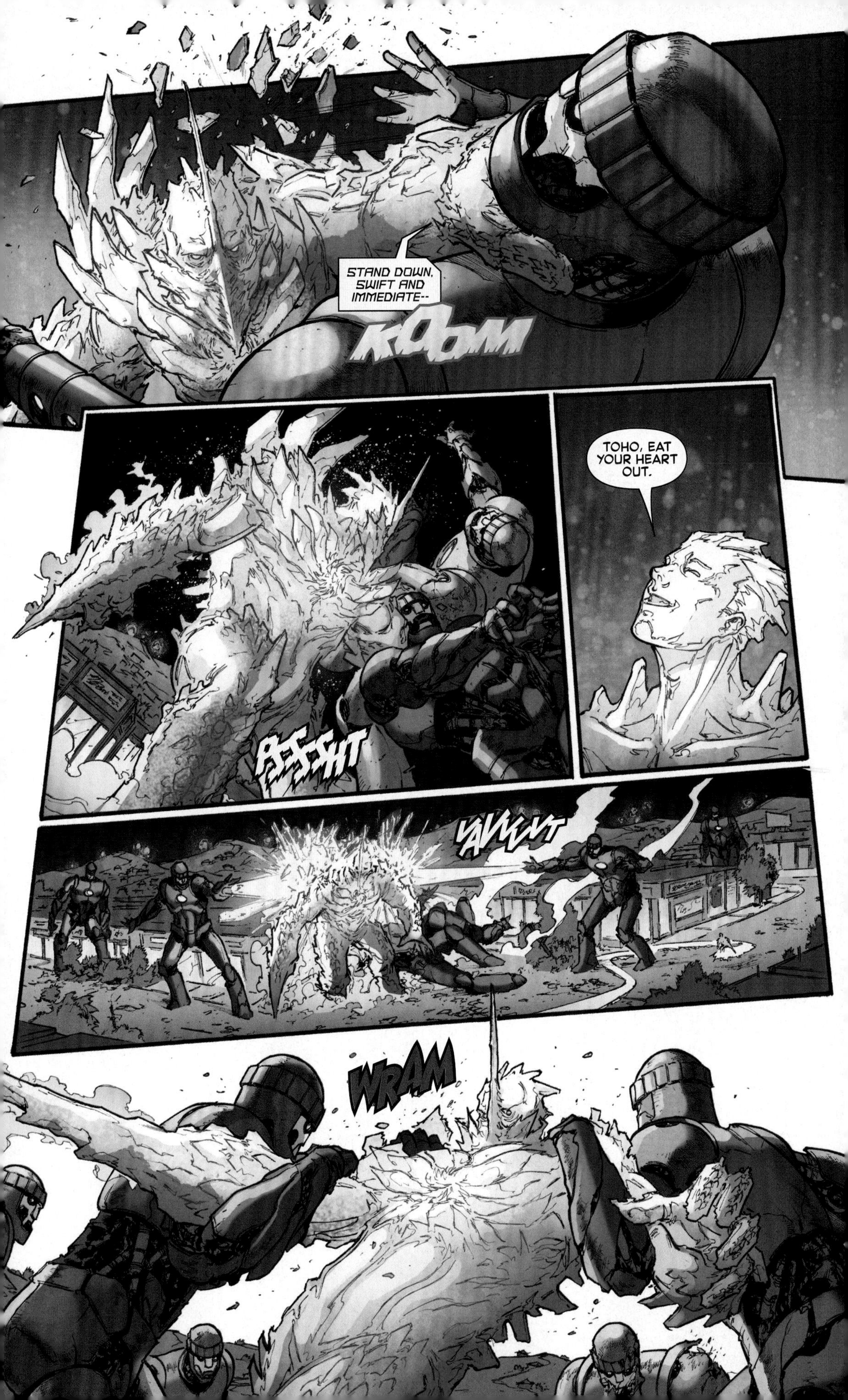
STAND DOWN, SWIFT AND IMMEDIATE--
KROOM
TOHO, EAT YOUR HEART OUT.
PFSSHT
VAVVVT
WRAM

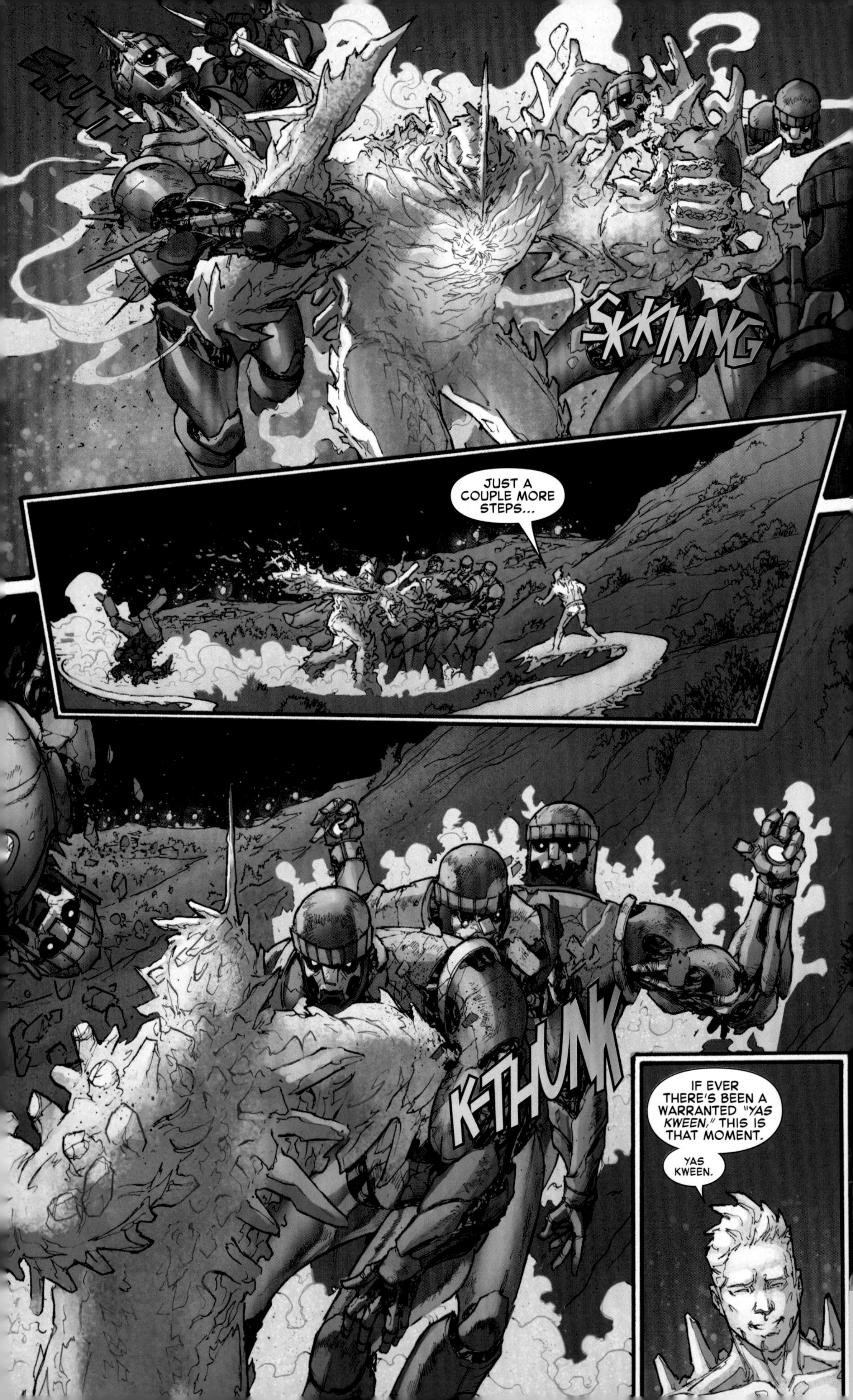
SHUNT
SKKINNG
JUST A COUPLE MORE STEPS...
K-THUNK
IF EVER THERE'S BEEN A WARRANTED *"YAS KWEEN,"* THIS IS THAT MOMENT.
YAS KWEEN.

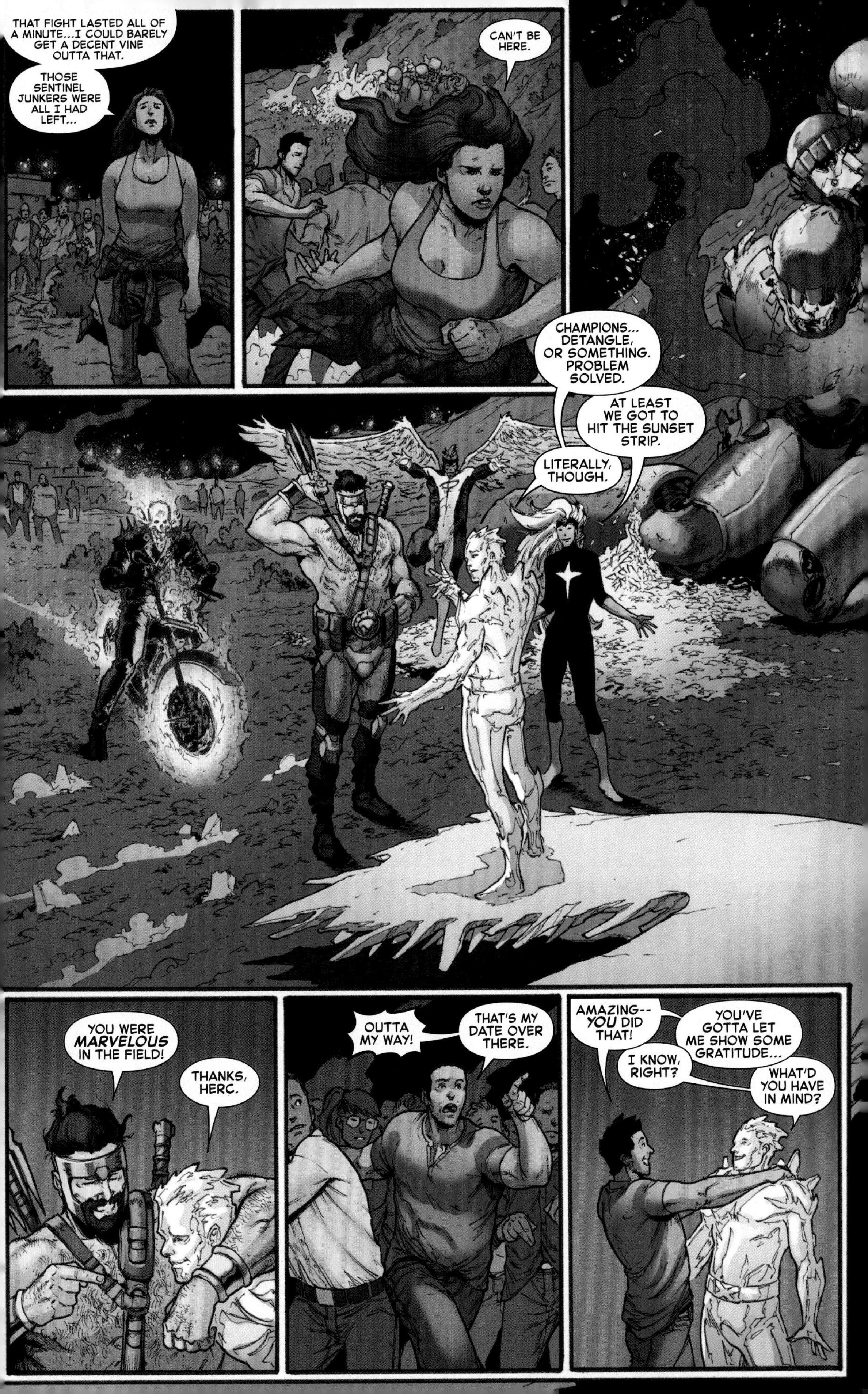
THAT FIGHT LASTED ALL OF A MINUTE...I COULD BARELY GET A DECENT VINE OUTTA THAT.
THOSE SENTINEL JUNKERS WERE ALL I HAD LEFT...
CAN'T BE HERE.
CHAMPIONS... DETANGLE, OR SOMETHING. PROBLEM SOLVED.
AT LEAST WE GOT TO HIT THE SUNSET STRIP.
LITERALLY, THOUGH.
YOU WERE MARVELOUS IN THE FIELD!
THANKS, HERC.
OUTTA MY WAY!
THAT'S MY DATE OVER THERE.
AMAZING-- YOU DID THAT!
YOU'VE GOTTA LET ME SHOW SOME GRATITUDE...
I KNOW, RIGHT?
WHAT'D YOU HAVE IN MIND?

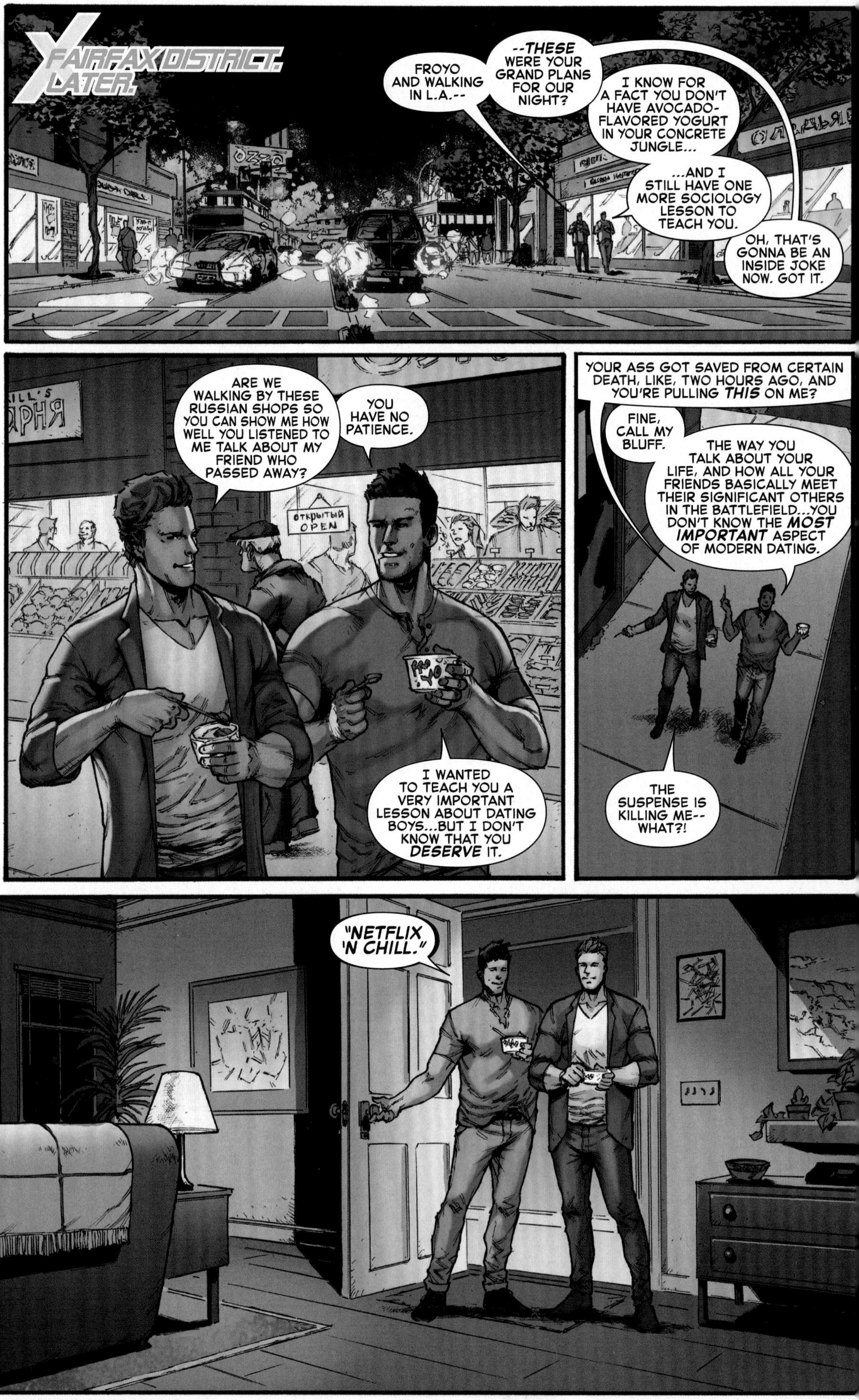
FAIRFAX DISTRICT. LATER.
FROYO AND WALKING IN L.A.--
--THESE WERE YOUR GRAND PLANS FOR OUR NIGHT?
I KNOW FOR A FACT YOU DON'T HAVE AVOCADO-FLAVORED YOGURT IN YOUR CONCRETE JUNGLE...
...AND I STILL HAVE ONE MORE SOCIOLOGY LESSON TO TEACH YOU.
OH, THAT'S GONNA BE AN INSIDE JOKE NOW. GOT IT.
ARE WE WALKING BY THESE RUSSIAN SHOPS SO YOU CAN SHOW ME HOW WELL YOU LISTENED TO ME TALK ABOUT MY FRIEND WHO PASSED AWAY?
YOU HAVE NO PATIENCE.
ОТКРЫТЫЙ OPEN
I WANTED TO TEACH YOU A VERY IMPORTANT LESSON ABOUT DATING BOYS...BUT I DON'T KNOW THAT YOU DESERVE IT.
YOUR ASS GOT SAVED FROM CERTAIN DEATH, LIKE, TWO HOURS AGO, AND YOU'RE PULLING THIS ON ME?
FINE, CALL MY BLUFF.
THE WAY YOU TALK ABOUT YOUR LIFE, AND HOW ALL YOUR FRIENDS BASICALLY MEET THEIR SIGNIFICANT OTHERS IN THE BATTLEFIELD...YOU DON'T KNOW THE MOST IMPORTANT ASPECT OF MODERN DATING.
THE SUSPENSE IS KILLING ME--WHAT?!
"NETFLIX 'N CHILL."

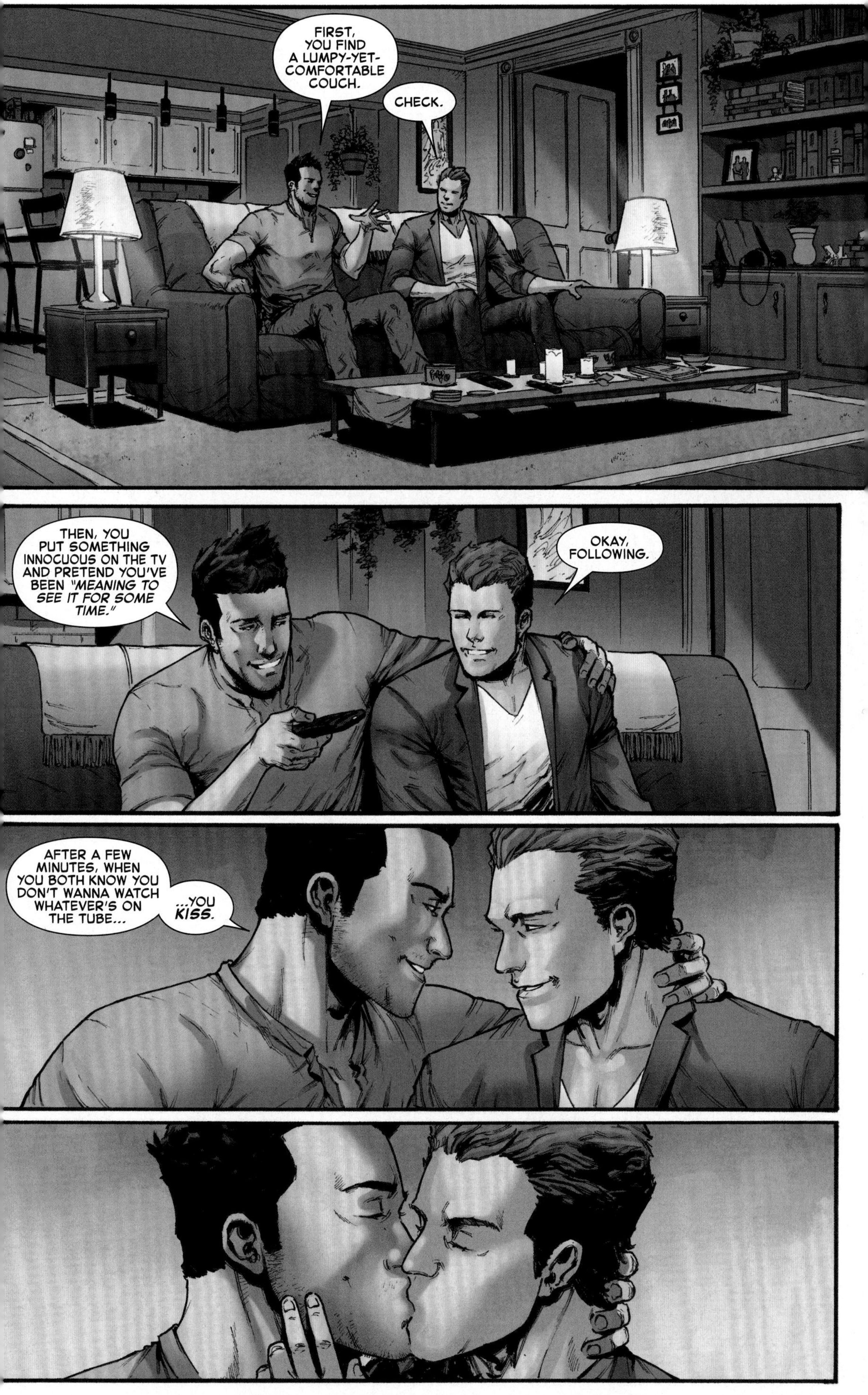
FIRST, YOU FIND A LUMPY-YET-COMFORTABLE COUCH.
CHECK.
THEN, YOU PUT SOMETHING INNOCUOUS ON THE TV AND PRETEND YOU'VE BEEN *"MEANING TO SEE IT FOR SOME TIME."*
OKAY, FOLLOWING.
AFTER A FEW MINUTES, WHEN YOU BOTH KNOW YOU DON'T WANNA WATCH WHATEVER'S ON THE TUBE...
...YOU ***KISS.***

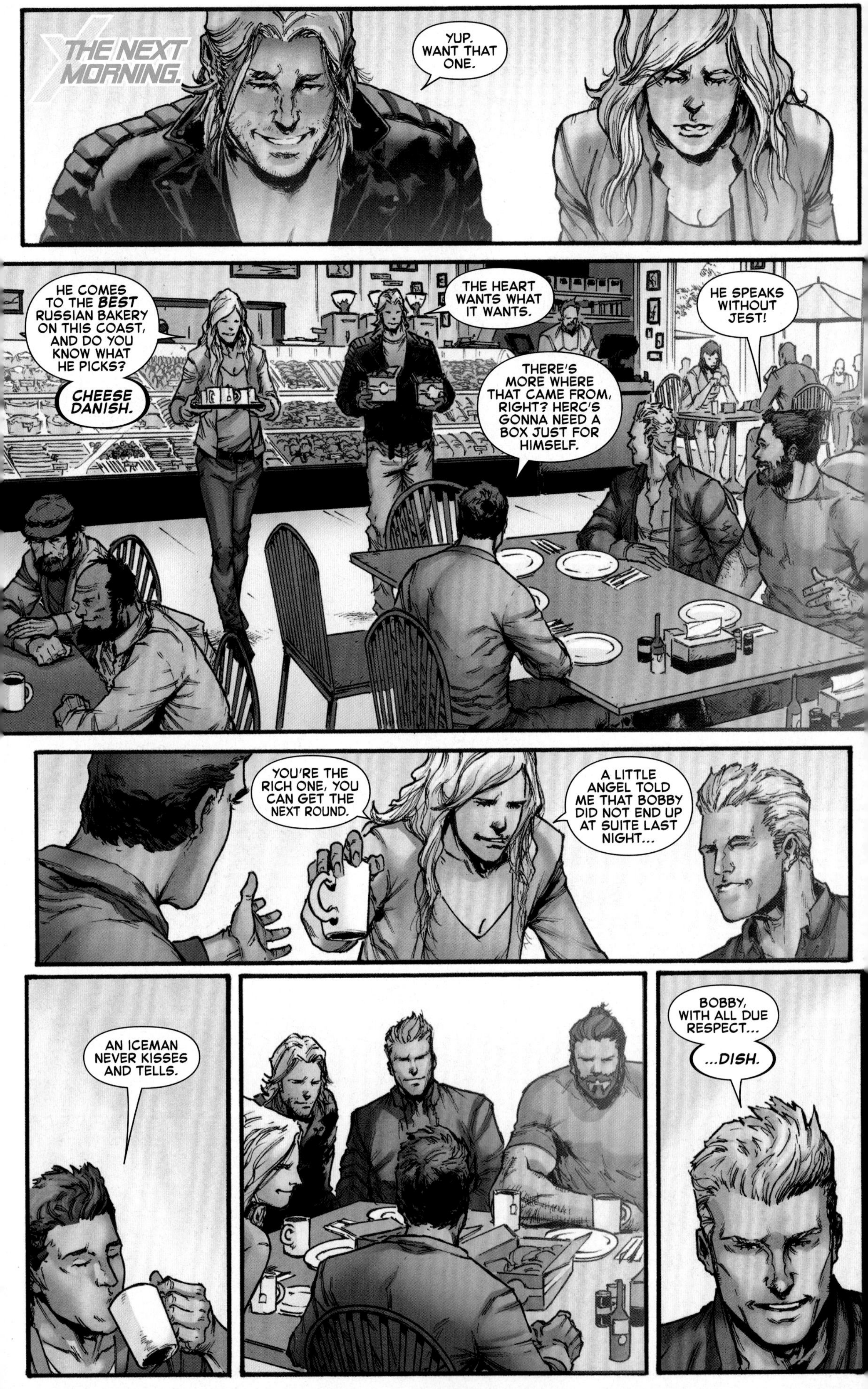
THE NEXT MORNING.
YUP. WANT THAT ONE.
HE COMES TO THE BEST RUSSIAN BAKERY ON THIS COAST, AND DO YOU KNOW WHAT HE PICKS?
CHEESE DANISH.
THE HEART WANTS WHAT IT WANTS.
THERE'S MORE WHERE THAT CAME FROM, RIGHT? HERC'S GONNA NEED A BOX JUST FOR HIMSELF.
HE SPEAKS WITHOUT JEST!
YOU'RE THE RICH ONE, YOU CAN GET THE NEXT ROUND.
A LITTLE ANGEL TOLD ME THAT BOBBY DID NOT END UP AT SUITE LAST NIGHT...
AN ICEMAN NEVER KISSES AND TELLS.
BOBBY, WITH ALL DUE RESPECT...
...DISH.

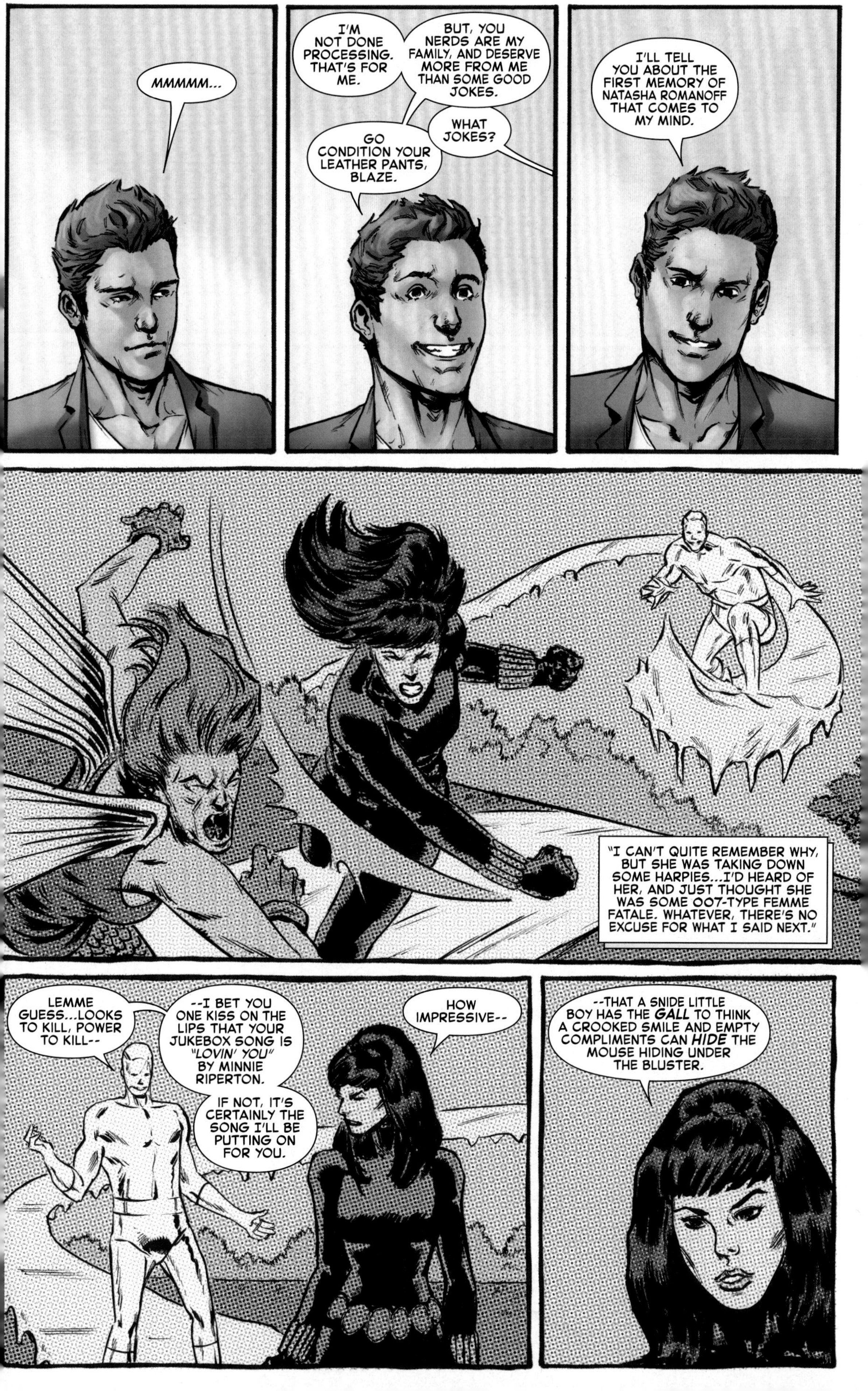
MMMMM...
I'M NOT DONE PROCESSING. THAT'S FOR ME.
BUT, YOU NERDS ARE MY FAMILY, AND DESERVE MORE FROM ME THAN SOME GOOD JOKES.
GO CONDITION YOUR LEATHER PANTS, BLAZE.
WHAT JOKES?
I'LL TELL YOU ABOUT THE FIRST MEMORY OF NATASHA ROMANOFF THAT COMES TO MY MIND.
"I CAN'T QUITE REMEMBER WHY, BUT SHE WAS TAKING DOWN SOME HARPIES...I'D HEARD OF HER, AND JUST THOUGHT SHE WAS SOME 007-TYPE FEMME FATALE. WHATEVER, THERE'S NO EXCUSE FOR WHAT I SAID NEXT."
LEMME GUESS...LOOKS TO KILL, POWER TO KILL--
--I BET YOU ONE KISS ON THE LIPS THAT YOUR JUKEBOX SONG IS *"LOVIN' YOU"* BY MINNIE RIPERTON.
IF NOT, IT'S CERTAINLY THE SONG I'LL BE PUTTING ON FOR YOU.
HOW IMPRESSIVE--
--THAT A SNIDE LITTLE BOY HAS THE ***GALL*** TO THINK A CROOKED SMILE AND EMPTY COMPLIMENTS CAN ***HIDE*** THE MOUSE HIDING UNDER THE BLUSTER.

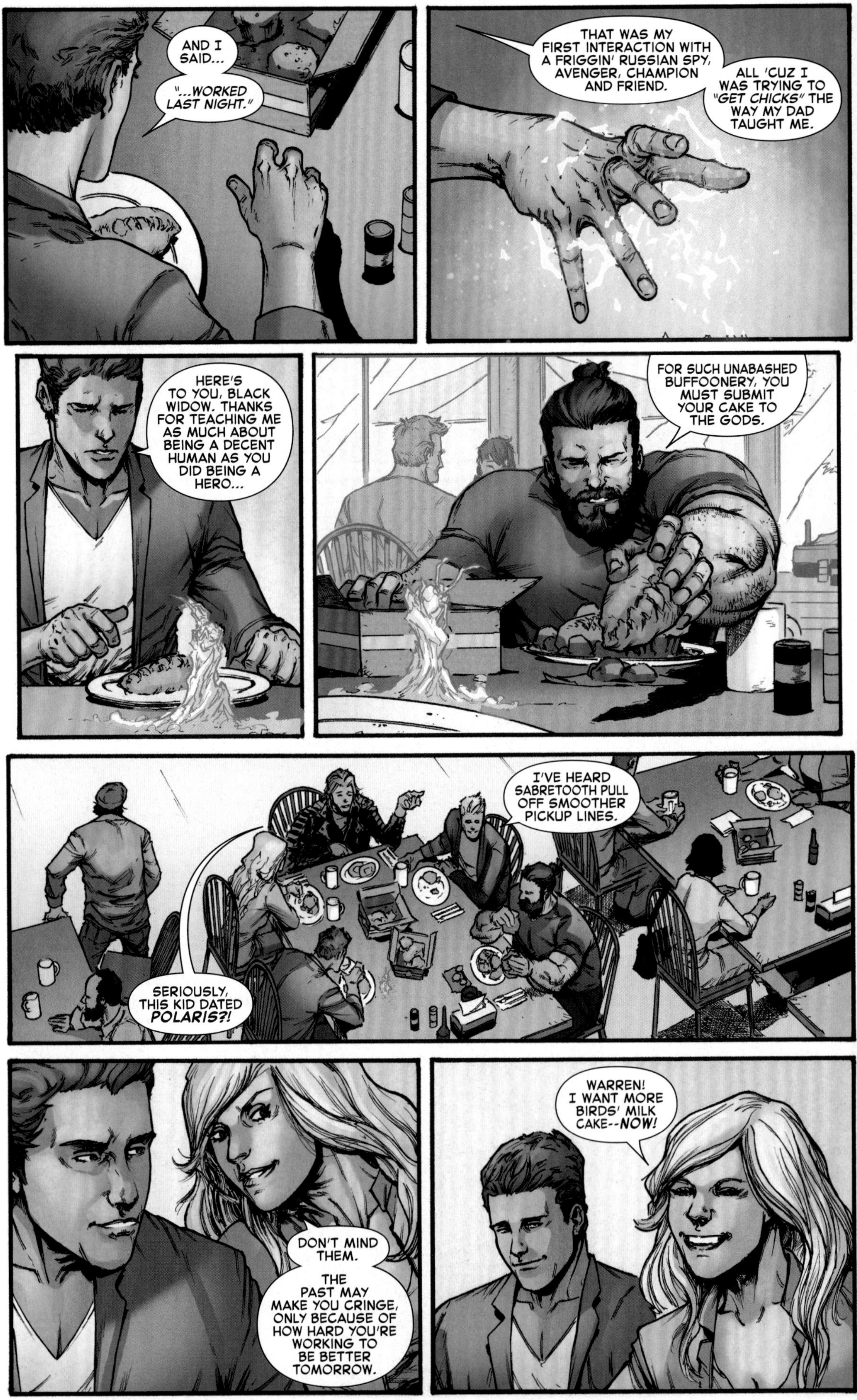

AND I SAID...
"...WORKED LAST NIGHT."
THAT WAS MY FIRST INTERACTION WITH A FRIGGIN' RUSSIAN SPY, AVENGER, CHAMPION AND FRIEND.
ALL 'CUZ I WAS TRYING TO "GET CHICKS" THE WAY MY DAD TAUGHT ME.
HERE'S TO YOU, BLACK WIDOW. THANKS FOR TEACHING ME AS MUCH ABOUT BEING A DECENT HUMAN AS YOU DID BEING A HERO...
FOR SUCH UNABASHED BUFFOONERY, YOU MUST SUBMIT YOUR CAKE TO THE GODS.
I'VE HEARD SABRETOOTH PULL OFF SMOOTHER PICKUP LINES.
SERIOUSLY, THIS KID DATED *POLARIS?!*
DON'T MIND THEM.
THE PAST MAY MAKE YOU CRINGE, ONLY BECAUSE OF HOW HARD YOU'RE WORKING TO BE BETTER TOMORROW.
WARREN! I WANT MORE BIRDS' MILK CAKE--*NOW!*

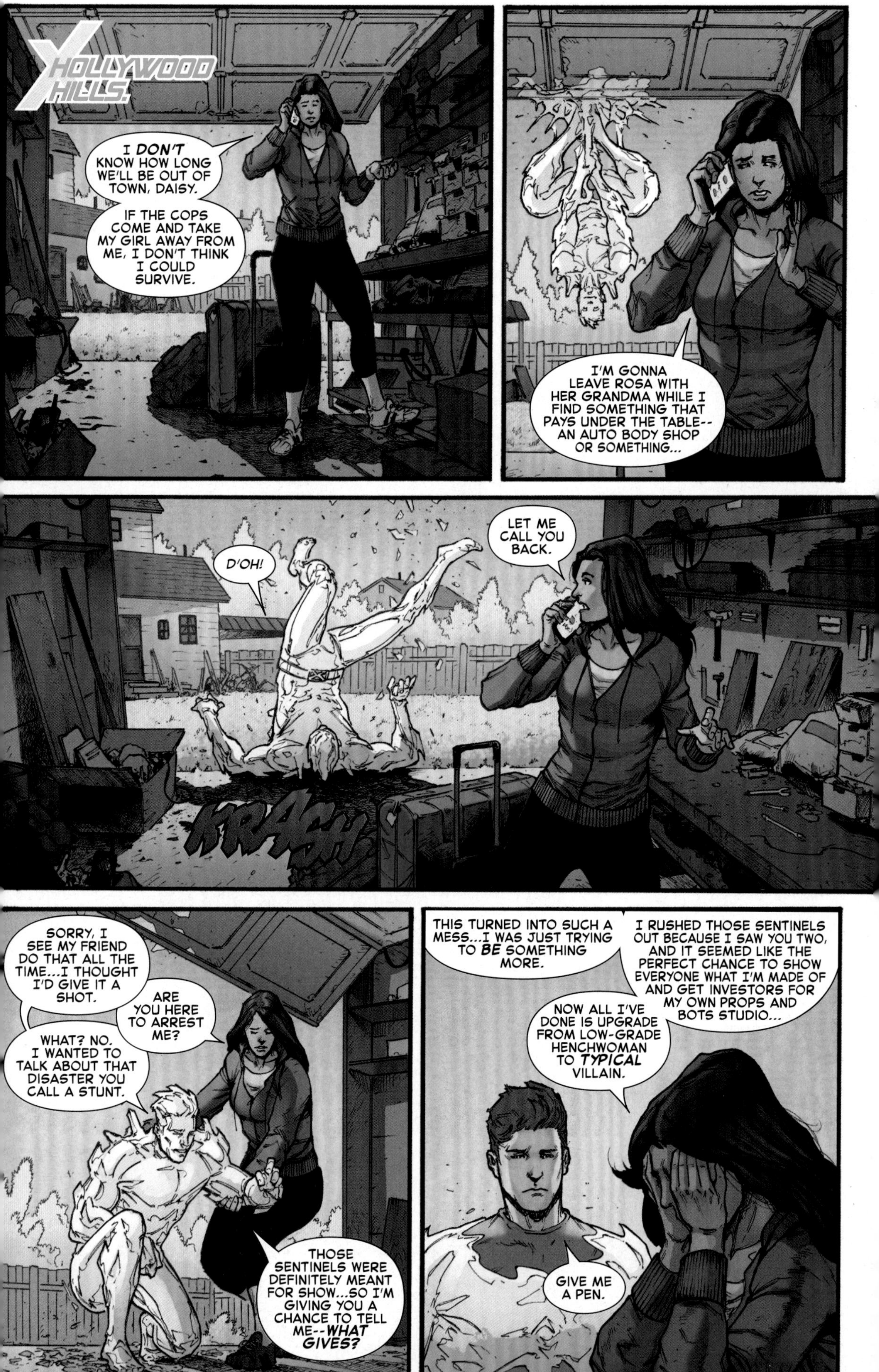
HOLLYWOOD HILLS.
I DON'T KNOW HOW LONG WE'LL BE OUT OF TOWN, DAISY.
IF THE COPS COME AND TAKE MY GIRL AWAY FROM ME, I DON'T THINK I COULD SURVIVE.
I'M GONNA LEAVE ROSA WITH HER GRANDMA WHILE I FIND SOMETHING THAT PAYS UNDER THE TABLE--AN AUTO BODY SHOP OR SOMETHING...
D'OH!
LET ME CALL YOU BACK.
KRASH
SORRY, I SEE MY FRIEND DO THAT ALL THE TIME...I THOUGHT I'D GIVE IT A SHOT.
ARE YOU HERE TO ARREST ME?
WHAT? NO. I WANTED TO TALK ABOUT THAT DISASTER YOU CALL A STUNT.
THOSE SENTINELS WERE DEFINITELY MEANT FOR SHOW...SO I'M GIVING YOU A CHANCE TO TELL ME--WHAT GIVES?
THIS TURNED INTO SUCH A MESS...I WAS JUST TRYING TO BE SOMETHING MORE.
I RUSHED THOSE SENTINELS OUT BECAUSE I SAW YOU TWO, AND IT SEEMED LIKE THE PERFECT CHANCE TO SHOW EVERYONE WHAT I'M MADE OF AND GET INVESTORS FOR MY OWN PROPS AND BOTS STUDIO...
NOW ALL I'VE DONE IS UPGRADE FROM LOW-GRADE HENCHWOMAN TO TYPICAL VILLAIN.
GIVE ME A PEN.

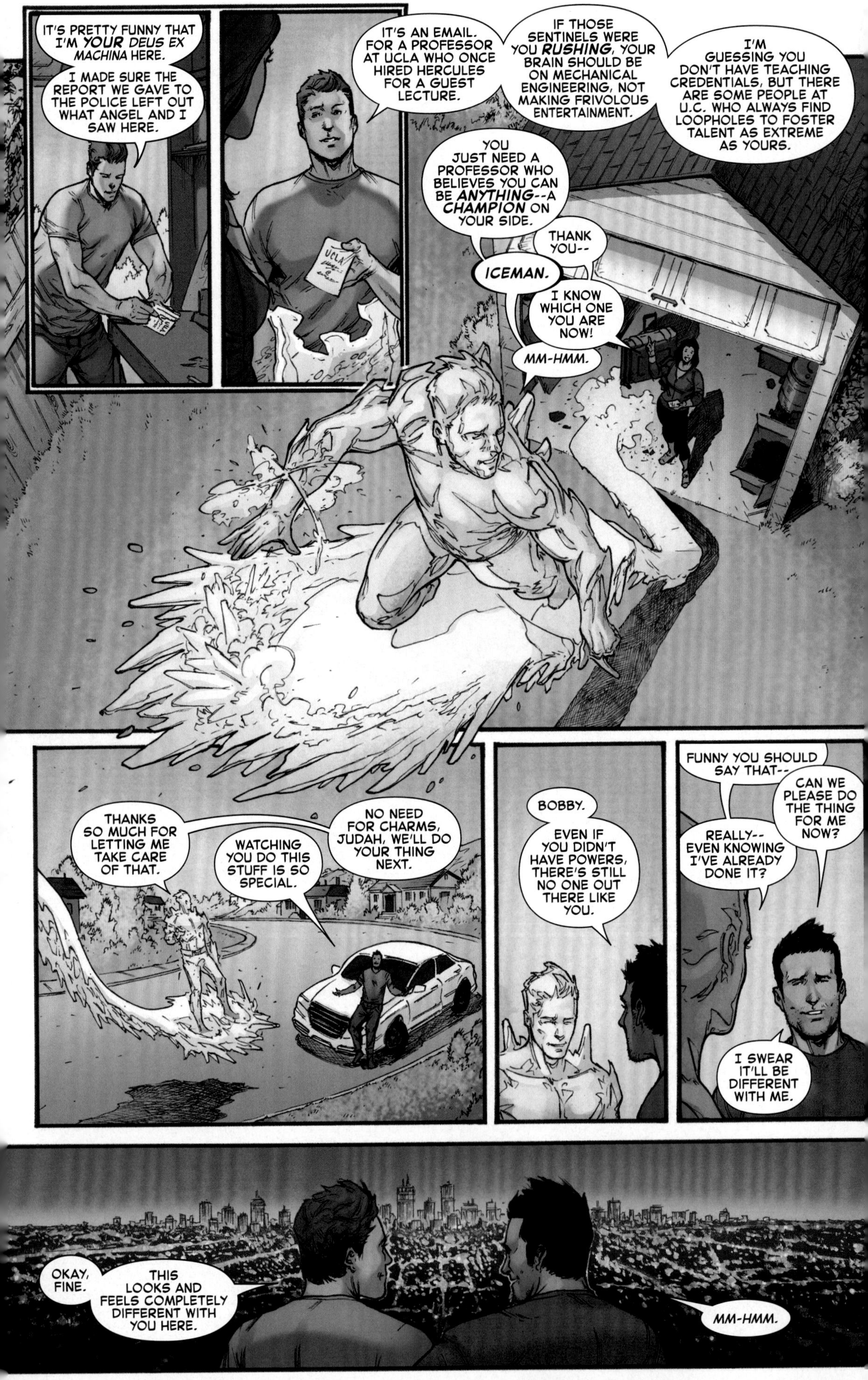

IT'S PRETTY FUNNY THAT I'M *YOUR* *DEUS EX MACHINA* HERE.
I MADE SURE THE REPORT WE GAVE TO THE POLICE LEFT OUT WHAT ANGEL AND I SAW HERE.
IT'S AN EMAIL. FOR A PROFESSOR AT UCLA WHO ONCE HIRED HERCULES FOR A GUEST LECTURE.
IF THOSE SENTINELS WERE YOU *RUSHING*, YOUR BRAIN SHOULD BE ON MECHANICAL ENGINEERING, NOT MAKING FRIVOLOUS ENTERTAINMENT.
I'M GUESSING YOU DON'T HAVE TEACHING CREDENTIALS, BUT THERE ARE SOME PEOPLE AT U.C. WHO ALWAYS FIND LOOPHOLES TO FOSTER TALENT AS EXTREME AS YOURS.
YOU JUST NEED A PROFESSOR WHO BELIEVES YOU CAN BE *ANYTHING*--A *CHAMPION* ON YOUR SIDE.
THANK YOU--
ICEMAN.
I KNOW WHICH ONE YOU ARE NOW!
MM-HMM.
THANKS SO MUCH FOR LETTING ME TAKE CARE OF THAT.
WATCHING YOU DO THIS STUFF IS SO SPECIAL.
NO NEED FOR CHARMS, JUDAH, WE'LL DO YOUR THING NEXT.
BOBBY.
EVEN IF YOU DIDN'T HAVE POWERS, THERE'S STILL NO ONE OUT THERE LIKE YOU.
FUNNY YOU SHOULD SAY THAT--
REALLY-- EVEN KNOWING I'VE ALREADY DONE IT?
CAN WE PLEASE DO THE THING FOR ME NOW?
I SWEAR IT'LL BE DIFFERENT WITH ME.
OKAY, FINE.
THIS LOOKS AND FEELS COMPLETELY DIFFERENT WITH YOU HERE.
MM-HMM.

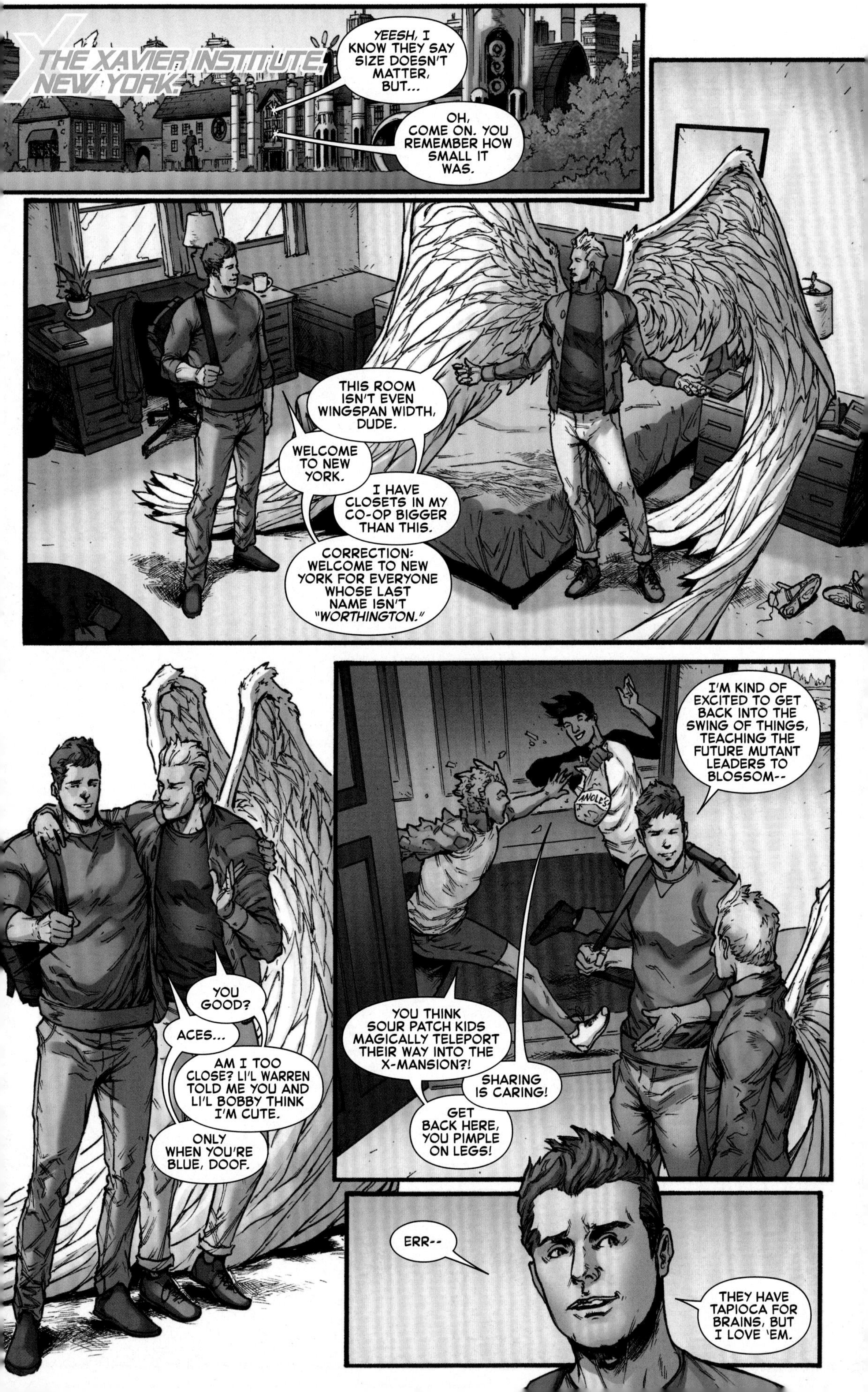
THE XAVIER INSTITUTE, NEW YORK.
YEESH, I KNOW THEY SAY SIZE DOESN'T MATTER, BUT...
OH, COME ON. YOU REMEMBER HOW SMALL IT WAS.
THIS ROOM ISN'T EVEN WINGSPAN WIDTH, DUDE.
WELCOME TO NEW YORK.
I HAVE CLOSETS IN MY CO-OP BIGGER THAN THIS.
CORRECTION: WELCOME TO NEW YORK FOR EVERYONE WHOSE LAST NAME ISN'T "WORTHINGTON."
YOU GOOD?
ACES...
AM I TOO CLOSE? LI'L WARREN TOLD ME YOU AND LI'L BOBBY THINK I'M CUTE.
ONLY WHEN YOU'RE BLUE, DOOF.
I'M KIND OF EXCITED TO GET BACK INTO THE SWING OF THINGS, TEACHING THE FUTURE MUTANT LEADERS TO BLOSSOM--
ANOLE'S
YOU THINK SOUR PATCH KIDS MAGICALLY TELEPORT THEIR WAY INTO THE X-MANSION?!
SHARING IS CARING!
GET BACK HERE, YOU PIMPLE ON LEGS!
ERR--
THEY HAVE TAPIOCA FOR BRAINS, BUT I LOVE 'EM.

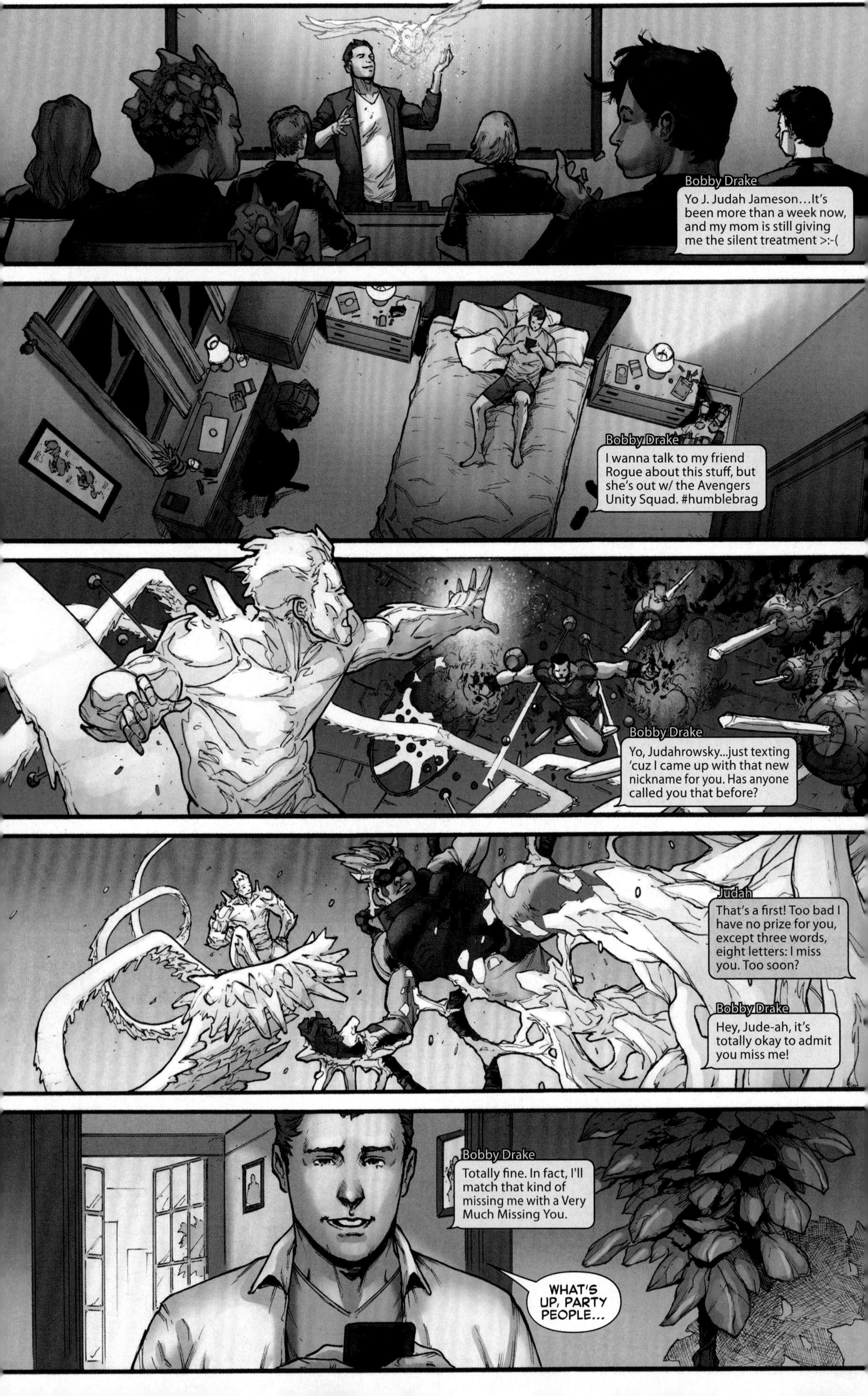
Bobby Drake
Yo J. Judah Jameson…It's been more than a week now, and my mom is still giving me the silent treatment >:-(
Bobby Drake
I wanna talk to my friend Rogue about this stuff, but she's out w/ the Avengers Unity Squad. #humblebrag
Bobby Drake
Yo, Judahrowsky…just texting 'cuz I came up with that new nickname for you. Has anyone called you that before?
Judah
That's a first! Too bad I have no prize for you, except three words, eight letters: I miss you. Too soon?
Bobby Drake
Hey, Jude-ah, it's totally okay to admit you miss me!
Bobby Drake
Totally fine. In fact, I'll match that kind of missing me with a Very Much Missing You.
WHAT'S UP, PARTY PEOPLE…

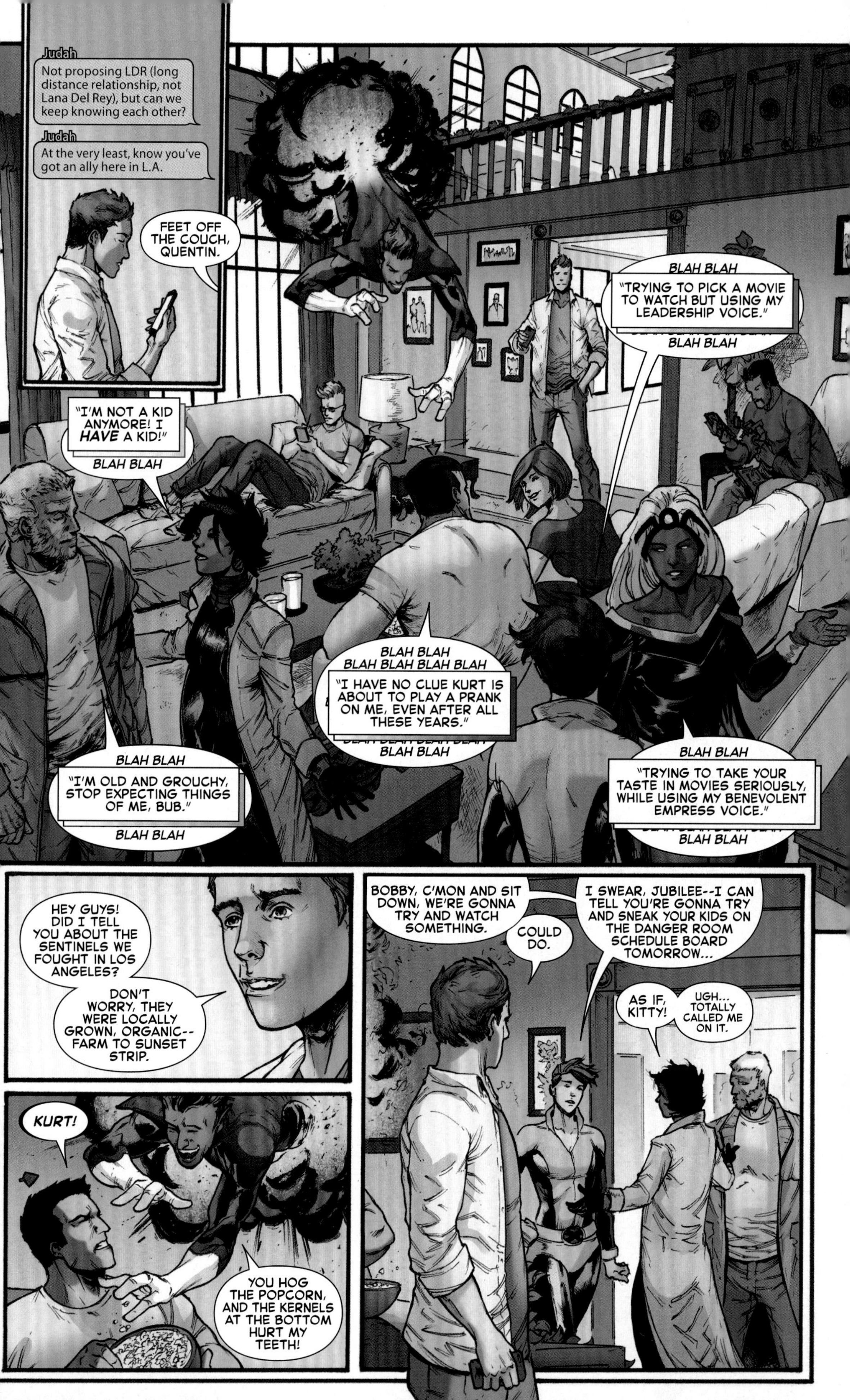

Judah
Not proposing LDR (long distance relationship, not Lana Del Rey), but can we keep knowing each other?
Judah
At the very least, know you've got an ally here in L.A.
FEET OFF THE COUCH, QUENTIN.
BLAH BLAH
"TRYING TO PICK A MOVIE TO WATCH BUT USING MY LEADERSHIP VOICE."
BLAH BLAH
"I'M NOT A KID ANYMORE! I HAVE A KID!"
BLAH BLAH
BLAH BLAH
BLAH BLAH BLAH BLAH
"I HAVE NO CLUE KURT IS ABOUT TO PLAY A PRANK ON ME, EVEN AFTER ALL THESE YEARS."
BLAH BLAH
BLAH BLAH
"I'M OLD AND GROUCHY, STOP EXPECTING THINGS OF ME, BUB."
BLAH BLAH
BLAH BLAH
"TRYING TO TAKE YOUR TASTE IN MOVIES SERIOUSLY, WHILE USING MY BENEVOLENT EMPRESS VOICE."
BLAH BLAH
HEY GUYS! DID I TELL YOU ABOUT THE SENTINELS WE FOUGHT IN LOS ANGELES?
DON'T WORRY, THEY WERE LOCALLY GROWN, ORGANIC--FARM TO SUNSET STRIP.
KURT!
YOU HOG THE POPCORN, AND THE KERNELS AT THE BOTTOM HURT MY TEETH!
BOBBY, C'MON AND SIT DOWN, WE'RE GONNA TRY AND WATCH SOMETHING.
COULD DO.
I SWEAR, JUBILEE--I CAN TELL YOU'RE GONNA TRY AND SNEAK YOUR KIDS ON THE DANGER ROOM SCHEDULE BOARD TOMORROW...
AS IF, KITTY!
UGH... TOTALLY CALLED ME ON IT.

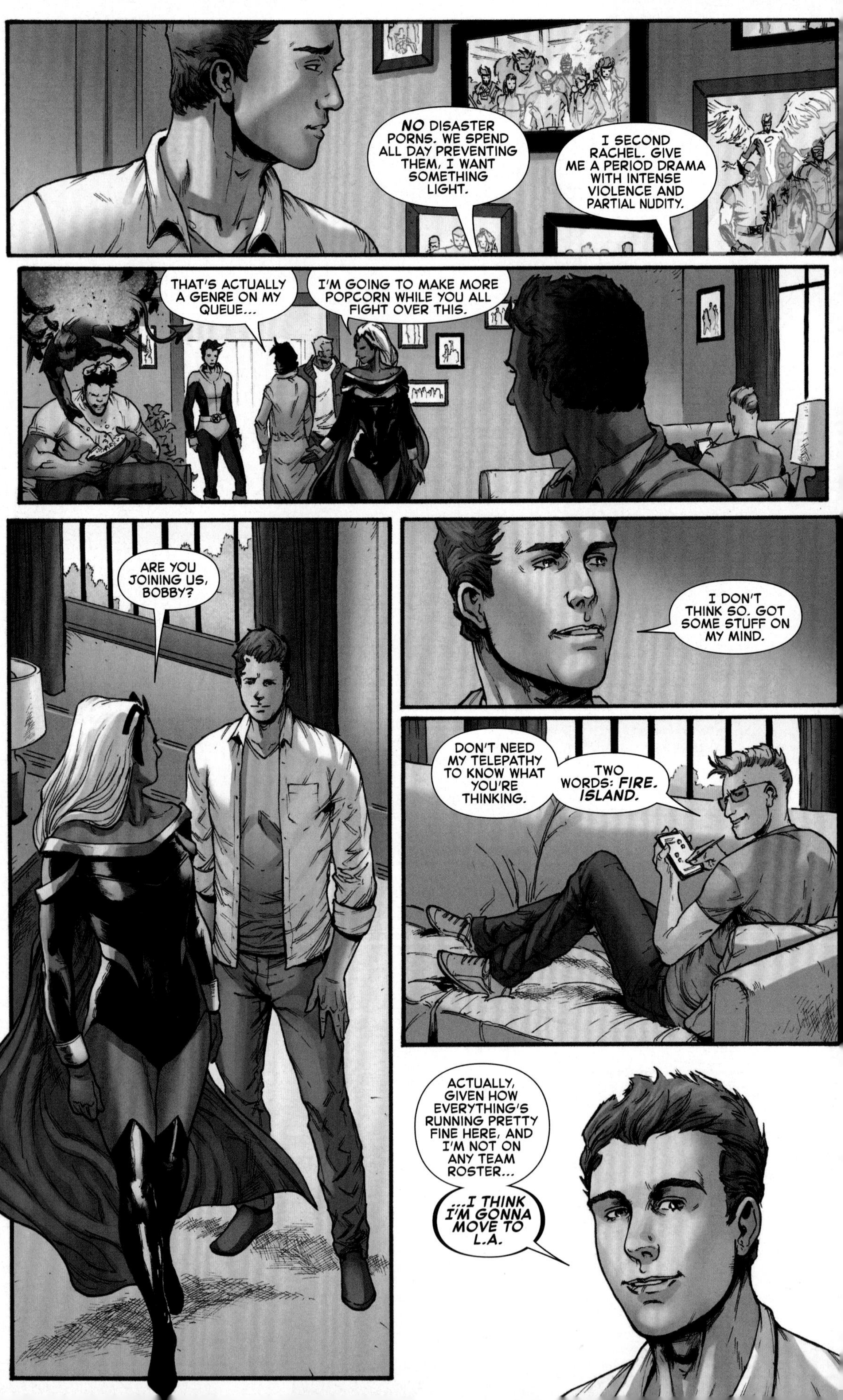
NO DISASTER PORNS. WE SPEND ALL DAY PREVENTING THEM, I WANT SOMETHING LIGHT.
I SECOND RACHEL. GIVE ME A PERIOD DRAMA WITH INTENSE VIOLENCE AND PARTIAL NUDITY.
THAT'S ACTUALLY A GENRE ON MY QUEUE...
I'M GOING TO MAKE MORE POPCORN WHILE YOU ALL FIGHT OVER THIS.
ARE YOU JOINING US, BOBBY?
I DON'T THINK SO. GOT SOME STUFF ON MY MIND.
DON'T NEED MY TELEPATHY TO KNOW WHAT YOU'RE THINKING.
TWO WORDS: FIRE. ISLAND.
ACTUALLY, GIVEN HOW EVERYTHING'S RUNNING PRETTY FINE HERE, AND I'M NOT ON ANY TEAM ROSTER...
...I THINK I'M GONNA MOVE TO L.A.

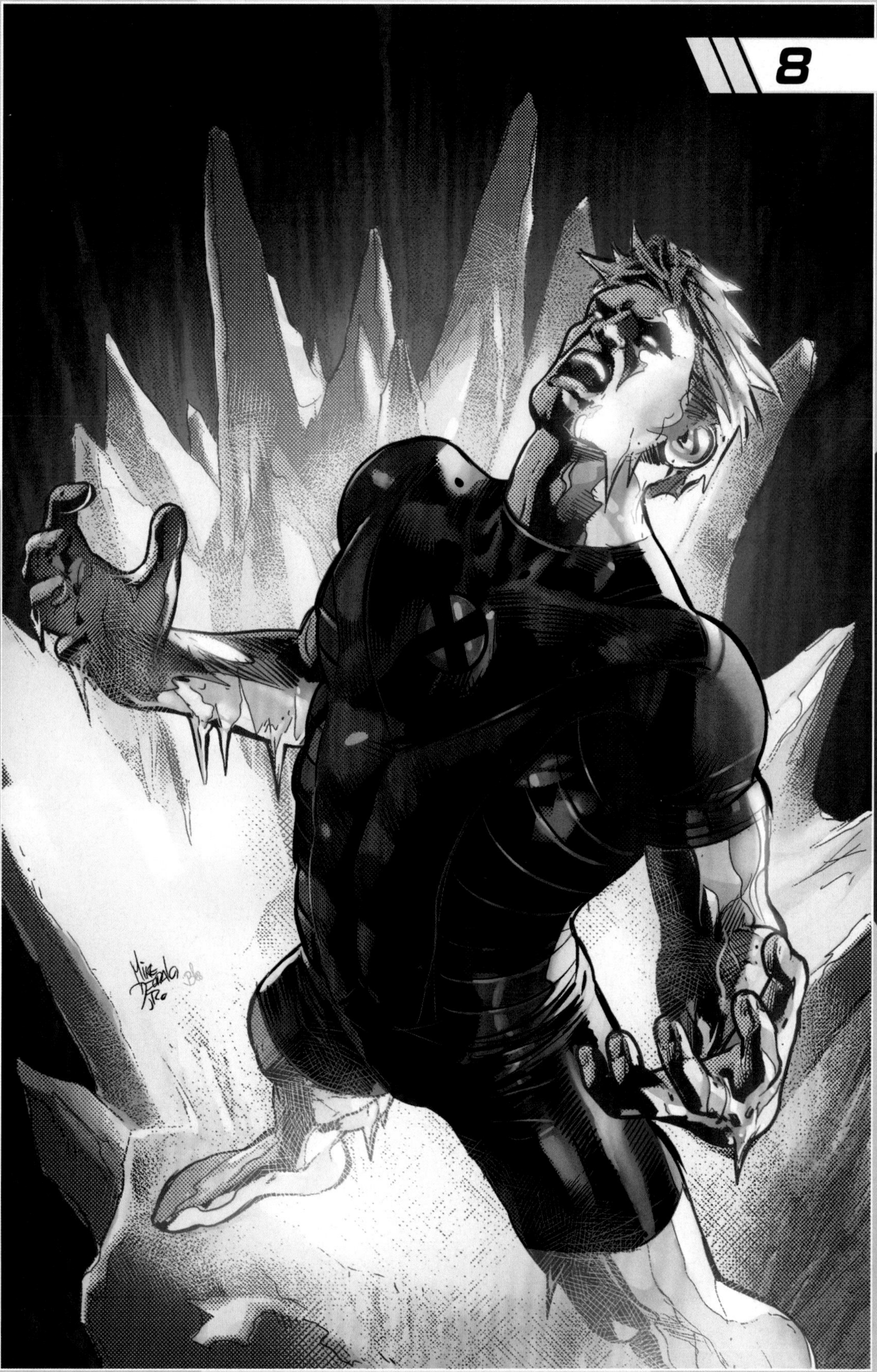
8

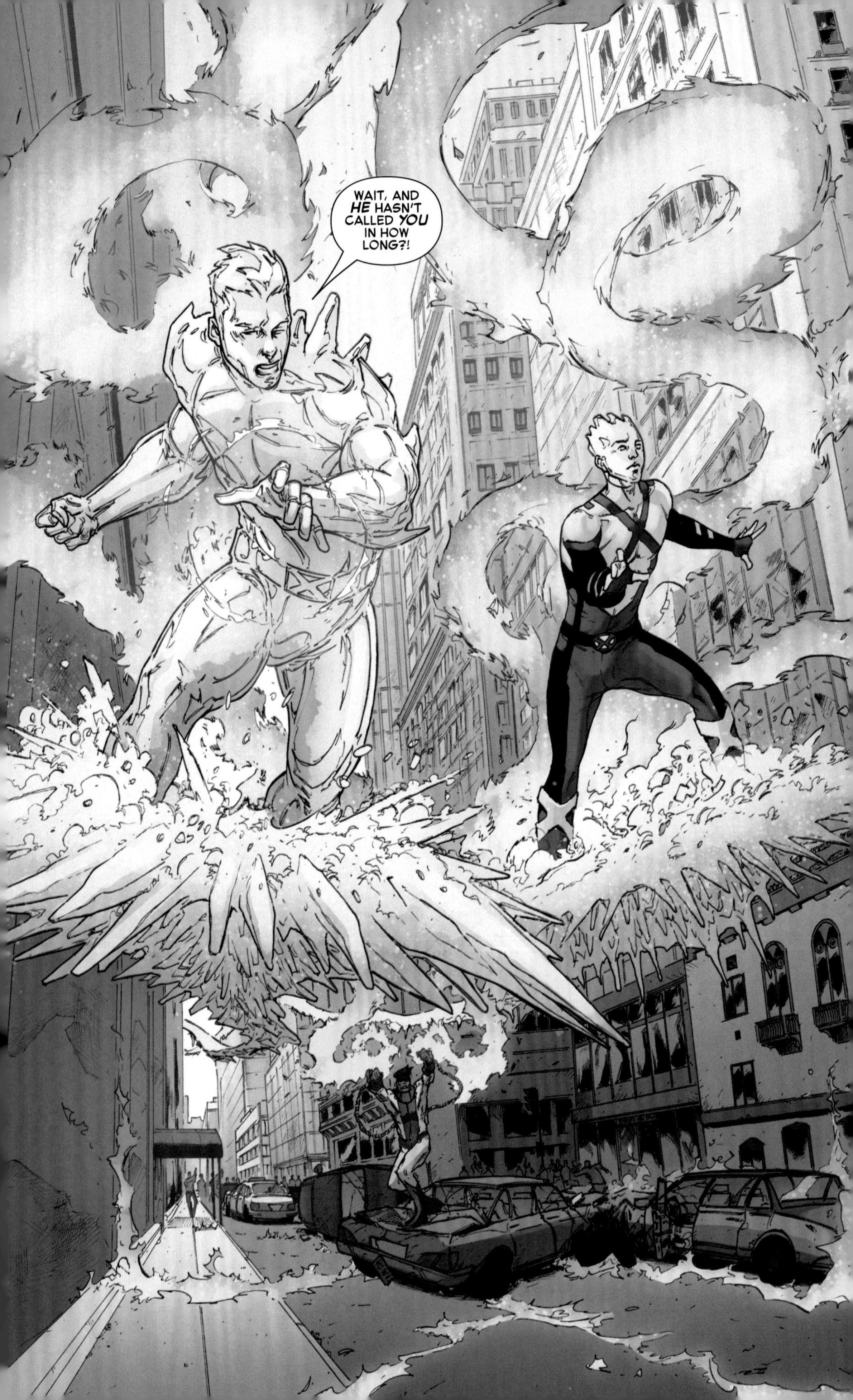
WAIT, AND HE HASN'T CALLED YOU IN HOW LONG?!

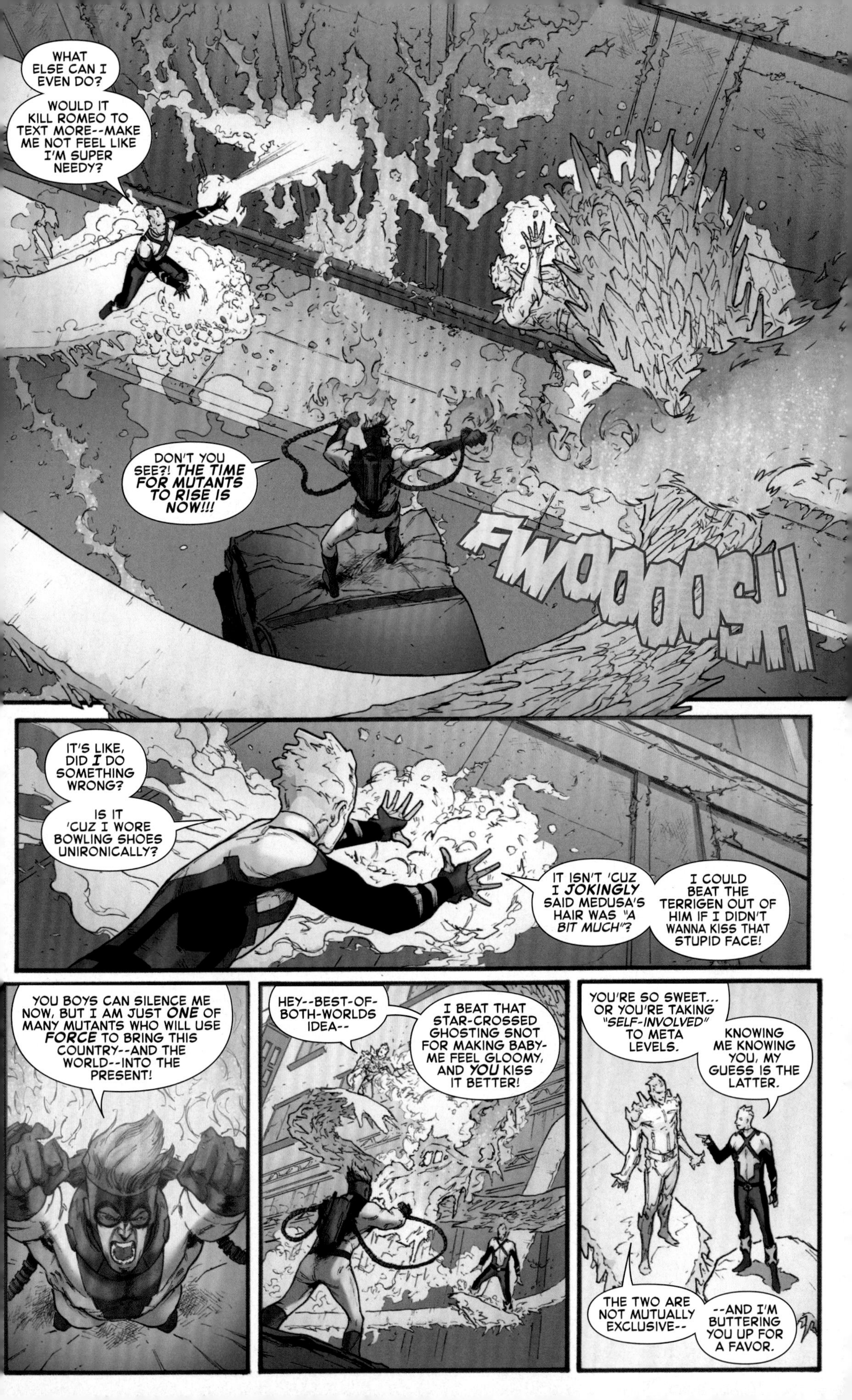
WHAT ELSE CAN I EVEN DO?
WOULD IT KILL ROMEO TO TEXT MORE--MAKE ME NOT FEEL LIKE I'M SUPER NEEDY?
DON'T YOU SEE?! THE TIME FOR MUTANTS TO RISE IS NOW!!!
FWOOOOSH
IT'S LIKE, DID I DO SOMETHING WRONG?
IS IT 'CUZ I WORE BOWLING SHOES UNIRONICALLY?
IT ISN'T 'CUZ I JOKINGLY SAID MEDUSA'S HAIR WAS "A BIT MUCH"?
I COULD BEAT THE TERRIGEN OUT OF HIM IF I DIDN'T WANNA KISS THAT STUPID FACE!
YOU BOYS CAN SILENCE ME NOW, BUT I AM JUST ONE OF MANY MUTANTS WHO WILL USE FORCE TO BRING THIS COUNTRY--AND THE WORLD--INTO THE PRESENT!
HEY--BEST-OF-BOTH-WORLDS IDEA--
I BEAT THAT STAR-CROSSED GHOSTING SNOT FOR MAKING BABY-ME FEEL GLOOMY, AND YOU KISS IT BETTER!
YOU'RE SO SWEET... OR YOU'RE TAKING "SELF-INVOLVED" TO META LEVELS.
KNOWING ME KNOWING YOU, MY GUESS IS THE LATTER.
THE TWO ARE NOT MUTUALLY EXCLUSIVE--
--AND I'M BUTTERING YOU UP FOR A FAVOR.

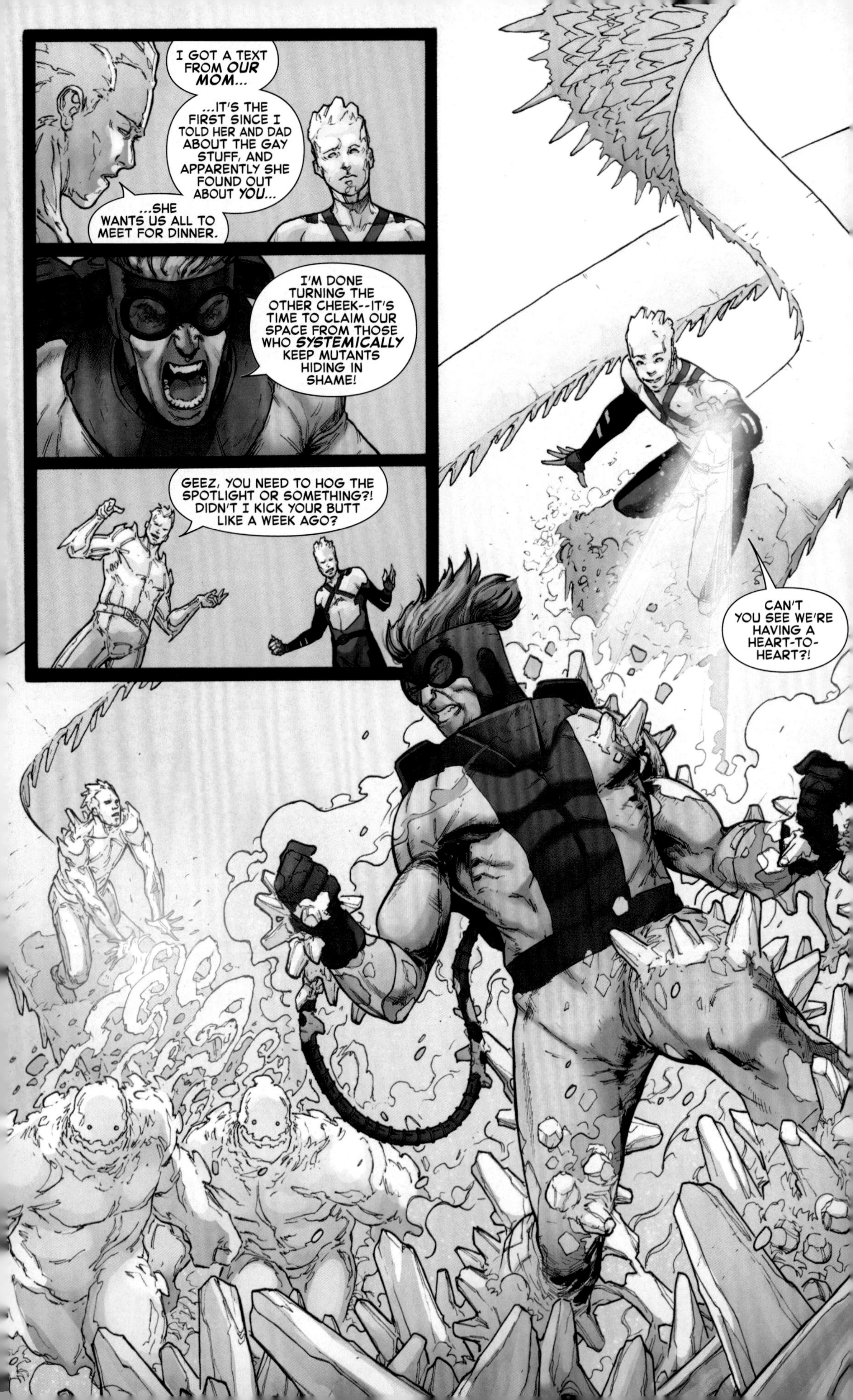

I GOT A TEXT FROM OUR MOM...
...IT'S THE FIRST SINCE I TOLD HER AND DAD ABOUT THE GAY STUFF, AND APPARENTLY SHE FOUND OUT ABOUT YOU...
...SHE WANTS US ALL TO MEET FOR DINNER.
I'M DONE TURNING THE OTHER CHEEK--IT'S TIME TO CLAIM OUR SPACE FROM THOSE WHO SYSTEMICALLY KEEP MUTANTS HIDING IN SHAME!
GEEZ, YOU NEED TO HOG THE SPOTLIGHT OR SOMETHING?! DIDN'T I KICK YOUR BUTT LIKE A WEEK AGO?
CAN'T YOU SEE WE'RE HAVING A HEART-TO-HEART?!

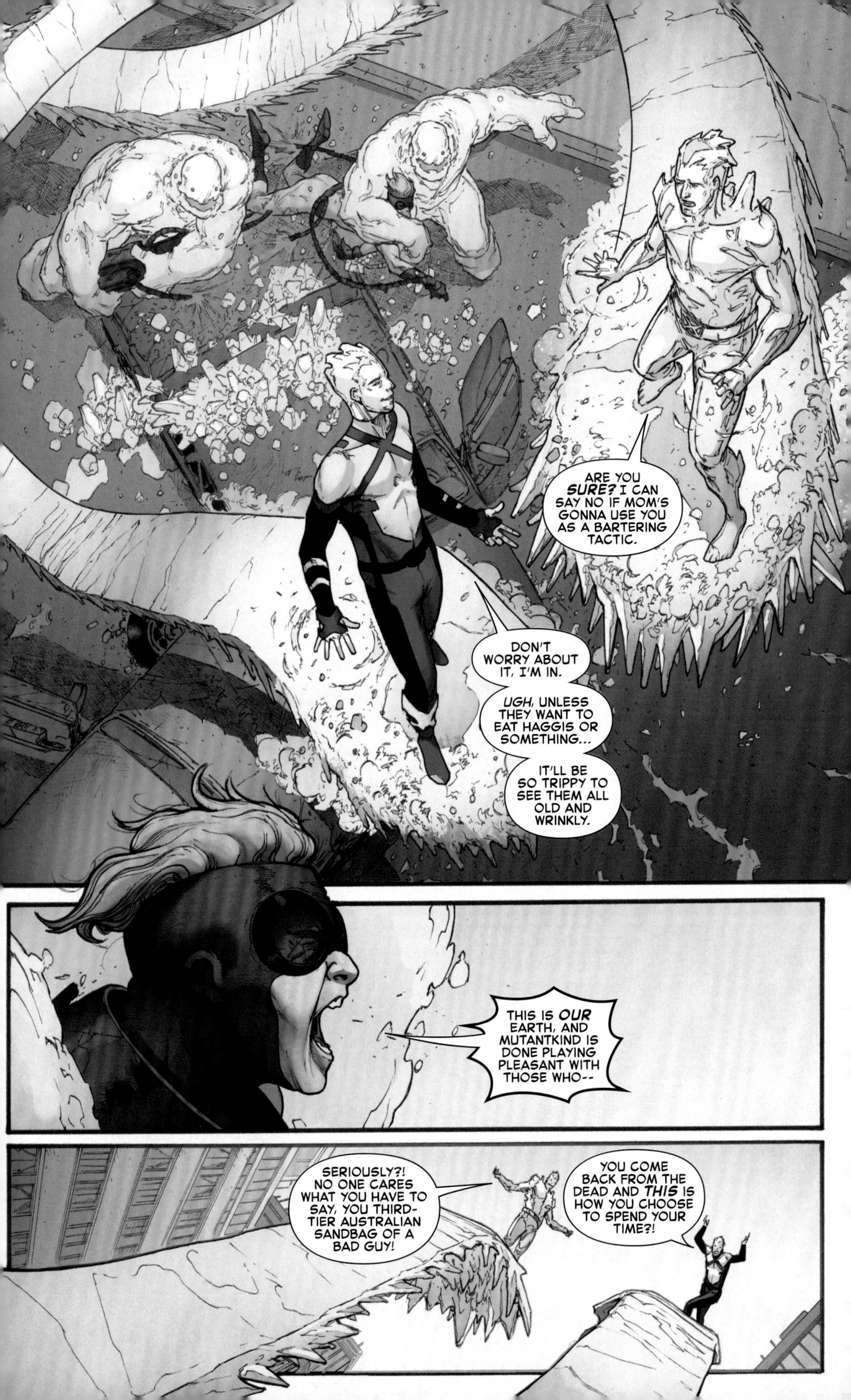
ARE YOU SURE? I CAN SAY NO IF MOM'S GONNA USE YOU AS A BARTERING TACTIC.
DON'T WORRY ABOUT IT, I'M IN.
UGH, UNLESS THEY WANT TO EAT HAGGIS OR SOMETHING...
IT'LL BE SO TRIPPY TO SEE THEM ALL OLD AND WRINKLY.
THIS IS OUR EARTH, AND MUTANTKIND IS DONE PLAYING PLEASANT WITH THOSE WHO--
SERIOUSLY?! NO ONE CARES WHAT YOU HAVE TO SAY, YOU THIRD-TIER AUSTRALIAN SANDBAG OF A BAD GUY!
YOU COME BACK FROM THE DEAD AND THIS IS HOW YOU CHOOSE TO SPEND YOUR TIME?!

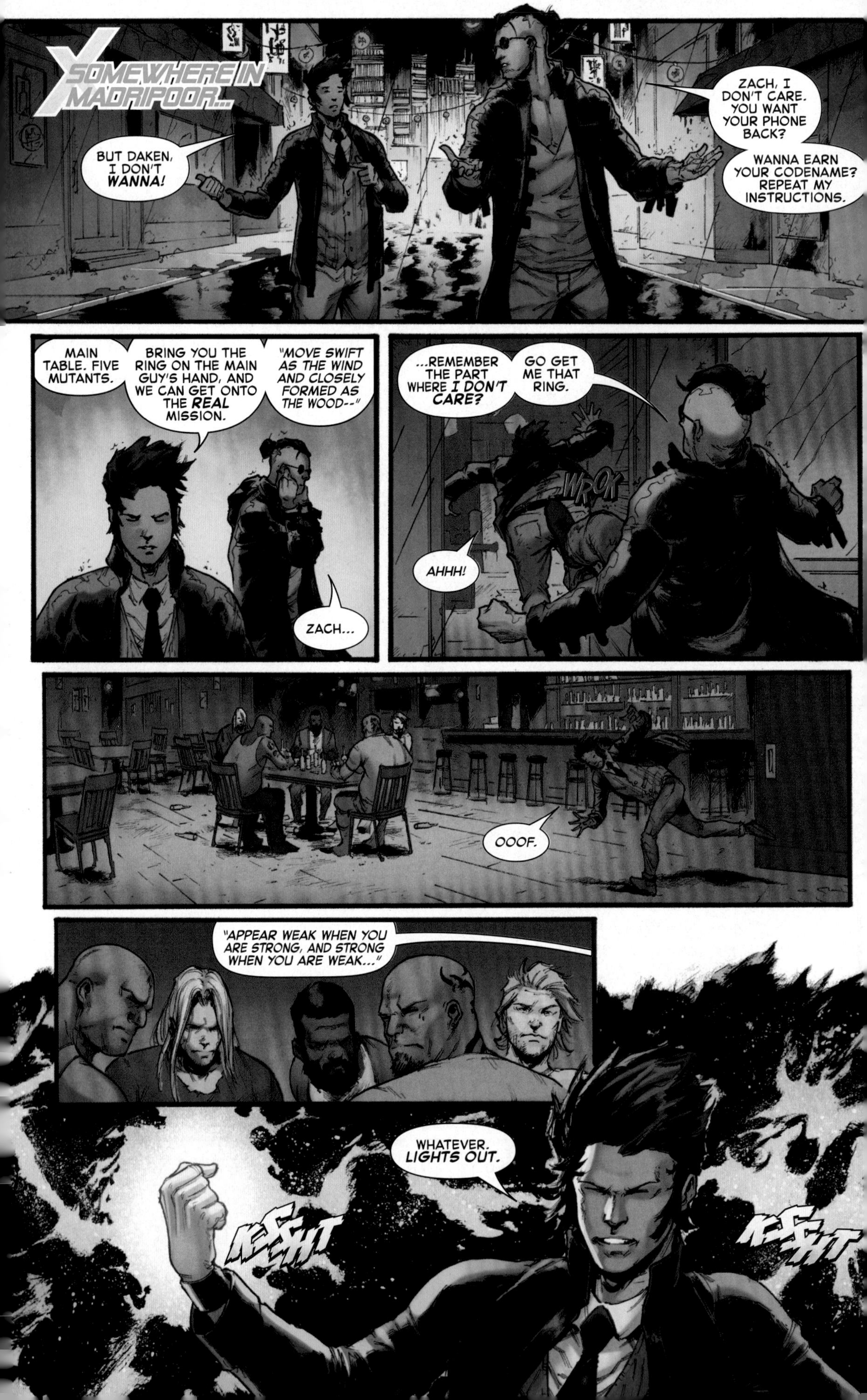
SOMEWHERE IN MADRIPOOR...
BUT DAKEN, I DON'T WANNA!
ZACH, I DON'T CARE. YOU WANT YOUR PHONE BACK?
WANNA EARN YOUR CODENAME? REPEAT MY INSTRUCTIONS.
MAIN TABLE. FIVE MUTANTS.
BRING YOU THE RING ON THE MAIN GUY'S HAND, AND WE CAN GET ONTO THE REAL MISSION.
"MOVE SWIFT AS THE WIND AND CLOSELY FORMED AS THE WOOD--"
ZACH...
...REMEMBER THE PART WHERE I DON'T CARE?
GO GET ME THAT RING.
WROK
AHHH!
OOOF.
"APPEAR WEAK WHEN YOU ARE STRONG, AND STRONG WHEN YOU ARE WEAK..."
WHATEVER. LIGHTS OUT.
K-SSHT
K-SSHT

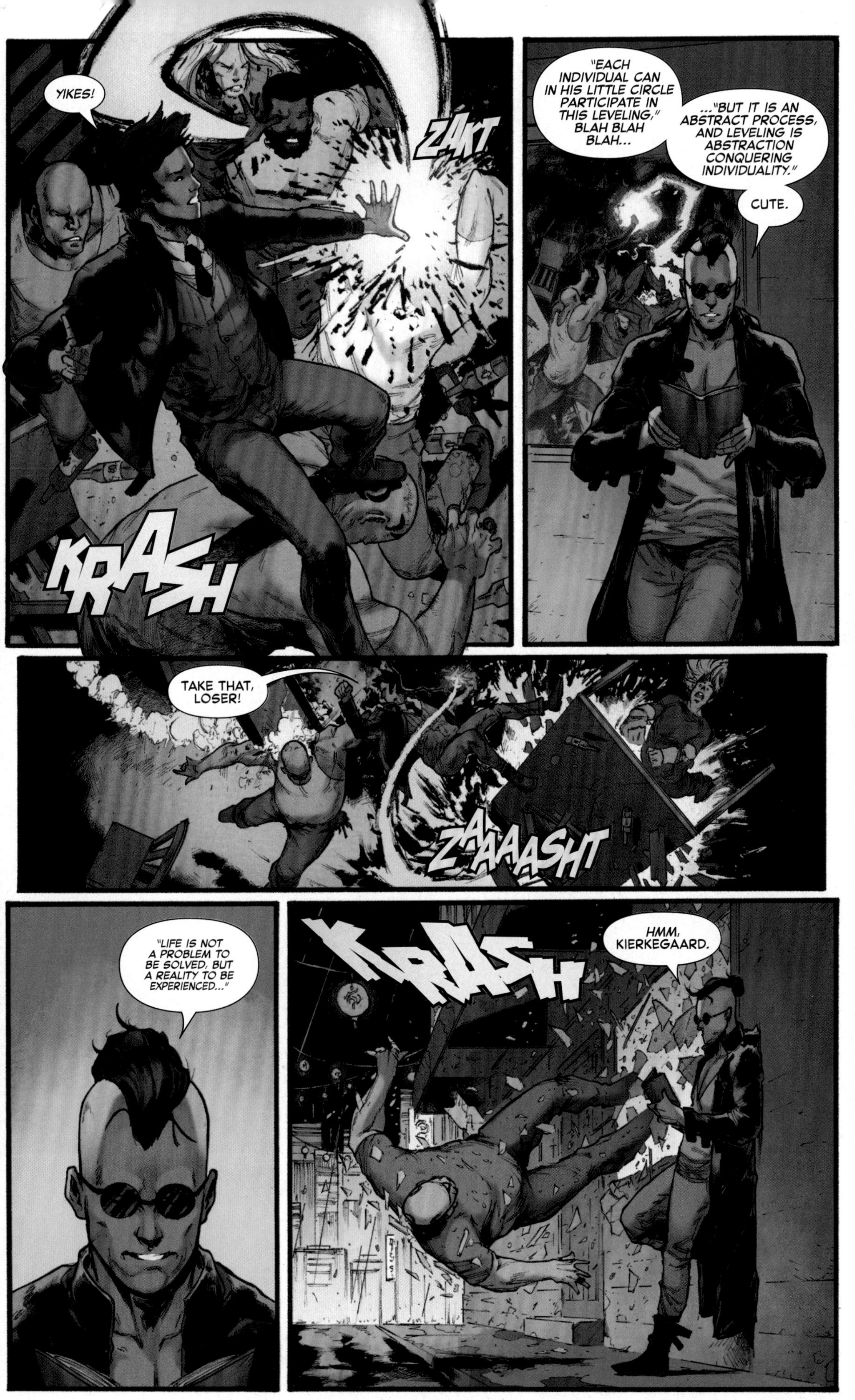

YIKES!
ZAKT
KRASH
"EACH INDIVIDUAL CAN IN HIS LITTLE CIRCLE PARTICIPATE IN THIS LEVELING," BLAH BLAH BLAH...
..."BUT IT IS AN ABSTRACT PROCESS, AND LEVELING IS ABSTRACTION CONQUERING INDIVIDUALITY."
CUTE.
TAKE THAT, LOSER!
ZAAAASHT
"LIFE IS NOT A PROBLEM TO BE SOLVED, BUT A REALITY TO BE EXPERIENCED..."
KRASH
HMM, KIERKEGAARD.

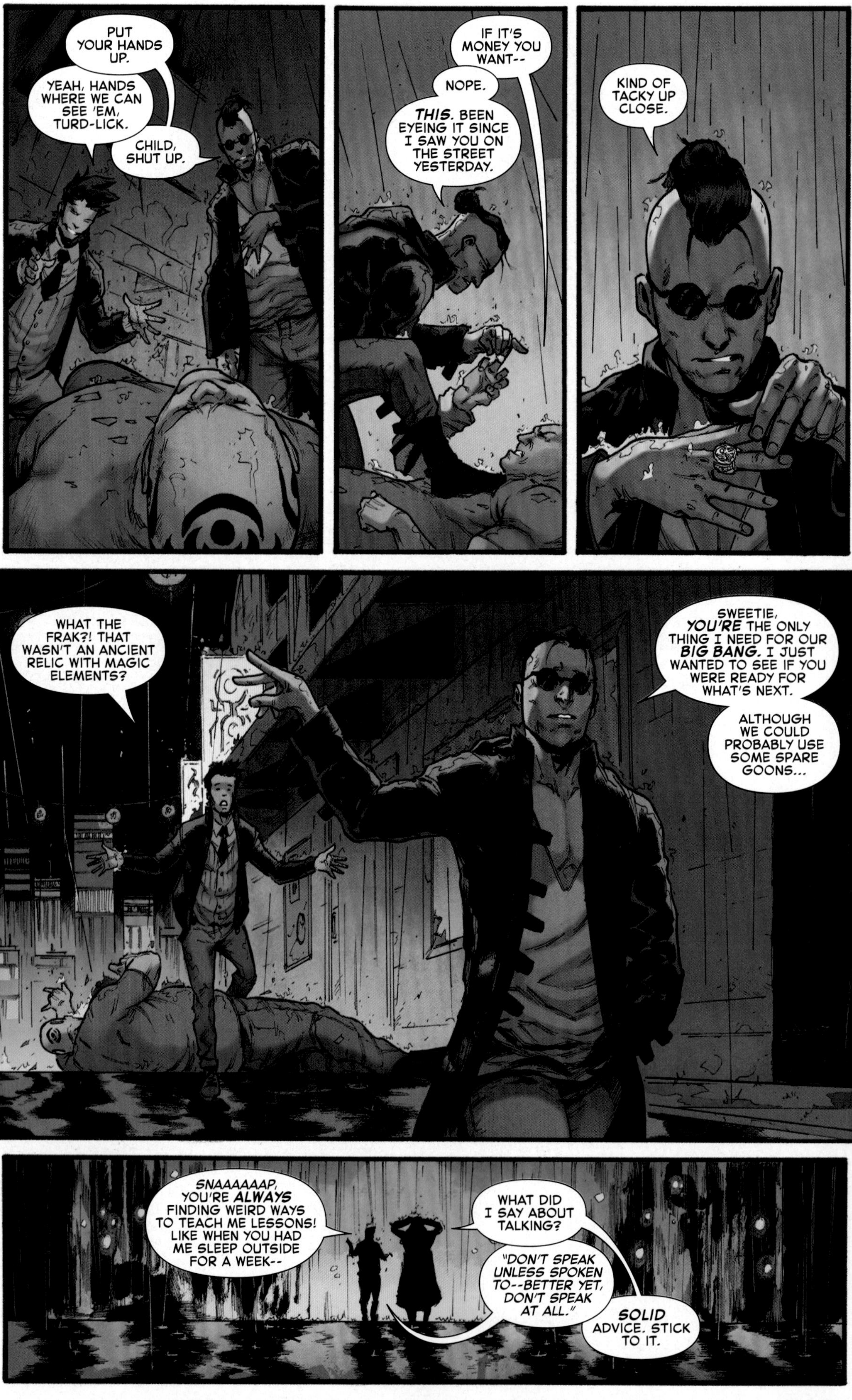
PUT YOUR HANDS UP.
YEAH, HANDS WHERE WE CAN SEE 'EM, TURD-LICK.
CHILD, SHUT UP.
IF IT'S MONEY YOU WANT--
NOPE.
THIS. BEEN EYEING IT SINCE I SAW YOU ON THE STREET YESTERDAY.
KIND OF TACKY UP CLOSE.
WHAT THE FRAK?! THAT WASN'T AN ANCIENT RELIC WITH MAGIC ELEMENTS?
SWEETIE, YOU'RE THE ONLY THING I NEED FOR OUR BIG BANG. I JUST WANTED TO SEE IF YOU WERE READY FOR WHAT'S NEXT.
ALTHOUGH WE COULD PROBABLY USE SOME SPARE GOONS...
SNAAAAAAP, YOU'RE ALWAYS FINDING WEIRD WAYS TO TEACH ME LESSONS! LIKE WHEN YOU HAD ME SLEEP OUTSIDE FOR A WEEK--
WHAT DID I SAY ABOUT TALKING?
"DON'T SPEAK UNLESS SPOKEN TO--BETTER YET, DON'T SPEAK AT ALL."
SOLID ADVICE. STICK TO IT.

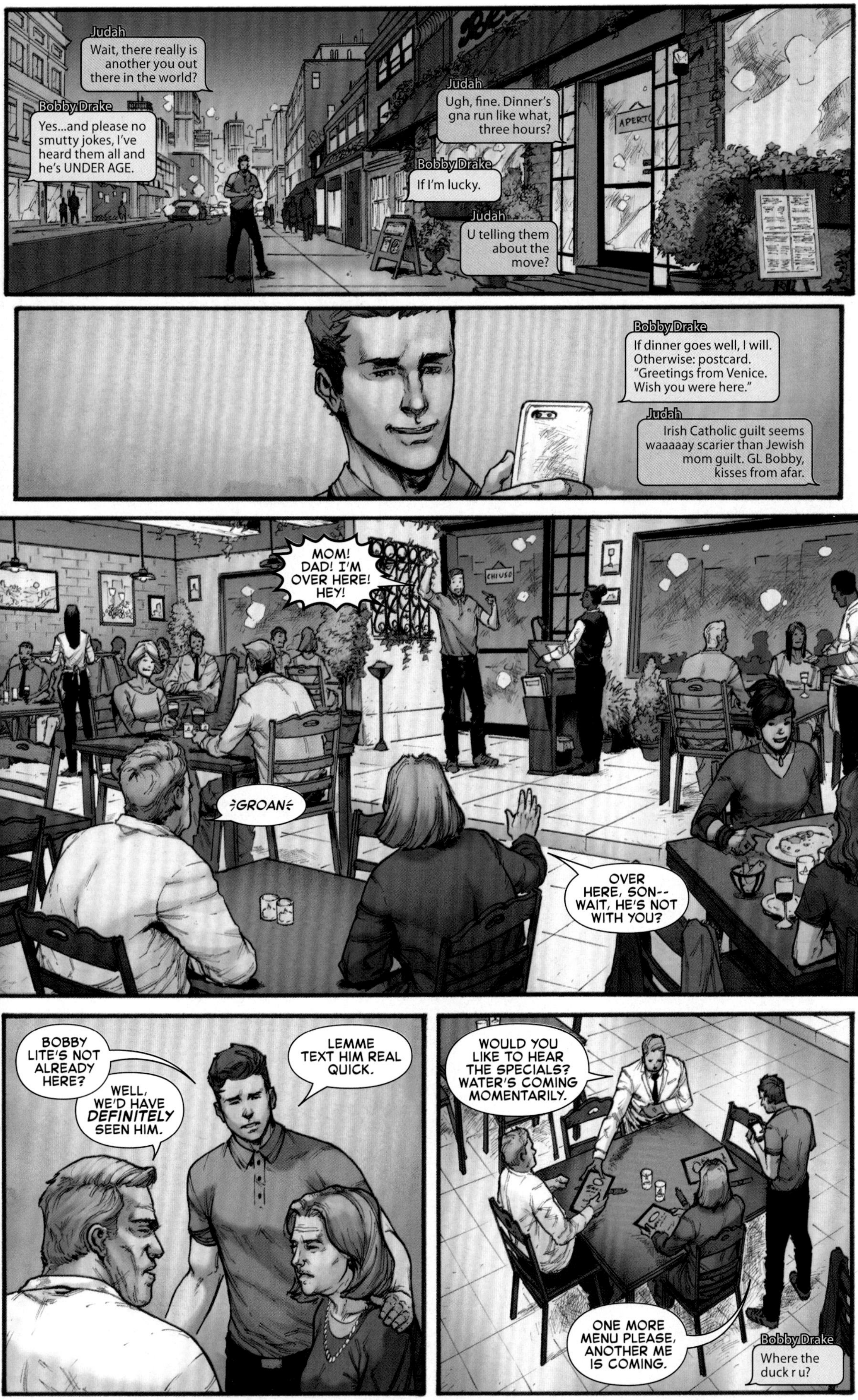
Judah
Wait, there really is another you out there in the world?
Bobby Drake
Yes...and please no smutty jokes, I've heard them all and he's UNDER AGE.
Judah
Ugh, fine. Dinner's gna run like what, three hours?
Bobby Drake
If I'm lucky.
Judah
U telling them about the move?
APERTO
Bobby Drake
If dinner goes well, I will. Otherwise: postcard. "Greetings from Venice. Wish you were here."
Judah
Irish Catholic guilt seems waaaaay scarier than Jewish mom guilt. GL Bobby, kisses from afar.
MOM! DAD! I'M OVER HERE! HEY!
CHIUSO
GROAN
OVER HERE, SON-- WAIT, HE'S NOT WITH YOU?
BOBBY LITE'S NOT ALREADY HERE?
WELL, WE'D HAVE *DEFINITELY* SEEN HIM.
LEMME TEXT HIM REAL QUICK.
WOULD YOU LIKE TO HEAR THE SPECIALS? WATER'S COMING MOMENTARILY.
ONE MORE MENU PLEASE, ANOTHER ME IS COMING.
Bobby Drake
Where the duck r u?

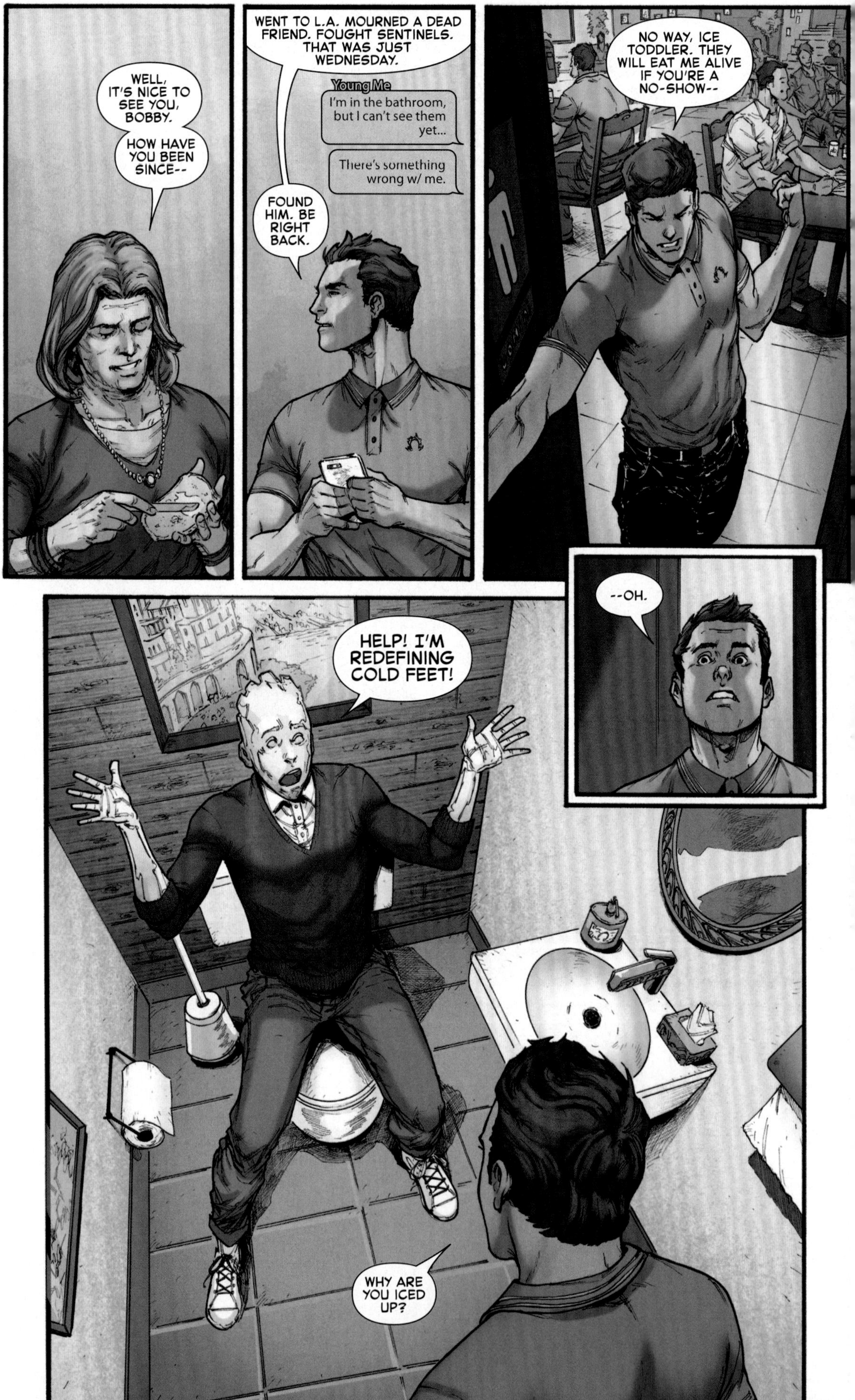
WELL, IT'S NICE TO SEE YOU, BOBBY.
HOW HAVE YOU BEEN SINCE--
WENT TO L.A. MOURNED A DEAD FRIEND. FOUGHT SENTINELS. THAT WAS JUST WEDNESDAY.
Young Me
I'm in the bathroom, but I can't see them yet...
There's something wrong w/ me.
FOUND HIM. BE RIGHT BACK.
NO WAY, ICE TODDLER. THEY WILL EAT ME ALIVE IF YOU'RE A NO-SHOW--
--OH.
HELP! I'M REDEFINING COLD FEET!
WHY ARE YOU ICED UP?

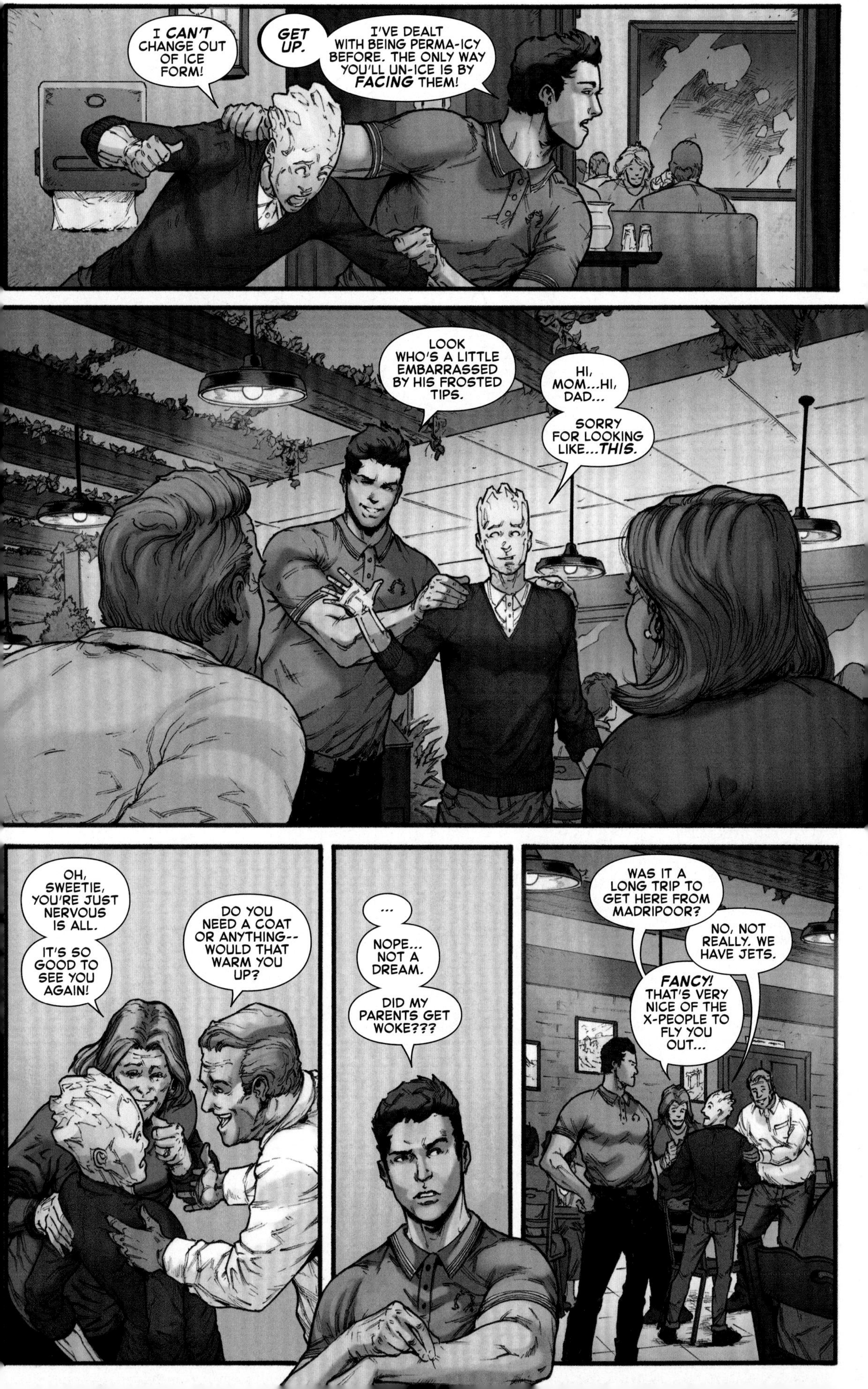
I CAN'T CHANGE OUT OF ICE FORM!
GET UP.
I'VE DEALT WITH BEING PERMA-ICY BEFORE. THE ONLY WAY YOU'LL UN-ICE IS BY FACING THEM!
LOOK WHO'S A LITTLE EMBARRASSED BY HIS FROSTED TIPS.
HI, MOM...HI, DAD...
SORRY FOR LOOKING LIKE...THIS.
OH, SWEETIE, YOU'RE JUST NERVOUS IS ALL.
IT'S SO GOOD TO SEE YOU AGAIN!
DO YOU NEED A COAT OR ANYTHING-- WOULD THAT WARM YOU UP?
...
NOPE... NOT A DREAM.
DID MY PARENTS GET WOKE???
WAS IT A LONG TRIP TO GET HERE FROM MADRIPOOR?
NO, NOT REALLY. WE HAVE JETS.
FANCY! THAT'S VERY NICE OF THE X-PEOPLE TO FLY YOU OUT...

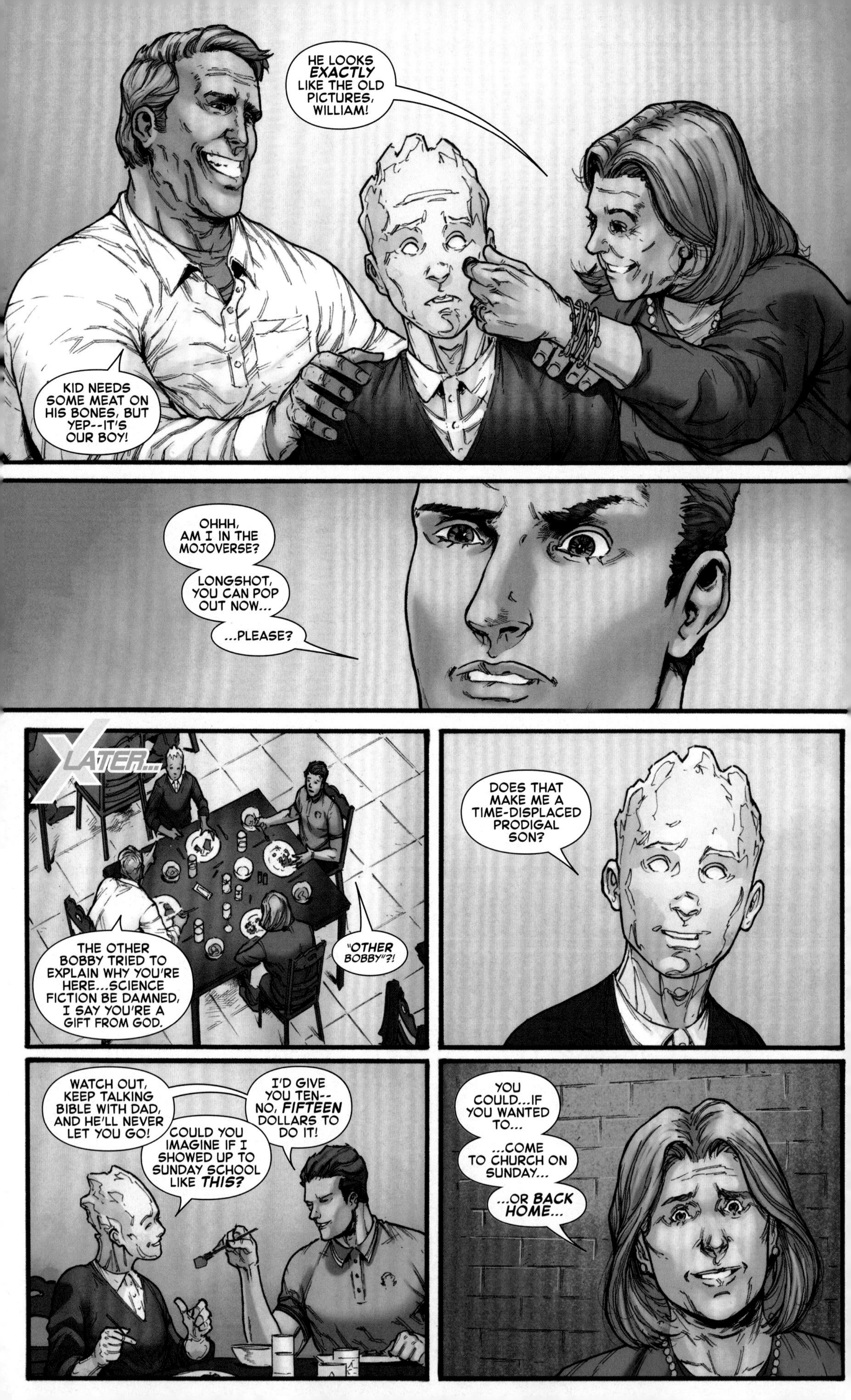
HE LOOKS EXACTLY LIKE THE OLD PICTURES, WILLIAM!
KID NEEDS SOME MEAT ON HIS BONES, BUT YEP--IT'S OUR BOY!
OHHH, AM I IN THE MOJOVERSE?
LONGSHOT, YOU CAN POP OUT NOW...
...PLEASE?
LATER...
THE OTHER BOBBY TRIED TO EXPLAIN WHY YOU'RE HERE...SCIENCE FICTION BE DAMNED, I SAY YOU'RE A GIFT FROM GOD.
"OTHER BOBBY"?!
DOES THAT MAKE ME A TIME-DISPLACED PRODIGAL SON?
WATCH OUT, KEEP TALKING BIBLE WITH DAD, AND HE'LL NEVER LET YOU GO!
COULD YOU IMAGINE IF I SHOWED UP TO SUNDAY SCHOOL LIKE THIS?
I'D GIVE YOU TEN-- NO, FIFTEEN DOLLARS TO DO IT!
YOU COULD...IF YOU WANTED TO...
...COME TO CHURCH ON SUNDAY...
...OR BACK HOME...

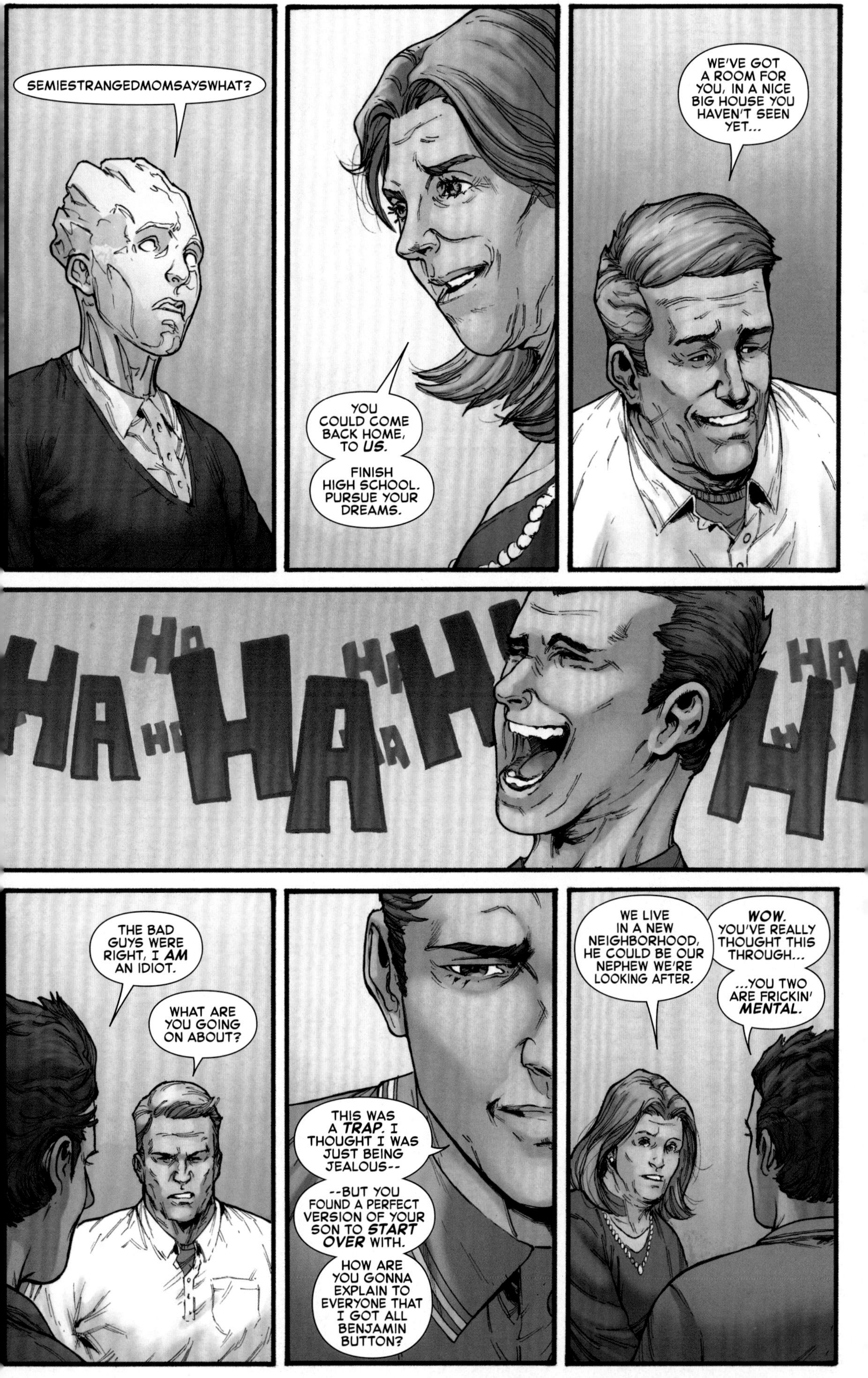
SEMIESTRANGEDMOMSAYSWHAT?
YOU COULD COME BACK HOME, TO US.
FINISH HIGH SCHOOL. PURSUE YOUR DREAMS.
WE'VE GOT A ROOM FOR YOU, IN A NICE BIG HOUSE YOU HAVEN'T SEEN YET...
HAHAHAHAHAHAHAHA
THE BAD GUYS WERE RIGHT, I AM AN IDIOT.
WHAT ARE YOU GOING ON ABOUT?
THIS WAS A TRAP. I THOUGHT I WAS JUST BEING JEALOUS--
--BUT YOU FOUND A PERFECT VERSION OF YOUR SON TO START OVER WITH.
HOW ARE YOU GONNA EXPLAIN TO EVERYONE THAT I GOT ALL BENJAMIN BUTTON?
WE LIVE IN A NEW NEIGHBORHOOD, HE COULD BE OUR NEPHEW WE'RE LOOKING AFTER.
WOW. YOU'VE REALLY THOUGHT THIS THROUGH...
...YOU TWO ARE FRICKIN' MENTAL.

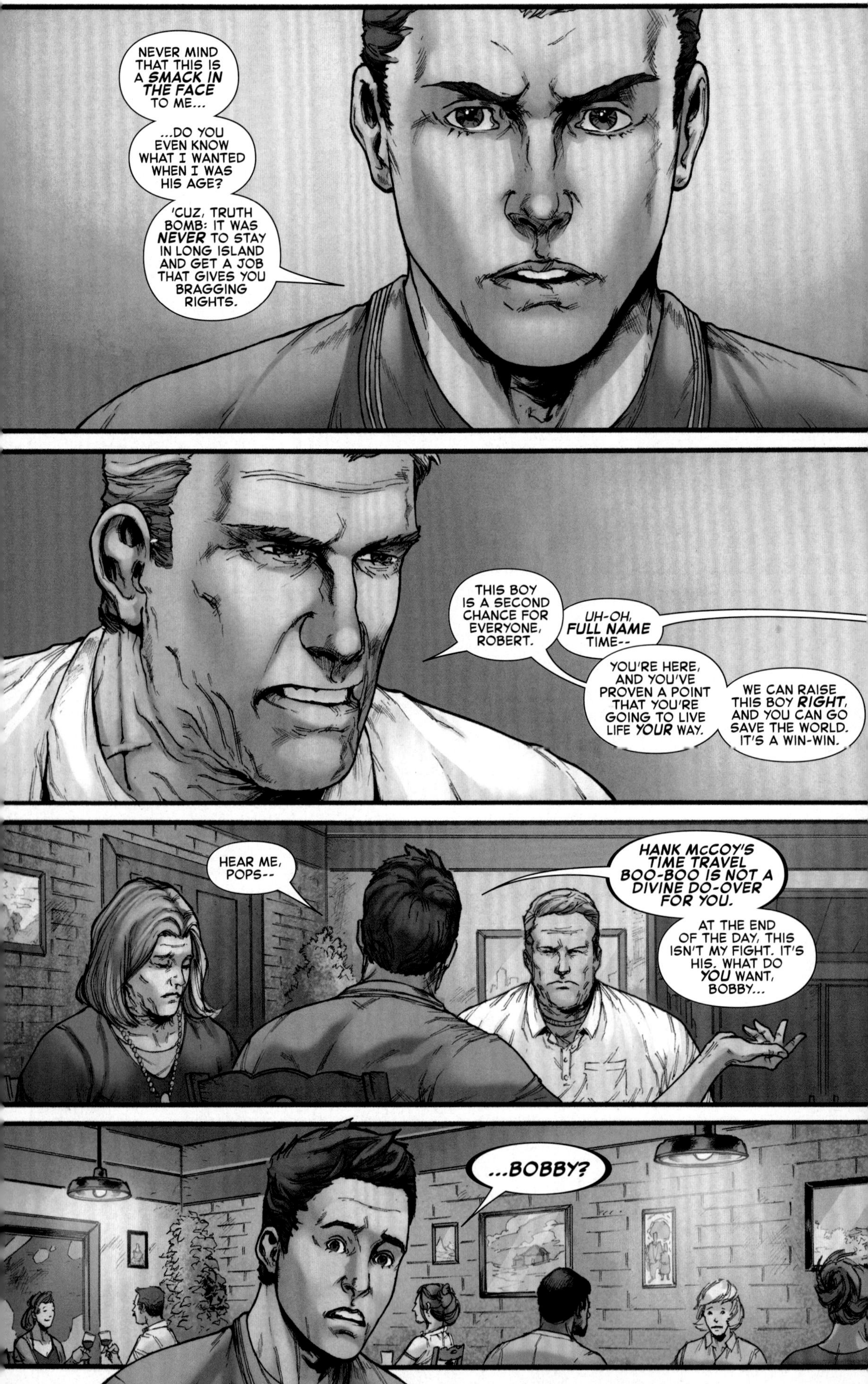
NEVER MIND THAT THIS IS A *SMACK IN THE FACE* TO ME...
...DO YOU EVEN KNOW WHAT I WANTED WHEN I WAS HIS AGE?
'CUZ, TRUTH BOMB: IT WAS *NEVER* TO STAY IN LONG ISLAND AND GET A JOB THAT GIVES YOU BRAGGING RIGHTS.
THIS BOY IS A SECOND CHANCE FOR EVERYONE, ROBERT.
UH-OH, *FULL NAME* TIME--
YOU'RE HERE, AND YOU'VE PROVEN A POINT THAT YOU'RE GOING TO LIVE LIFE *YOUR* WAY.
WE CAN RAISE THIS BOY *RIGHT*, AND YOU CAN GO SAVE THE WORLD. IT'S A WIN-WIN.
HEAR ME, POPS--
HANK McCOY'S TIME TRAVEL BOO-BOO IS NOT A DIVINE DO-OVER FOR YOU.
AT THE END OF THE DAY, THIS ISN'T MY FIGHT. IT'S HIS. WHAT DO *YOU* WANT, BOBBY...
...BOBBY?

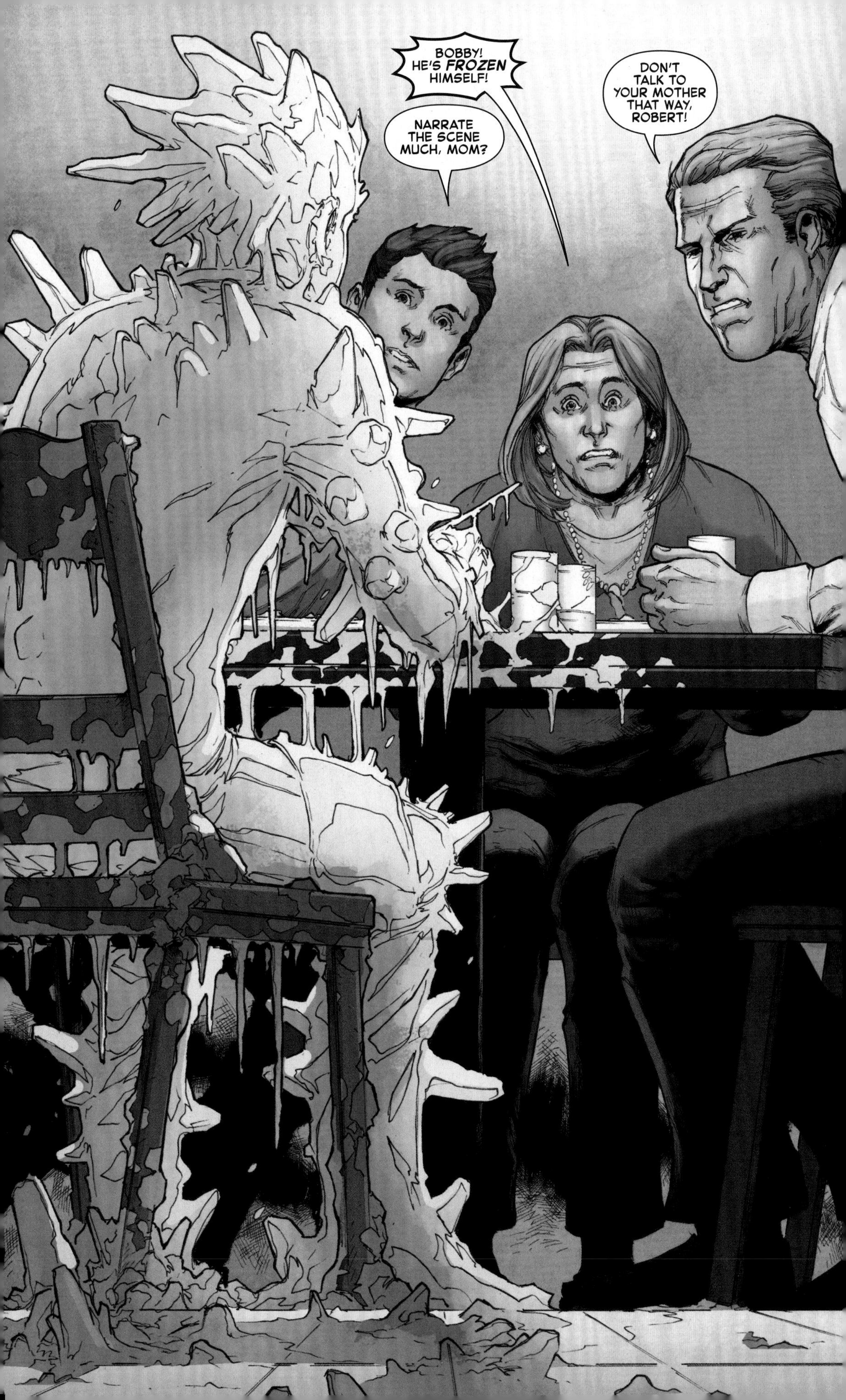
BOBBY! HE'S FROZEN HIMSELF!
NARRATE THE SCENE MUCH, MOM?
DON'T TALK TO YOUR MOTHER THAT WAY, ROBERT!

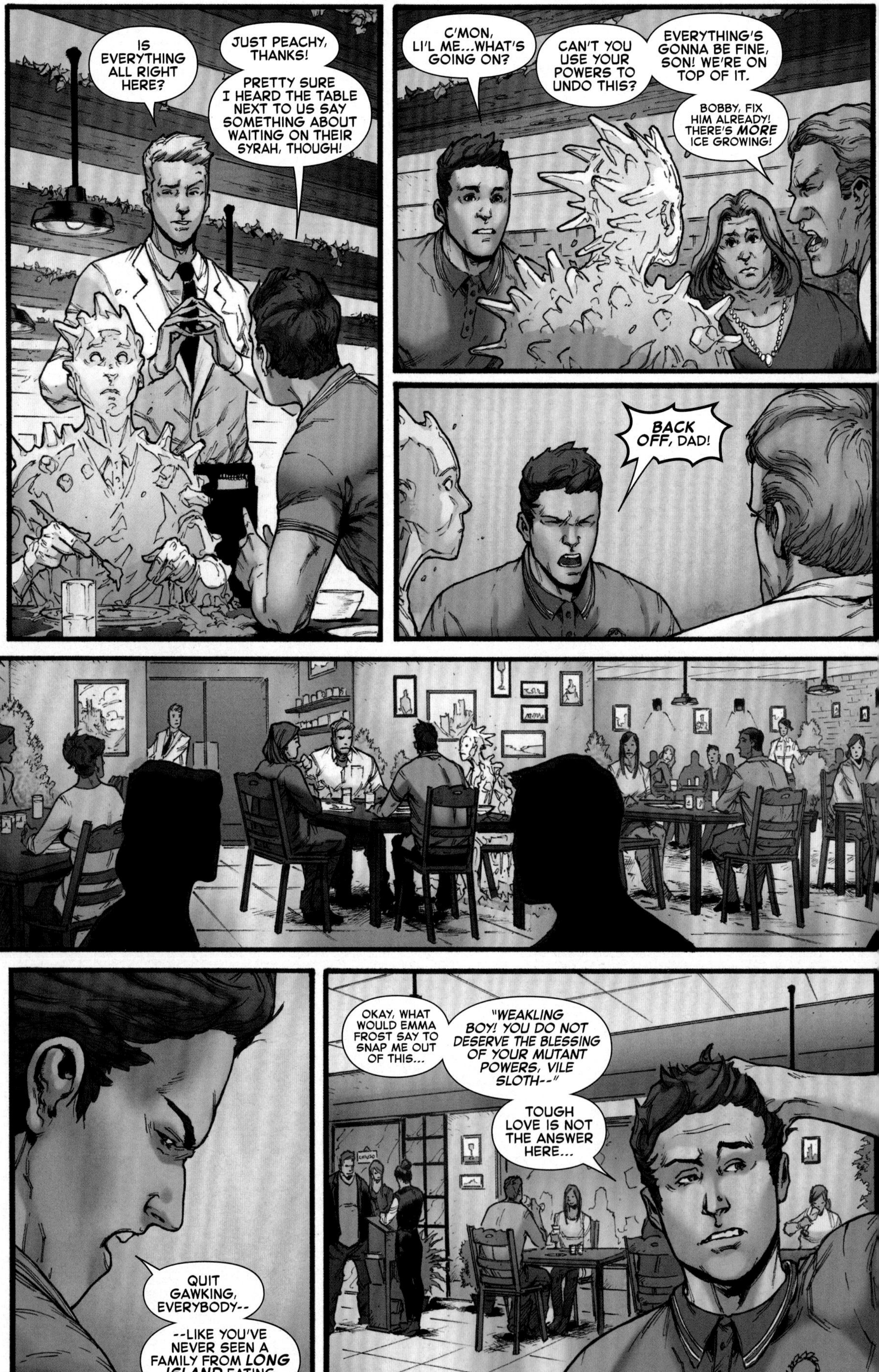
IS EVERYTHING ALL RIGHT HERE?
JUST PEACHY, THANKS!
PRETTY SURE I HEARD THE TABLE NEXT TO US SAY SOMETHING ABOUT WAITING ON THEIR SYRAH, THOUGH!
C'MON, LI'L ME...WHAT'S GOING ON?
CAN'T YOU USE YOUR POWERS TO UNDO THIS?
EVERYTHING'S GONNA BE FINE, SON! WE'RE ON TOP OF IT.
BOBBY, FIX HIM ALREADY! THERE'S MORE ICE GROWING!
BACK OFF, DAD!
QUIT GAWKING, EVERYBODY--
--LIKE YOU'VE NEVER SEEN A FAMILY FROM LONG ISLAND EATING DINNER!
OKAY, WHAT WOULD EMMA FROST SAY TO SNAP ME OUT OF THIS...
"WEAKLING BOY! YOU DO NOT DESERVE THE BLESSING OF YOUR MUTANT POWERS, VILE SLOTH--"
TOUGH LOVE IS NOT THE ANSWER HERE...

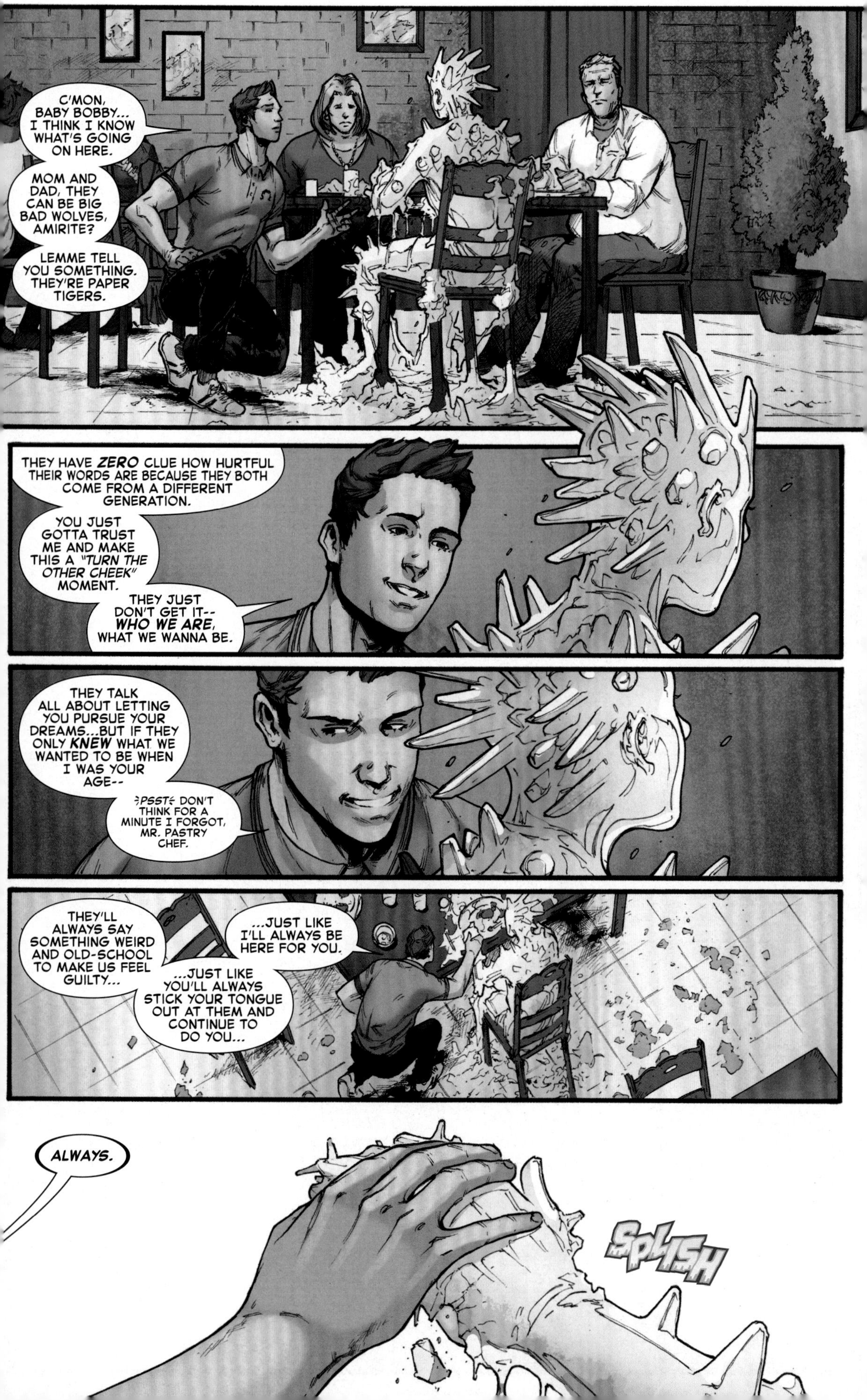
C'MON, BABY BOBBY... I THINK I KNOW WHAT'S GOING ON HERE.
MOM AND DAD, THEY CAN BE BIG BAD WOLVES, AMIRITE?
LEMME TELL YOU SOMETHING. THEY'RE PAPER TIGERS.
THEY HAVE ZERO CLUE HOW HURTFUL THEIR WORDS ARE BECAUSE THEY BOTH COME FROM A DIFFERENT GENERATION.
YOU JUST GOTTA TRUST ME AND MAKE THIS A "TURN THE OTHER CHEEK" MOMENT.
THEY JUST DON'T GET IT-- WHO WE ARE, WHAT WE WANNA BE.
THEY TALK ALL ABOUT LETTING YOU PURSUE YOUR DREAMS...BUT IF THEY ONLY KNEW WHAT WE WANTED TO BE WHEN I WAS YOUR AGE--
PSST DON'T THINK FOR A MINUTE I FORGOT, MR. PASTRY CHEF.
THEY'LL ALWAYS SAY SOMETHING WEIRD AND OLD-SCHOOL TO MAKE US FEEL GUILTY...
...JUST LIKE YOU'LL ALWAYS STICK YOUR TONGUE OUT AT THEM AND CONTINUE TO DO YOU...
...JUST LIKE I'LL ALWAYS BE HERE FOR YOU.
ALWAYS.
SPLISH

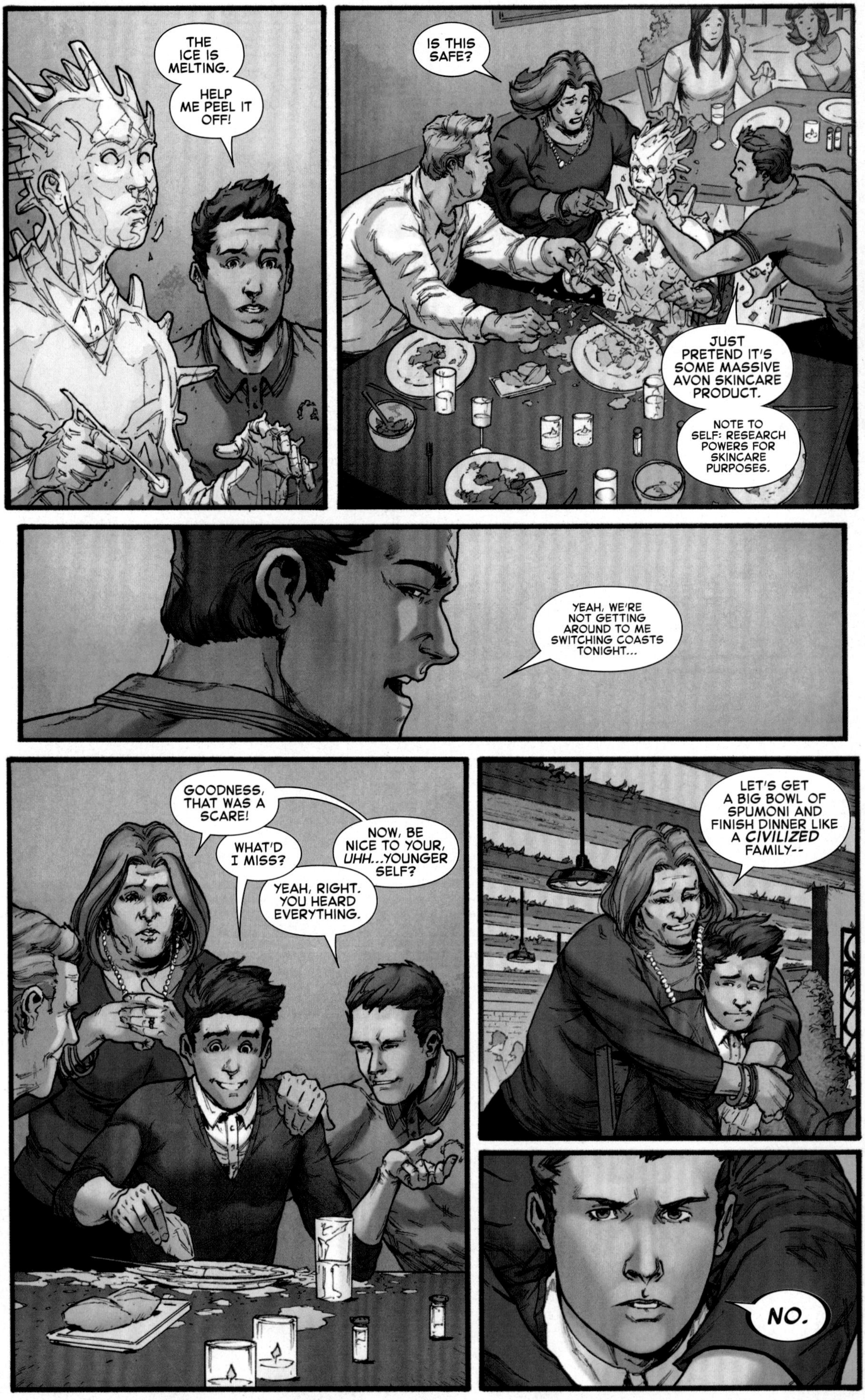
THE ICE IS MELTING.
HELP ME PEEL IT OFF!
IS THIS SAFE?
JUST PRETEND IT'S SOME MASSIVE AVON SKINCARE PRODUCT.
NOTE TO SELF: RESEARCH POWERS FOR SKINCARE PURPOSES.
YEAH, WE'RE NOT GETTING AROUND TO ME SWITCHING COASTS TONIGHT...
GOODNESS, THAT WAS A SCARE!
WHAT'D I MISS?
NOW, BE NICE TO YOUR, *UHH*...YOUNGER SELF?
YEAH, RIGHT. YOU HEARD EVERYTHING.
LET'S GET A BIG BOWL OF SPUMONI AND FINISH DINNER LIKE A *CIVILIZED* FAMILY--
NO.

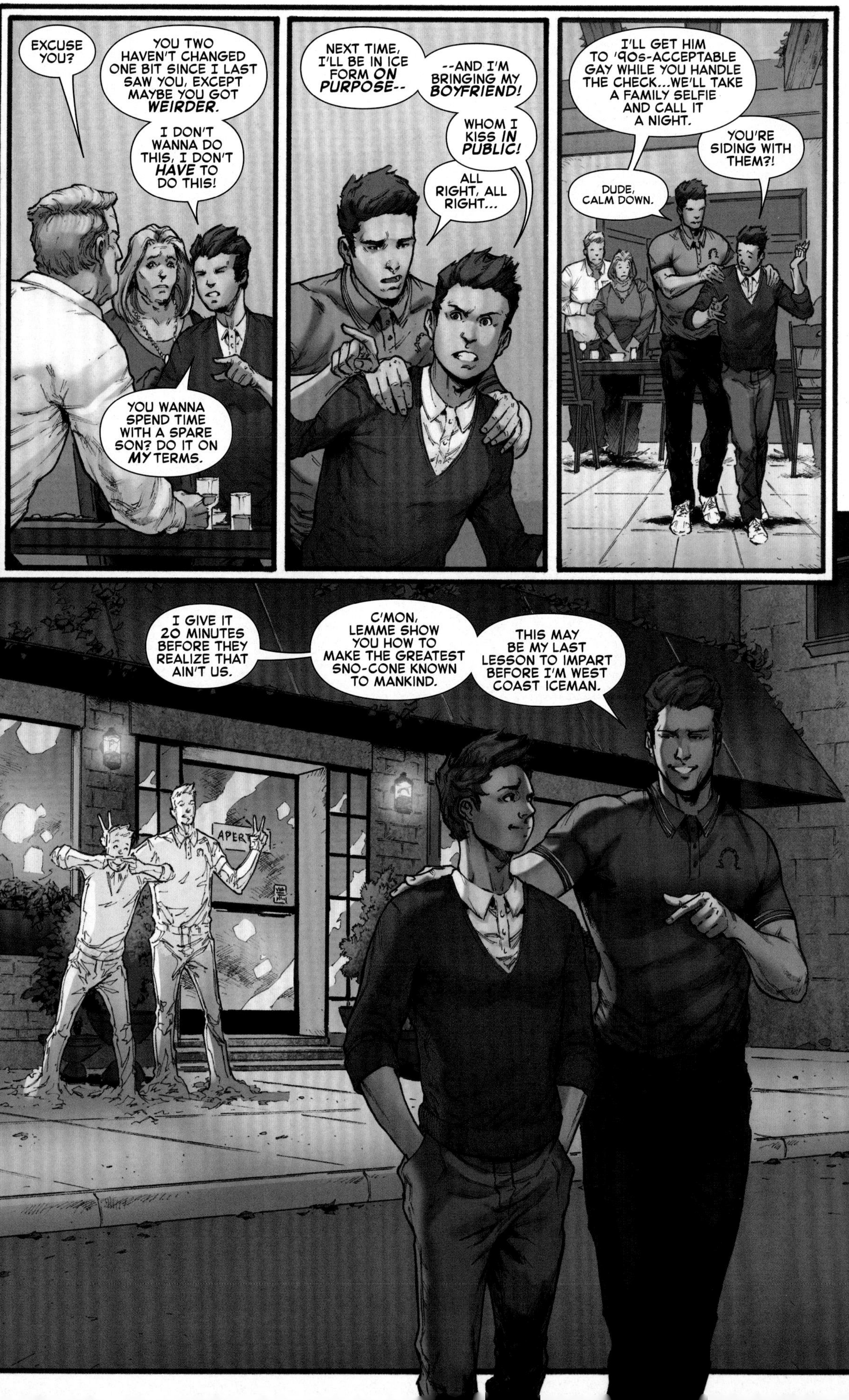
EXCUSE YOU?
YOU TWO HAVEN'T CHANGED ONE BIT SINCE I LAST SAW YOU, EXCEPT MAYBE YOU GOT WEIRDER.
I DON'T WANNA DO THIS, I DON'T HAVE TO DO THIS!
YOU WANNA SPEND TIME WITH A SPARE SON? DO IT ON MY TERMS.
NEXT TIME, I'LL BE IN ICE FORM ON PURPOSE--
--AND I'M BRINGING MY BOYFRIEND!
WHOM I KISS IN PUBLIC!
ALL RIGHT, ALL RIGHT...
I'LL GET HIM TO '90s-ACCEPTABLE GAY WHILE YOU HANDLE THE CHECK...WE'LL TAKE A FAMILY SELFIE AND CALL IT A NIGHT.
YOU'RE SIDING WITH THEM?!
DUDE, CALM DOWN.
I GIVE IT 20 MINUTES BEFORE THEY REALIZE THAT AIN'T US.
C'MON, LEMME SHOW YOU HOW TO MAKE THE GREATEST SNO-CONE KNOWN TO MANKIND.
THIS MAY BE MY LAST LESSON TO IMPART BEFORE I'M WEST COAST ICEMAN.
APERT

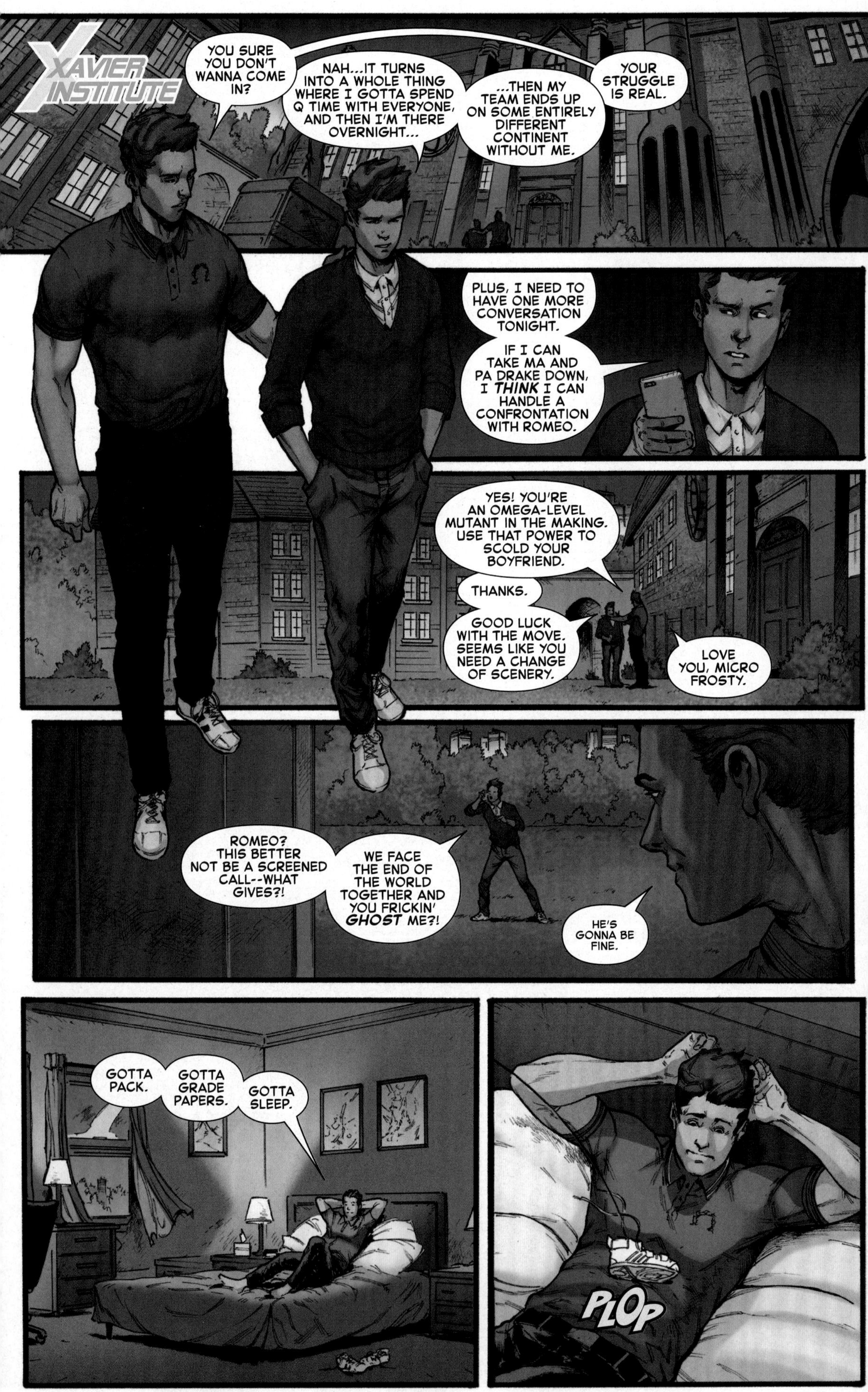
XAVIER INSTITUTE
YOU SURE YOU DON'T WANNA COME IN?
NAH...IT TURNS INTO A WHOLE THING WHERE I GOTTA SPEND Q TIME WITH EVERYONE, AND THEN I'M THERE OVERNIGHT...
...THEN MY TEAM ENDS UP ON SOME ENTIRELY DIFFERENT CONTINENT WITHOUT ME.
YOUR STRUGGLE IS REAL.
PLUS, I NEED TO HAVE ONE MORE CONVERSATION TONIGHT.
IF I CAN TAKE MA AND PA DRAKE DOWN, I THINK I CAN HANDLE A CONFRONTATION WITH ROMEO.
YES! YOU'RE AN OMEGA-LEVEL MUTANT IN THE MAKING. USE THAT POWER TO SCOLD YOUR BOYFRIEND.
THANKS.
GOOD LUCK WITH THE MOVE. SEEMS LIKE YOU NEED A CHANGE OF SCENERY.
LOVE YOU, MICRO FROSTY.
ROMEO? THIS BETTER NOT BE A SCREENED CALL--WHAT GIVES?!
WE FACE THE END OF THE WORLD TOGETHER AND YOU FRICKIN' GHOST ME?!
HE'S GONNA BE FINE.
GOTTA PACK.
GOTTA GRADE PAPERS.
GOTTA SLEEP.
PLOP

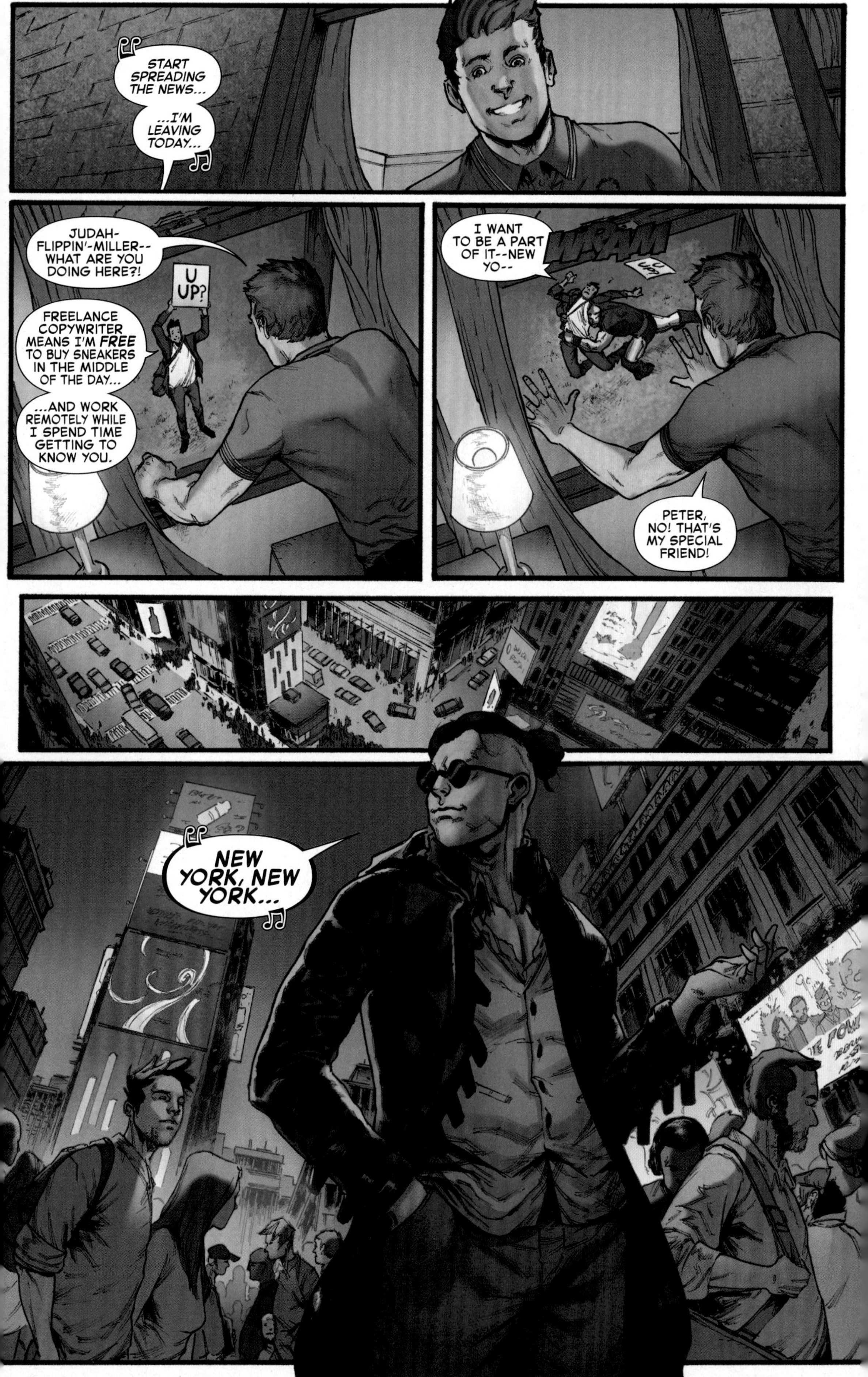
START SPREADING THE NEWS...
...I'M LEAVING TODAY...
JUDAH-FLIPPIN'-MILLER--WHAT ARE YOU DOING HERE?!
U UP?
FREELANCE COPYWRITER MEANS I'M FREE TO BUY SNEAKERS IN THE MIDDLE OF THE DAY...
...AND WORK REMOTELY WHILE I SPEND TIME GETTING TO KNOW YOU.
I WANT TO BE A PART OF IT--NEW YO--
WHAM
U UP?
PETER, NO! THAT'S MY SPECIAL FRIEND!
NEW YORK, NEW YORK...

9

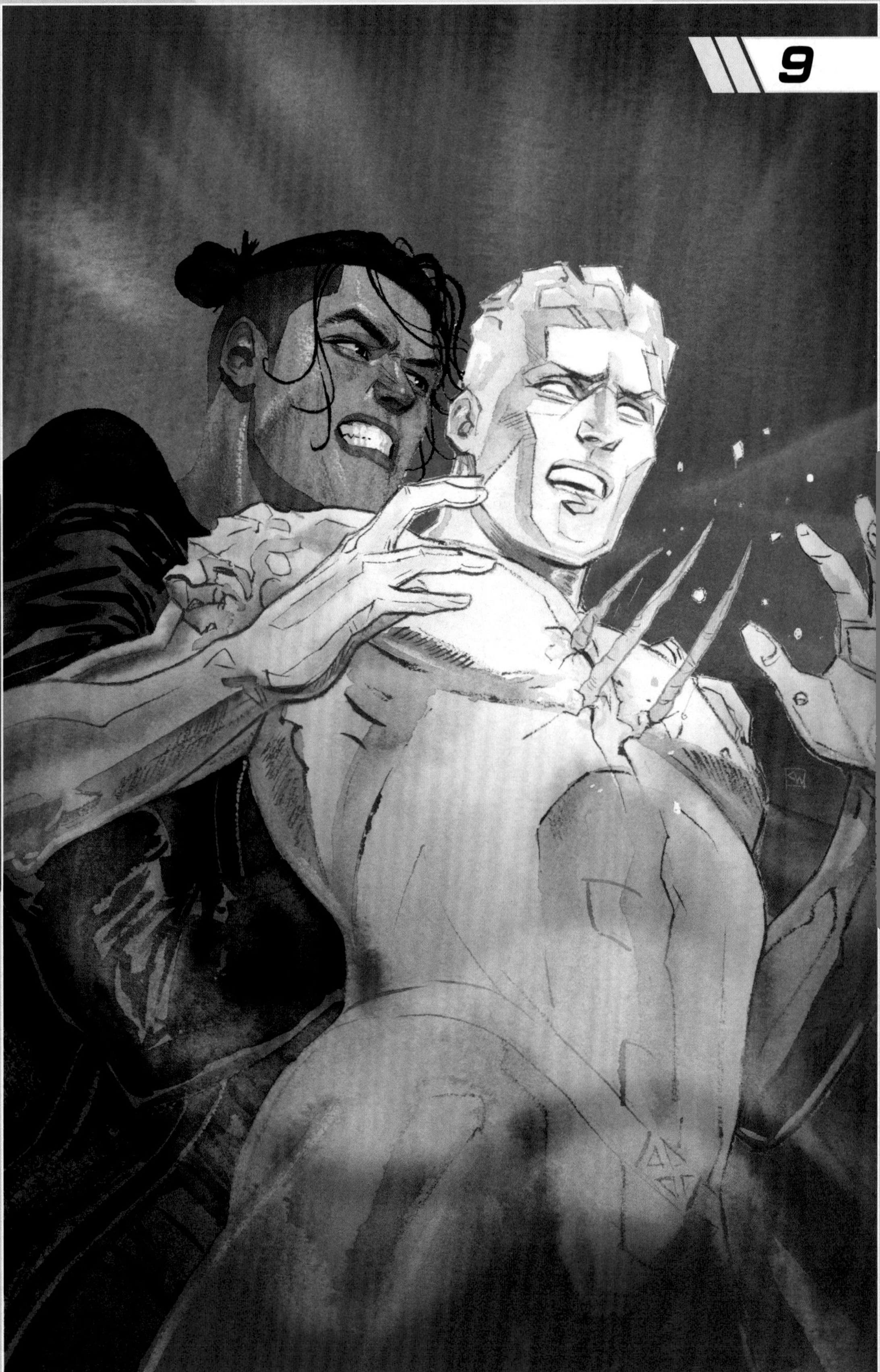

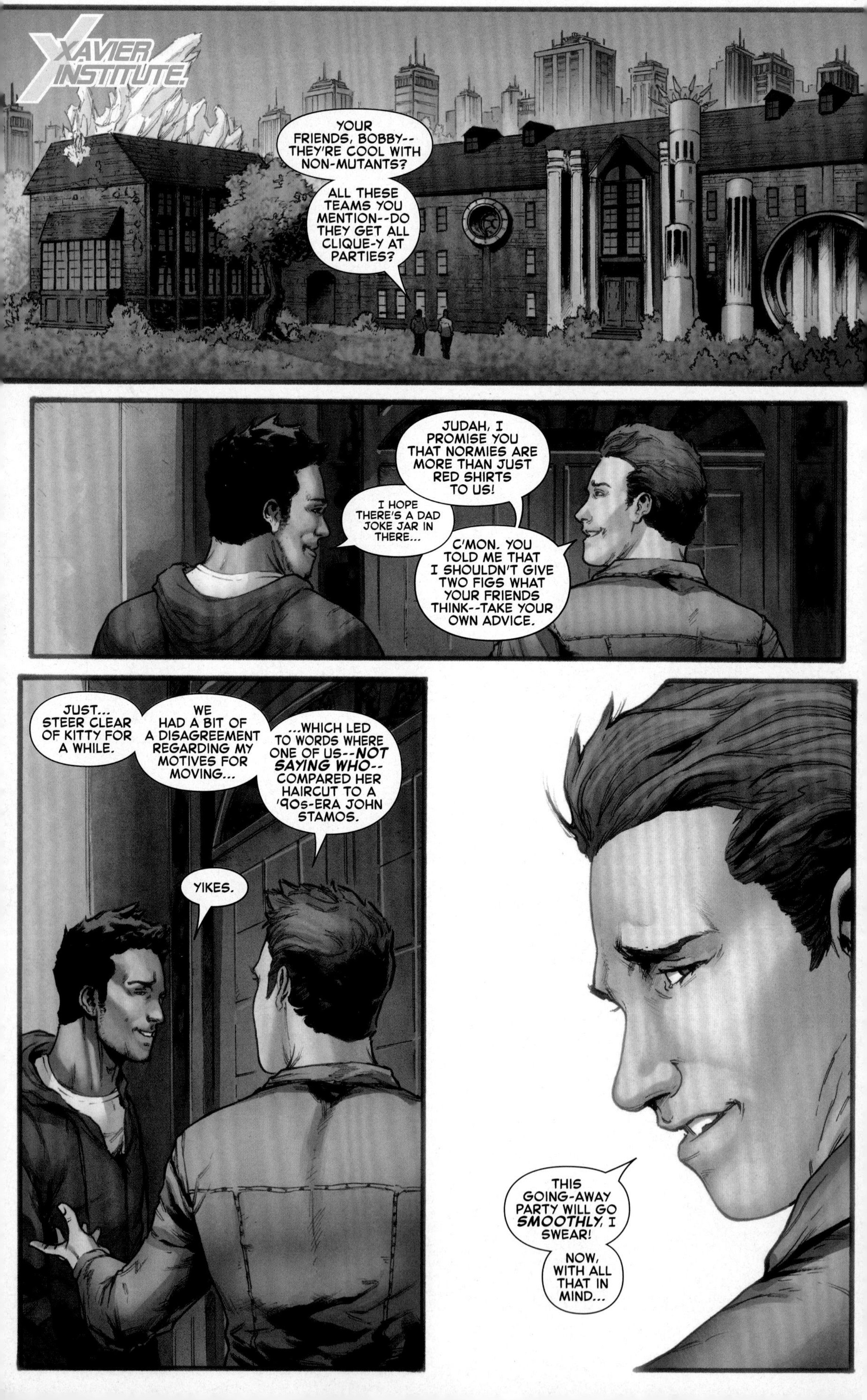
XAVIER INSTITUTE
YOUR FRIENDS, BOBBY-- THEY'RE COOL WITH NON-MUTANTS?
ALL THESE TEAMS YOU MENTION--DO THEY GET ALL CLIQUE-Y AT PARTIES?
JUDAH, I PROMISE YOU THAT NORMIES ARE MORE THAN JUST RED SHIRTS TO US!
I HOPE THERE'S A DAD JOKE JAR IN THERE...
C'MON. YOU TOLD ME THAT I SHOULDN'T GIVE TWO FIGS WHAT YOUR FRIENDS THINK--TAKE YOUR OWN ADVICE.
JUST... STEER CLEAR OF KITTY FOR A WHILE.
WE HAD A BIT OF A DISAGREEMENT REGARDING MY MOTIVES FOR MOVING...
...WHICH LED TO WORDS WHERE ONE OF US--NOT SAYING WHO--COMPARED HER HAIRCUT TO A '90s-ERA JOHN STAMOS.
YIKES.
THIS GOING-AWAY PARTY WILL GO SMOOTHLY, I SWEAR!
NOW, WITH ALL THAT IN MIND...

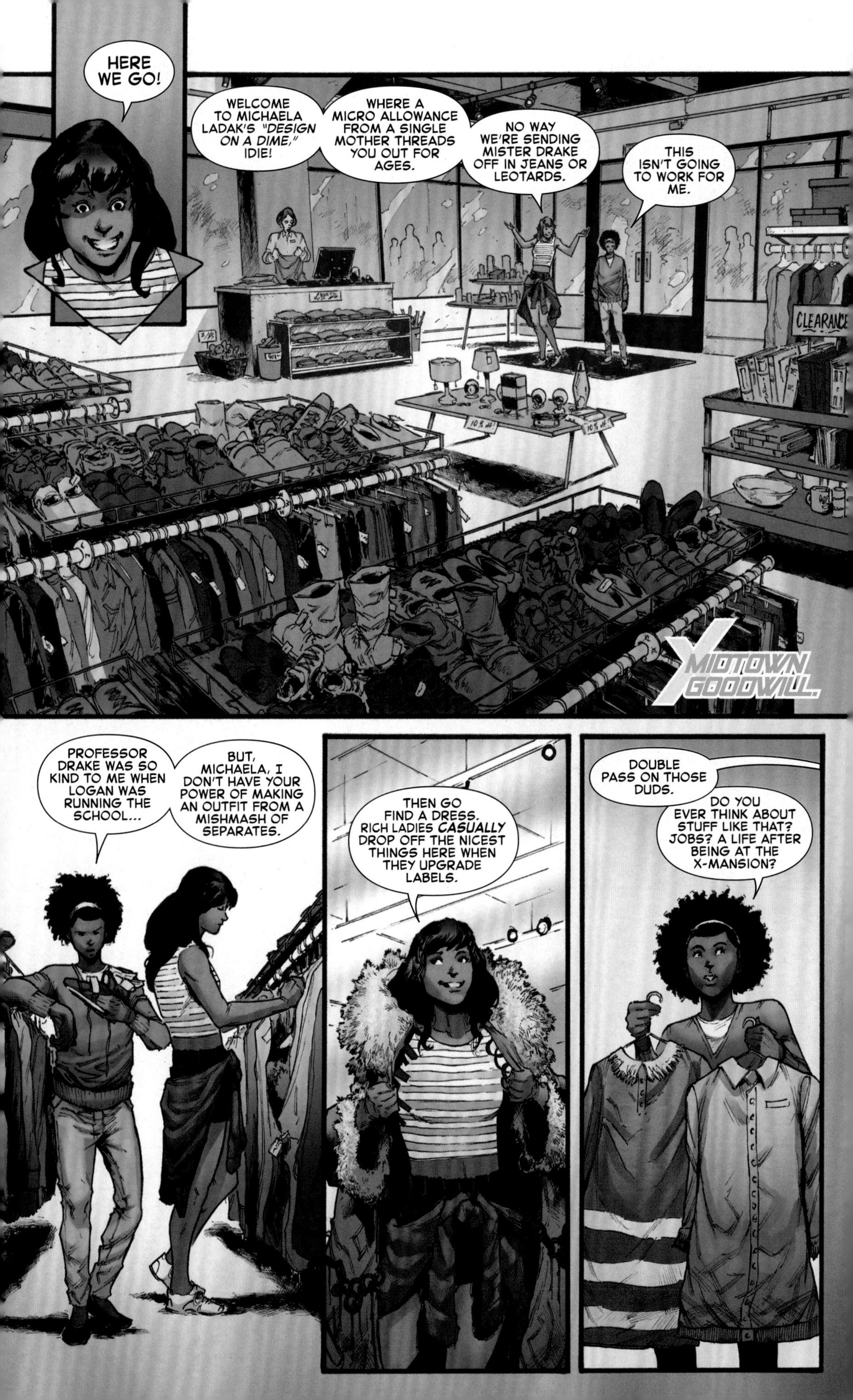
HERE WE GO!
WELCOME TO MICHAELA LADAK'S "DESIGN ON A DIME," IDIE!
WHERE A MICRO ALLOWANCE FROM A SINGLE MOTHER THREADS YOU OUT FOR AGES.
NO WAY WE'RE SENDING MISTER DRAKE OFF IN JEANS OR LEOTARDS.
THIS ISN'T GOING TO WORK FOR ME.
CLEARANCE
MIDTOWN GOODWILL.
PROFESSOR DRAKE WAS SO KIND TO ME WHEN LOGAN WAS RUNNING THE SCHOOL...
BUT, MICHAELA, I DON'T HAVE YOUR POWER OF MAKING AN OUTFIT FROM A MISHMASH OF SEPARATES.
THEN GO FIND A DRESS. RICH LADIES CASUALLY DROP OFF THE NICEST THINGS HERE WHEN THEY UPGRADE LABELS.
DOUBLE PASS ON THOSE DUDS.
DO YOU EVER THINK ABOUT STUFF LIKE THAT? JOBS? A LIFE AFTER BEING AT THE X-MANSION?

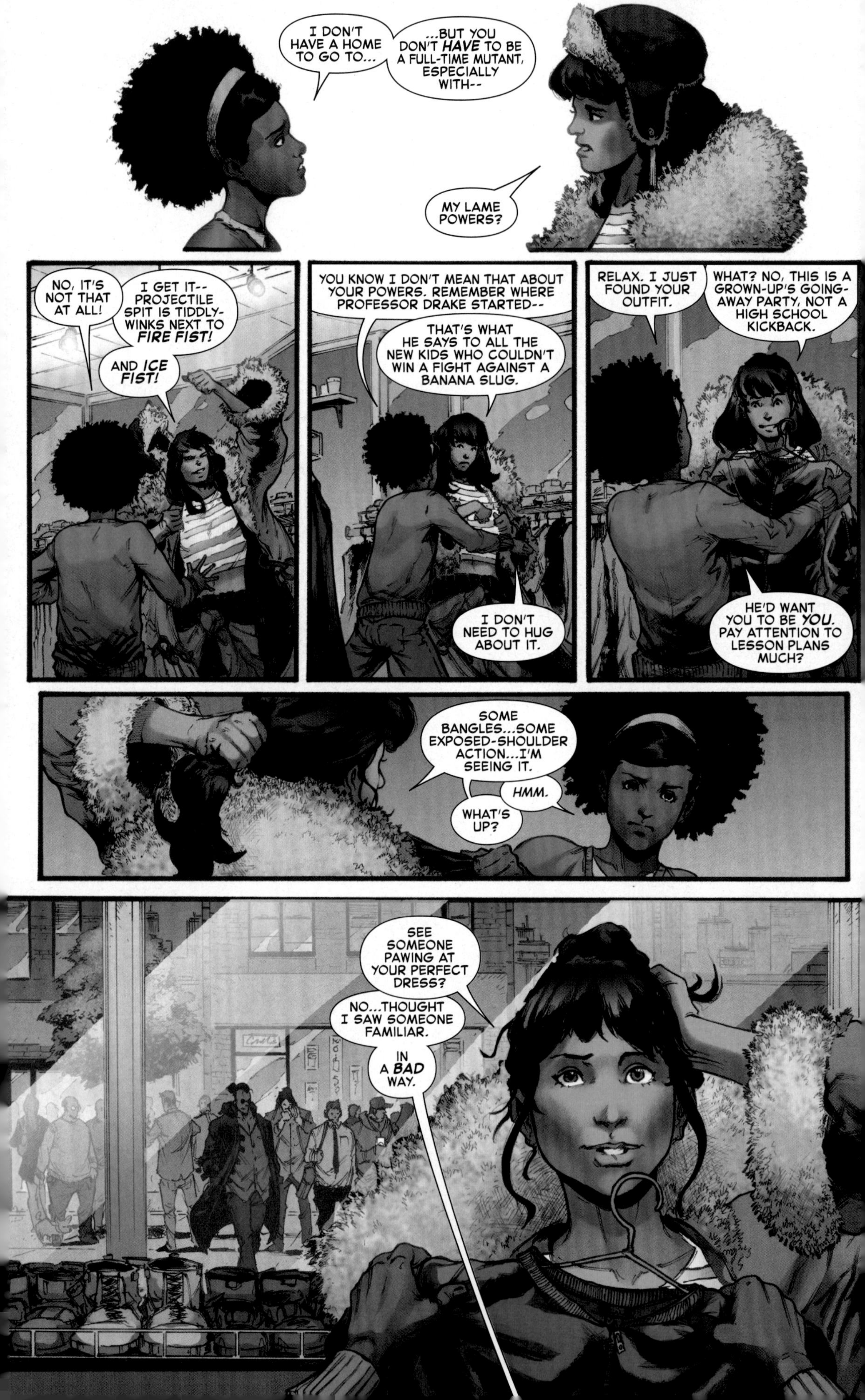
I DON'T HAVE A HOME TO GO TO...
...BUT YOU DON'T HAVE TO BE A FULL-TIME MUTANT, ESPECIALLY WITH--
MY LAME POWERS?
NO, IT'S NOT THAT AT ALL!
I GET IT-- PROJECTILE SPIT IS TIDDLY-WINKS NEXT TO FIRE FIST!
AND ICE FIST!
YOU KNOW I DON'T MEAN THAT ABOUT YOUR POWERS. REMEMBER WHERE PROFESSOR DRAKE STARTED--
THAT'S WHAT HE SAYS TO ALL THE NEW KIDS WHO COULDN'T WIN A FIGHT AGAINST A BANANA SLUG.
I DON'T NEED TO HUG ABOUT IT.
RELAX. I JUST FOUND YOUR OUTFIT.
WHAT? NO, THIS IS A GROWN-UP'S GOING-AWAY PARTY, NOT A HIGH SCHOOL KICKBACK.
HE'D WANT YOU TO BE YOU. PAY ATTENTION TO LESSON PLANS MUCH?
SOME BANGLES...SOME EXPOSED-SHOULDER ACTION...I'M SEEING IT.
HMM.
WHAT'S UP?
SEE SOMEONE PAWING AT YOUR PERFECT DRESS?
NO...THOUGHT I SAW SOMEONE FAMILIAR.
IN A BAD WAY.

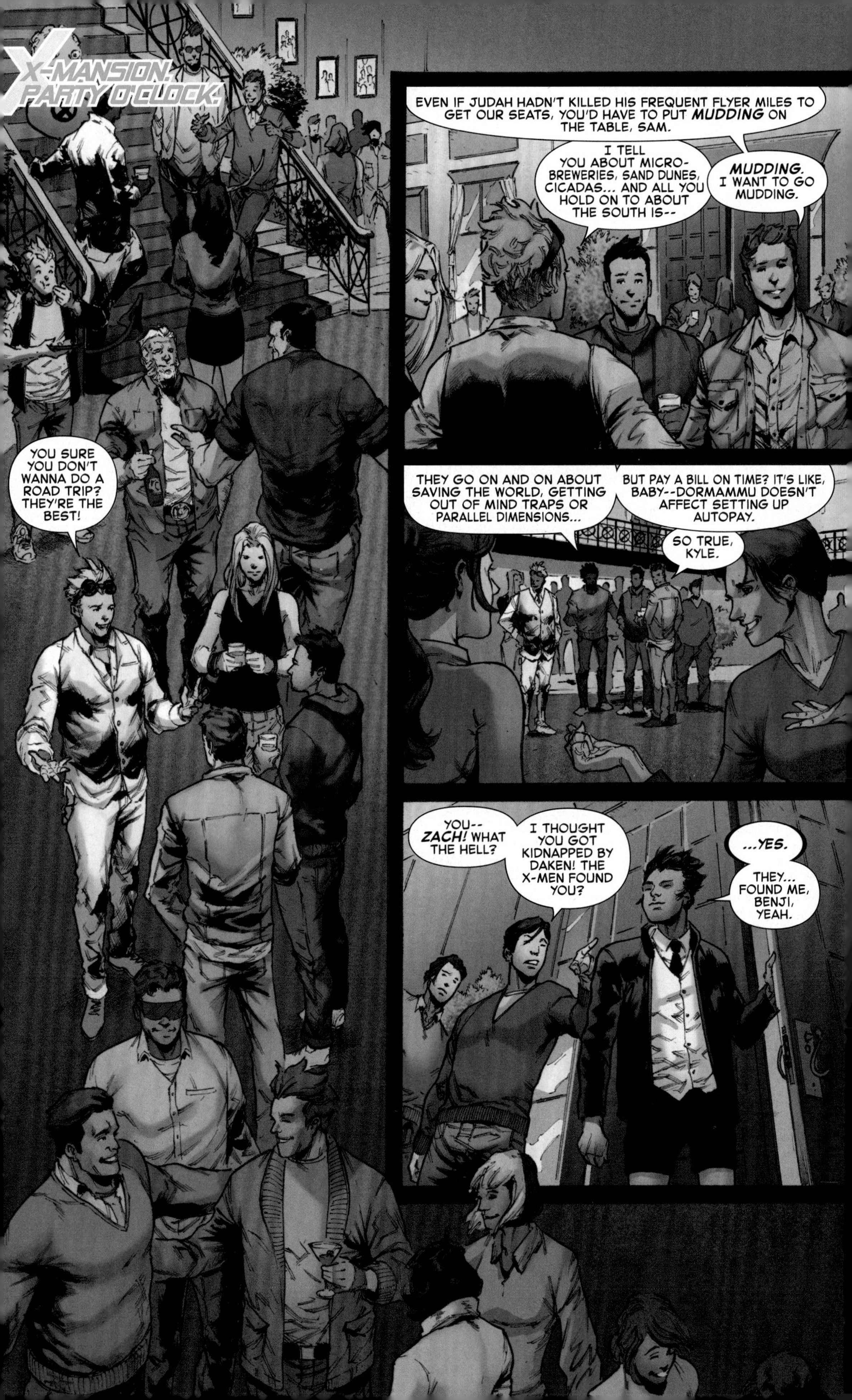
X-MANSION. PARTY O'CLOCK.
YOU SURE YOU DON'T WANNA DO A ROAD TRIP? THEY'RE THE BEST!
EVEN IF JUDAH HADN'T KILLED HIS FREQUENT FLYER MILES TO GET OUR SEATS, YOU'D HAVE TO PUT MUDDING ON THE TABLE, SAM.
I TELL YOU ABOUT MICRO-BREWERIES, SAND DUNES, CICADAS... AND ALL YOU HOLD ON TO ABOUT THE SOUTH IS--
MUDDING. I WANT TO GO MUDDING.
THEY GO ON AND ON ABOUT SAVING THE WORLD, GETTING OUT OF MIND TRAPS OR PARALLEL DIMENSIONS...
BUT PAY A BILL ON TIME? IT'S LIKE, BABY--DORMAMMU DOESN'T AFFECT SETTING UP AUTOPAY.
SO TRUE, KYLE.
YOU-- ZACH! WHAT THE HELL?
I THOUGHT YOU GOT KIDNAPPED BY DAKEN! THE X-MEN FOUND YOU?
...YES.
THEY... FOUND ME, BENJI, YEAH.

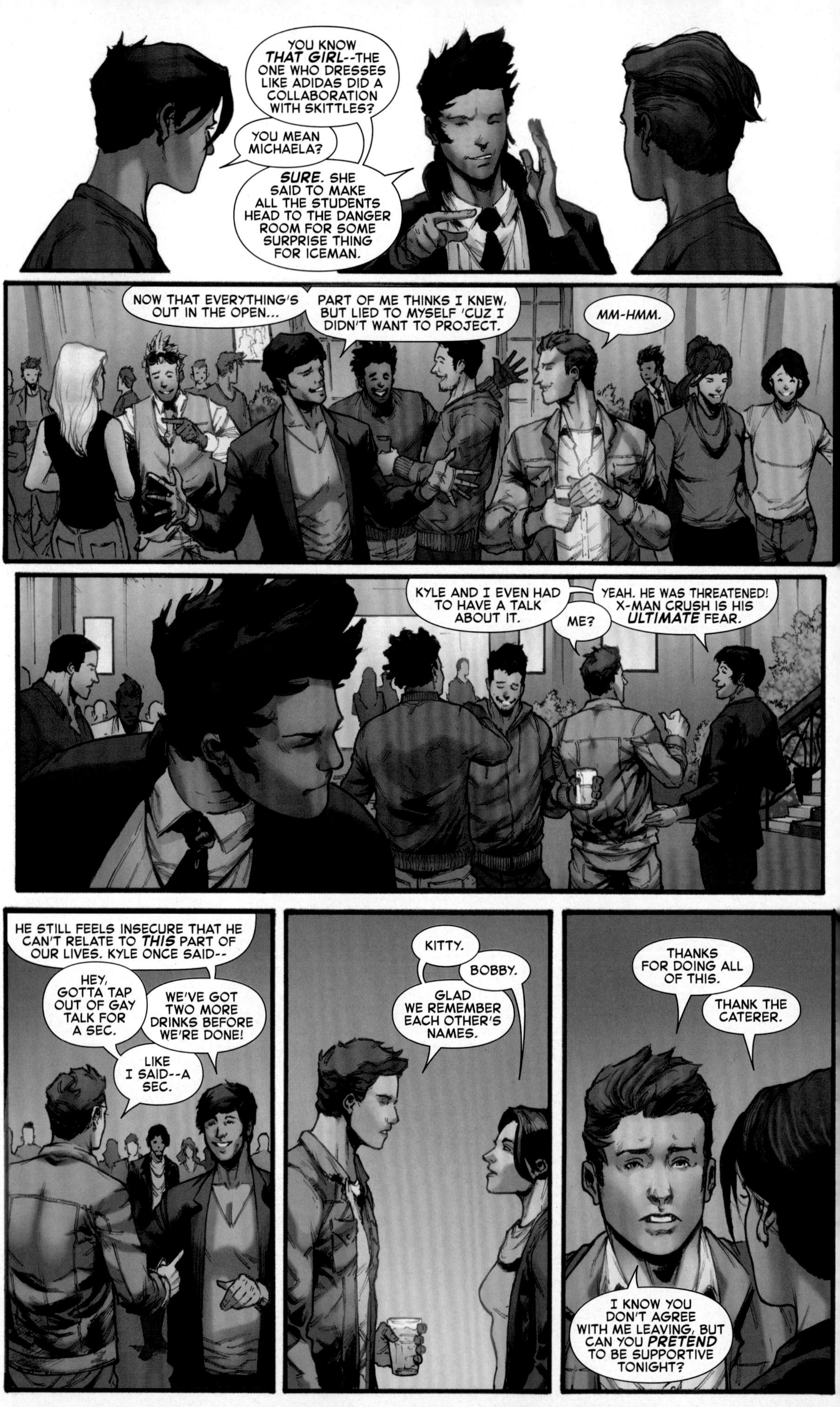
YOU KNOW THAT GIRL--THE ONE WHO DRESSES LIKE ADIDAS DID A COLLABORATION WITH SKITTLES?
YOU MEAN MICHAELA?
SURE. SHE SAID TO MAKE ALL THE STUDENTS HEAD TO THE DANGER ROOM FOR SOME SURPRISE THING FOR ICEMAN.
NOW THAT EVERYTHING'S OUT IN THE OPEN...
PART OF ME THINKS I KNEW, BUT LIED TO MYSELF 'CUZ I DIDN'T WANT TO PROJECT.
MM-HMM.
KYLE AND I EVEN HAD TO HAVE A TALK ABOUT IT.
ME?
YEAH. HE WAS THREATENED! X-MAN CRUSH IS HIS ULTIMATE FEAR.
HE STILL FEELS INSECURE THAT HE CAN'T RELATE TO THIS PART OF OUR LIVES. KYLE ONCE SAID--
HEY, GOTTA TAP OUT OF GAY TALK FOR A SEC.
WE'VE GOT TWO MORE DRINKS BEFORE WE'RE DONE!
LIKE I SAID--A SEC.
KITTY.
BOBBY.
GLAD WE REMEMBER EACH OTHER'S NAMES.
THANKS FOR DOING ALL OF THIS.
THANK THE CATERER.
I KNOW YOU DON'T AGREE WITH ME LEAVING, BUT CAN YOU PRETEND TO BE SUPPORTIVE TONIGHT?

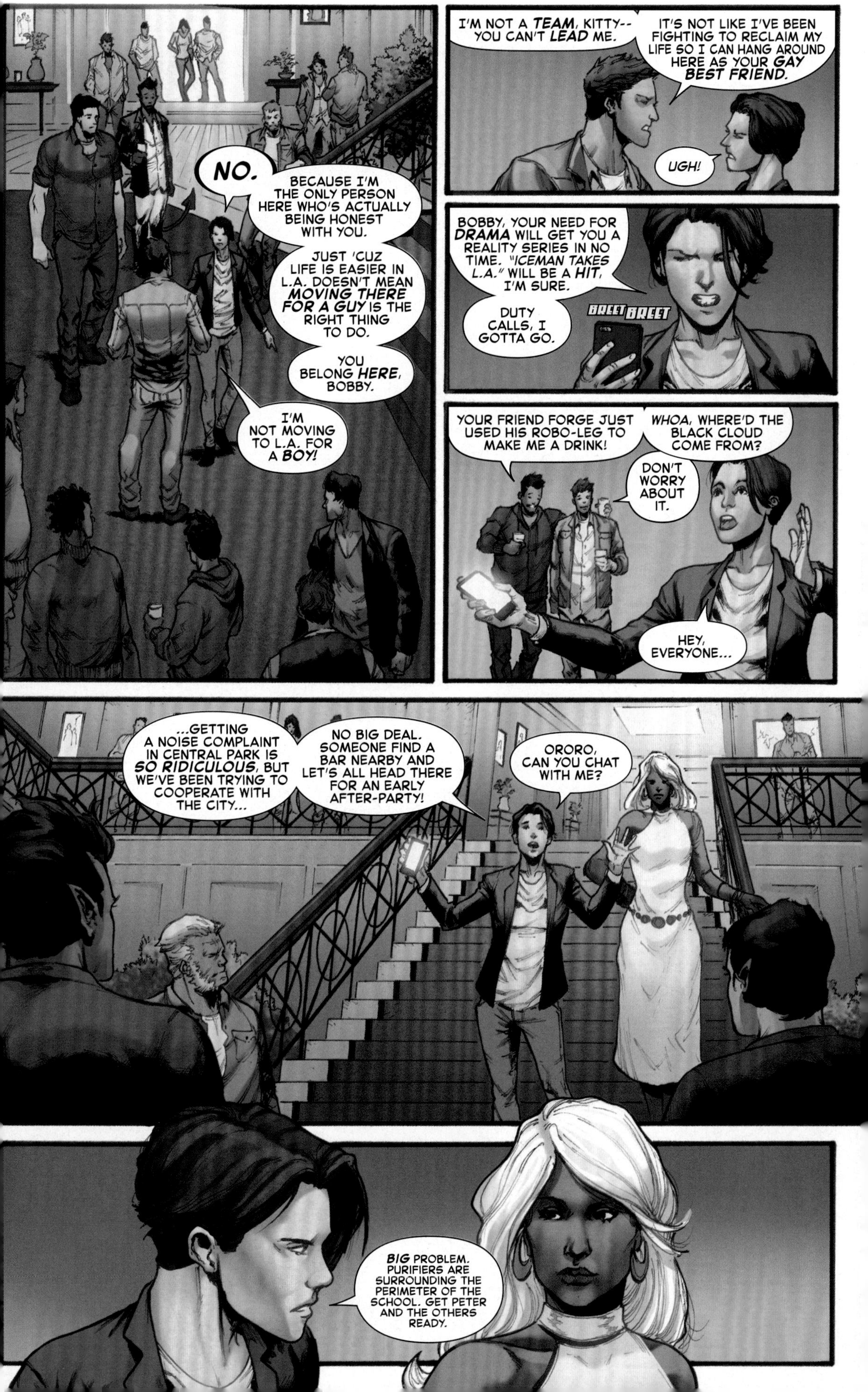
NO.
BECAUSE I'M THE ONLY PERSON HERE WHO'S ACTUALLY BEING HONEST WITH YOU.
JUST 'CUZ LIFE IS EASIER IN L.A. DOESN'T MEAN MOVING THERE FOR A GUY IS THE RIGHT THING TO DO.
YOU BELONG HERE, BOBBY.
I'M NOT MOVING TO L.A. FOR A BOY!
I'M NOT A TEAM, KITTY-- YOU CAN'T LEAD ME.
IT'S NOT LIKE I'VE BEEN FIGHTING TO RECLAIM MY LIFE SO I CAN HANG AROUND HERE AS YOUR GAY BEST FRIEND.
UGH!
BOBBY, YOUR NEED FOR DRAMA WILL GET YOU A REALITY SERIES IN NO TIME. "ICEMAN TAKES L.A." WILL BE A HIT, I'M SURE.
BREET BREET
DUTY CALLS, I GOTTA GO.
YOUR FRIEND FORGE JUST USED HIS ROBO-LEG TO MAKE ME A DRINK!
WHOA, WHERE'D THE BLACK CLOUD COME FROM?
DON'T WORRY ABOUT IT.
HEY, EVERYONE...
...GETTING A NOISE COMPLAINT IN CENTRAL PARK IS SO RIDICULOUS, BUT WE'VE BEEN TRYING TO COOPERATE WITH THE CITY...
NO BIG DEAL. SOMEONE FIND A BAR NEARBY AND LET'S ALL HEAD THERE FOR AN EARLY AFTER-PARTY!
ORORO, CAN YOU CHAT WITH ME?
BIG PROBLEM. PURIFIERS ARE SURROUNDING THE PERIMETER OF THE SCHOOL. GET PETER AND THE OTHERS READY.

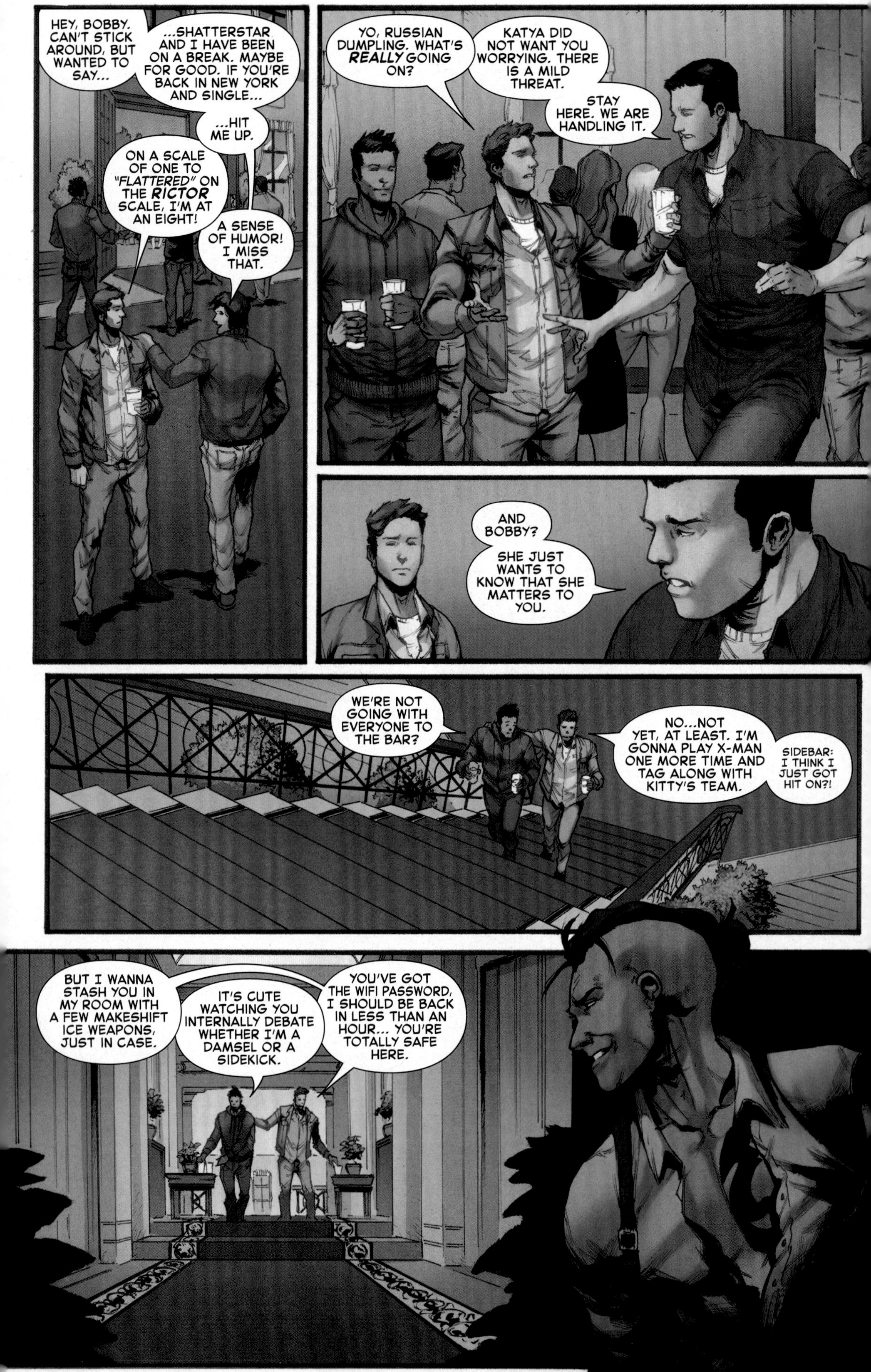
HEY, BOBBY. CAN'T STICK AROUND, BUT WANTED TO SAY...
...SHATTERSTAR AND I HAVE BEEN ON A BREAK. MAYBE FOR GOOD. IF YOU'RE BACK IN NEW YORK AND SINGLE...
...HIT ME UP.
ON A SCALE OF ONE TO "FLATTERED" ON THE RICTOR SCALE, I'M AT AN EIGHT!
A SENSE OF HUMOR! I MISS THAT.
YO, RUSSIAN DUMPLING. WHAT'S REALLY GOING ON?
KATYA DID NOT WANT YOU WORRYING. THERE IS A MILD THREAT.
STAY HERE. WE ARE HANDLING IT.
AND BOBBY?
SHE JUST WANTS TO KNOW THAT SHE MATTERS TO YOU.
WE'RE NOT GOING WITH EVERYONE TO THE BAR?
NO...NOT YET, AT LEAST. I'M GONNA PLAY X-MAN ONE MORE TIME AND TAG ALONG WITH KITTY'S TEAM.
SIDEBAR: I THINK I JUST GOT HIT ON?!
BUT I WANNA STASH YOU IN MY ROOM WITH A FEW MAKESHIFT ICE WEAPONS, JUST IN CASE.
IT'S CUTE WATCHING YOU INTERNALLY DEBATE WHETHER I'M A DAMSEL OR A SIDEKICK.
YOU'VE GOT THE WIFI PASSWORD, I SHOULD BE BACK IN LESS THAN AN HOUR... YOU'RE TOTALLY SAFE HERE.

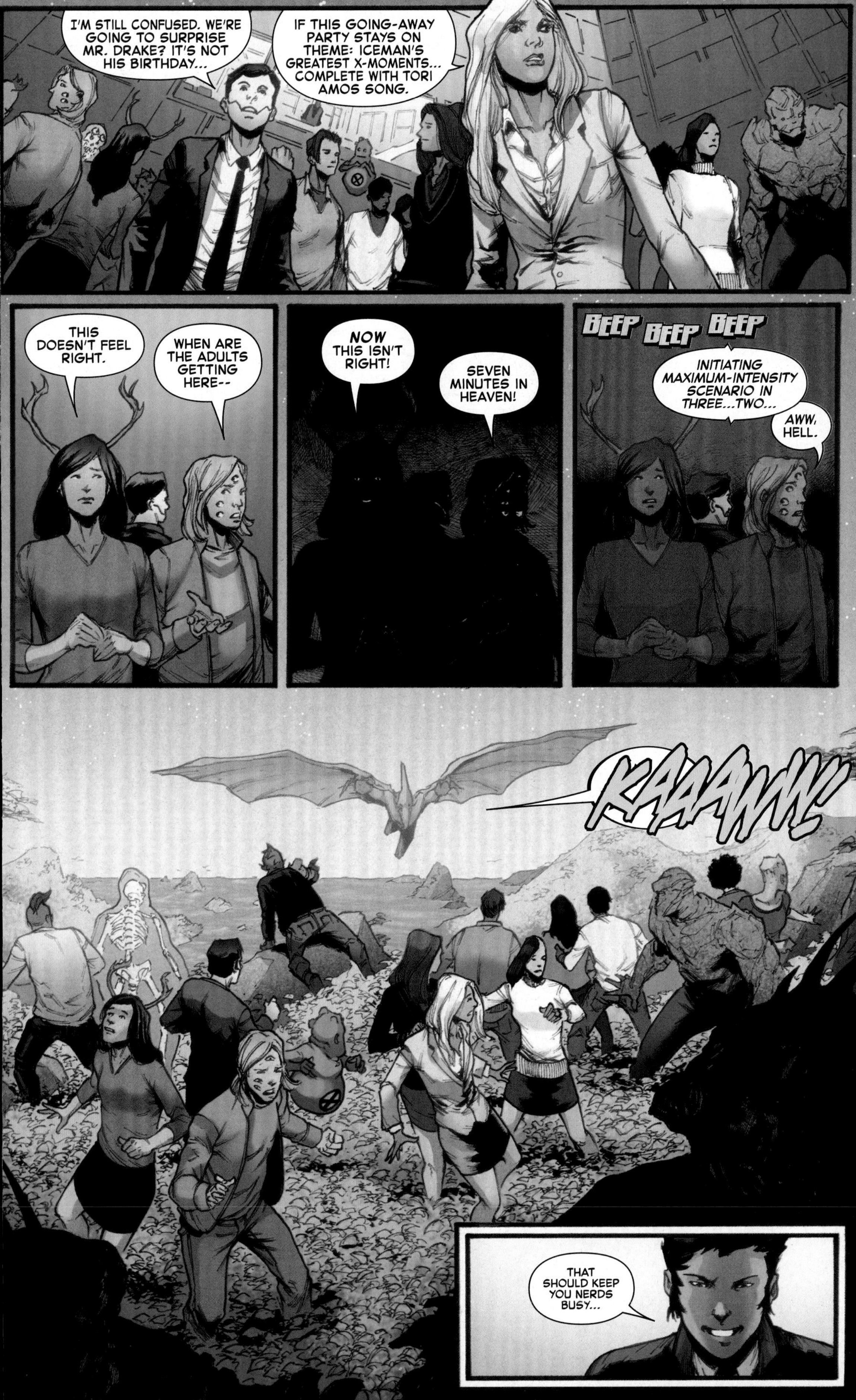
I'M STILL CONFUSED. WE'RE GOING TO SURPRISE MR. DRAKE? IT'S NOT HIS BIRTHDAY...
IF THIS GOING-AWAY PARTY STAYS ON THEME: ICEMAN'S GREATEST X-MOMENTS... COMPLETE WITH TORI AMOS SONG.
THIS DOESN'T FEEL RIGHT.
WHEN ARE THE ADULTS GETTING HERE--
NOW THIS ISN'T RIGHT!
SEVEN MINUTES IN HEAVEN!
BEEP BEEP BEEP
INITIATING MAXIMUM-INTENSITY SCENARIO IN THREE...TWO...
AWW, HELL.
KAAAWW!
THAT SHOULD KEEP YOU NERDS BUSY...

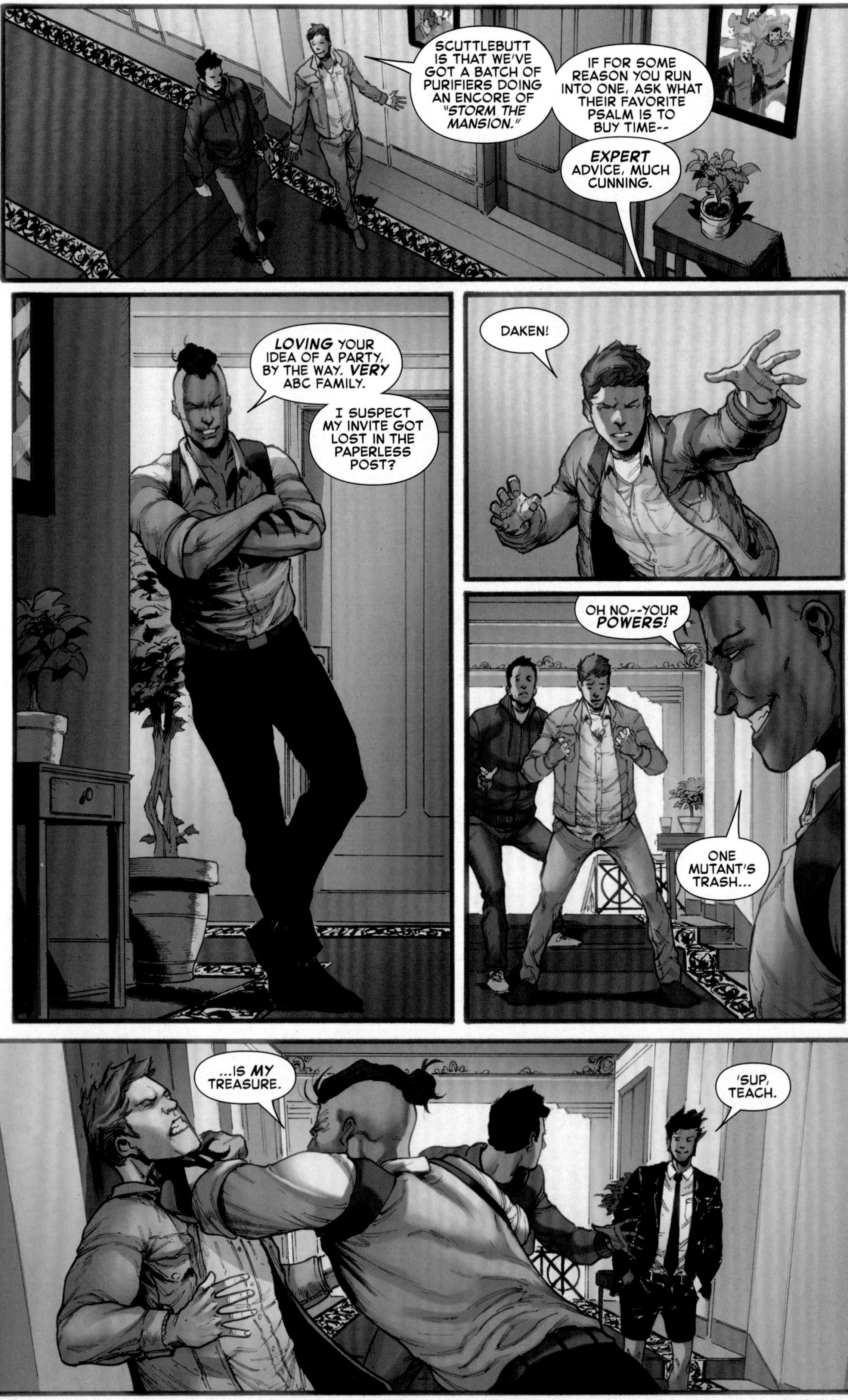

SCUTTLEBUTT IS THAT WE'VE GOT A BATCH OF PURIFIERS DOING AN ENCORE OF "STORM THE MANSION."
IF FOR SOME REASON YOU RUN INTO ONE, ASK WHAT THEIR FAVORITE PSALM IS TO BUY TIME--
EXPERT ADVICE, MUCH CUNNING.
LOVING YOUR IDEA OF A PARTY, BY THE WAY. VERY ABC FAMILY.
I SUSPECT MY INVITE GOT LOST IN THE PAPERLESS POST?
DAKEN!
OH NO--YOUR POWERS!
ONE MUTANT'S TRASH...
...IS MY TREASURE.
'SUP, TEACH.

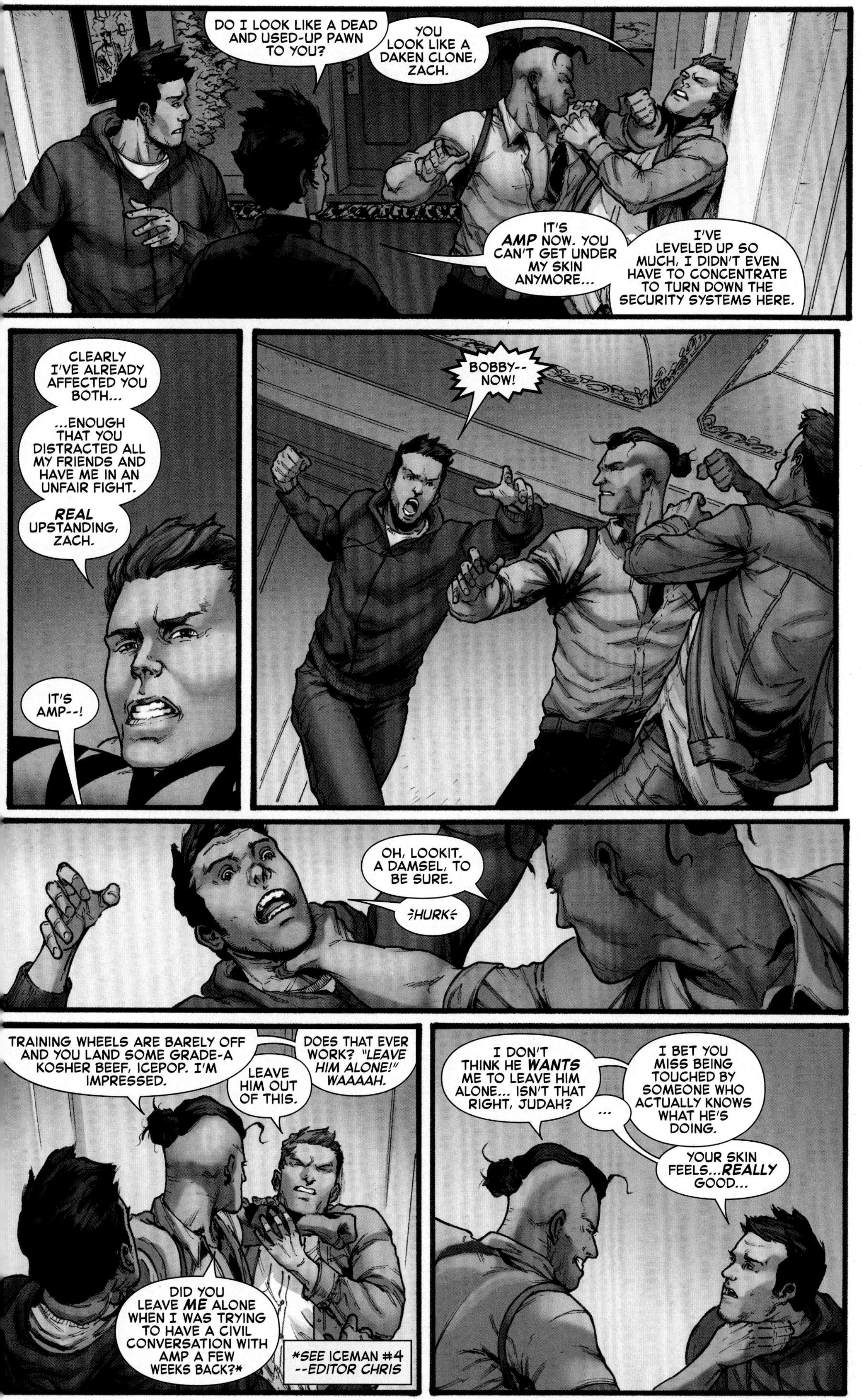
DO I LOOK LIKE A DEAD AND USED-UP PAWN TO YOU?
YOU LOOK LIKE A DAKEN CLONE, ZACH.
IT'S AMP NOW. YOU CAN'T GET UNDER MY SKIN ANYMORE...
I'VE LEVELED UP SO MUCH, I DIDN'T EVEN HAVE TO CONCENTRATE TO TURN DOWN THE SECURITY SYSTEMS HERE.
CLEARLY I'VE ALREADY AFFECTED YOU BOTH...
...ENOUGH THAT YOU DISTRACTED ALL MY FRIENDS AND HAVE ME IN AN UNFAIR FIGHT.
REAL UPSTANDING, ZACH.
IT'S AMP--!
BOBBY-- NOW!
OH, LOOKIT. A DAMSEL, TO BE SURE.
HURK
TRAINING WHEELS ARE BARELY OFF AND YOU LAND SOME GRADE-A KOSHER BEEF, ICEPOP. I'M IMPRESSED.
LEAVE HIM OUT OF THIS.
DOES THAT EVER WORK? "LEAVE HIM ALONE!" WAAAAH.
DID YOU LEAVE ME ALONE WHEN I WAS TRYING TO HAVE A CIVIL CONVERSATION WITH AMP A FEW WEEKS BACK?*
*SEE ICEMAN #4 --EDITOR CHRIS
I DON'T THINK HE WANTS ME TO LEAVE HIM ALONE... ISN'T THAT RIGHT, JUDAH?
...
I BET YOU MISS BEING TOUCHED BY SOMEONE WHO ACTUALLY KNOWS WHAT HE'S DOING.
YOUR SKIN FEELS...REALLY GOOD...

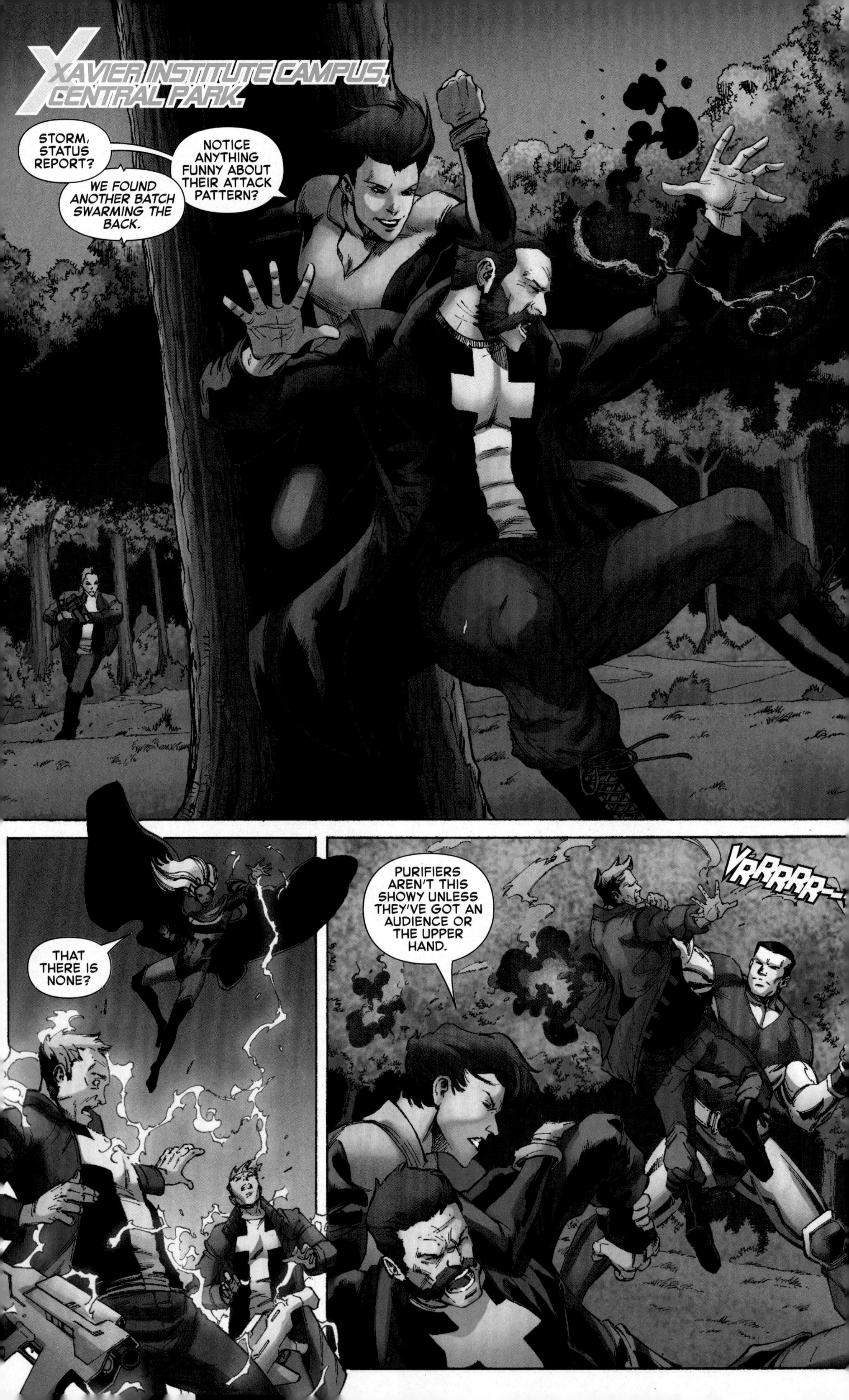
XAVIER INSTITUTE CAMPUS, CENTRAL PARK.
STORM, STATUS REPORT?
WE FOUND ANOTHER BATCH SWARMING THE BACK.
NOTICE ANYTHING FUNNY ABOUT THEIR ATTACK PATTERN?
THAT THERE IS NONE?
PURIFIERS AREN'T THIS SHOWY UNLESS THEY'VE GOT AN AUDIENCE OR THE UPPER HAND.
VRRRRR--

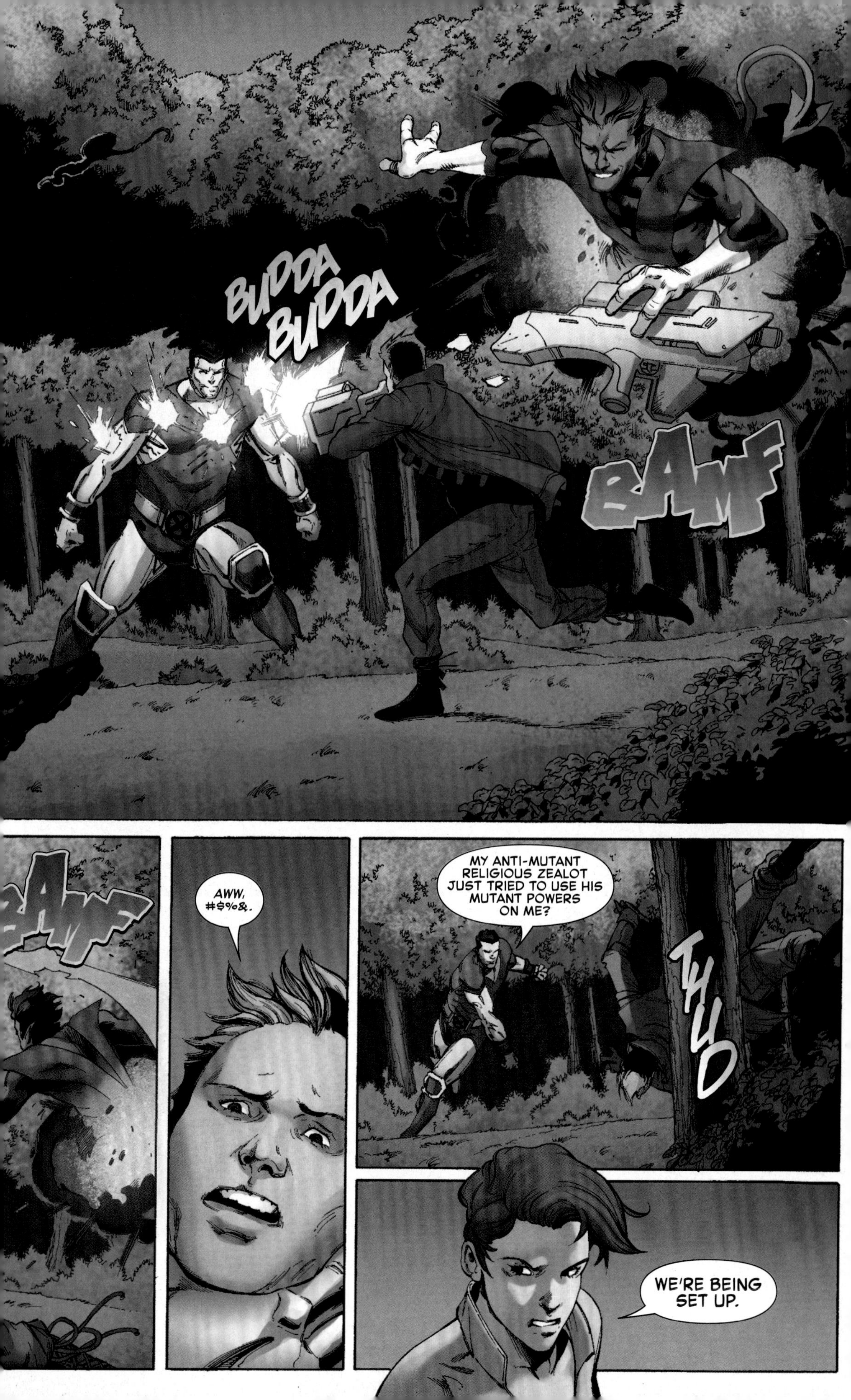

BUDDA BUDDA
BAMF
BAMF
AWW, #$%&.
MY ANTI-MUTANT RELIGIOUS ZEALOT JUST TRIED TO USE HIS MUTANT POWERS ON ME?
THUD
WE'RE BEING SET UP.

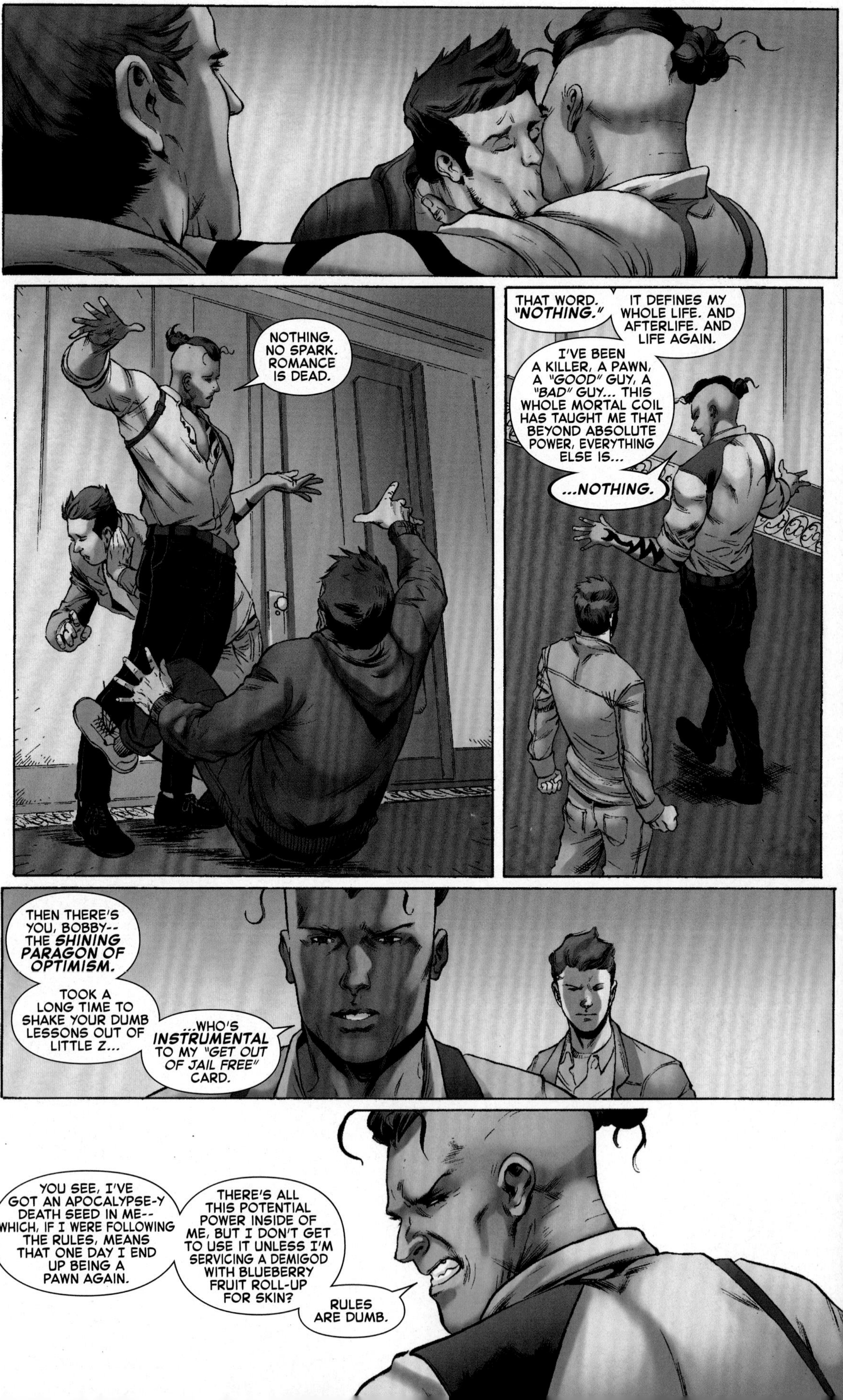

NOTHING. NO SPARK. ROMANCE IS DEAD.
THAT WORD. "NOTHING."
IT DEFINES MY WHOLE LIFE. AND AFTERLIFE. AND LIFE AGAIN.
I'VE BEEN A KILLER, A PAWN, A "GOOD" GUY, A "BAD" GUY... THIS WHOLE MORTAL COIL HAS TAUGHT ME THAT BEYOND ABSOLUTE POWER, EVERYTHING ELSE IS...
...NOTHING.
THEN THERE'S YOU, BOBBY-- THE SHINING PARAGON OF OPTIMISM.
TOOK A LONG TIME TO SHAKE YOUR DUMB LESSONS OUT OF LITTLE Z...
...WHO'S INSTRUMENTAL TO MY "GET OUT OF JAIL FREE" CARD.
YOU SEE, I'VE GOT AN APOCALYPSE-Y DEATH SEED IN ME-- WHICH, IF I WERE FOLLOWING THE RULES, MEANS THAT ONE DAY I END UP BEING A PAWN AGAIN.
THERE'S ALL THIS POTENTIAL POWER INSIDE OF ME, BUT I DON'T GET TO USE IT UNLESS I'M SERVICING A DEMIGOD WITH BLUEBERRY FRUIT ROLL-UP FOR SKIN?
RULES ARE DUMB.

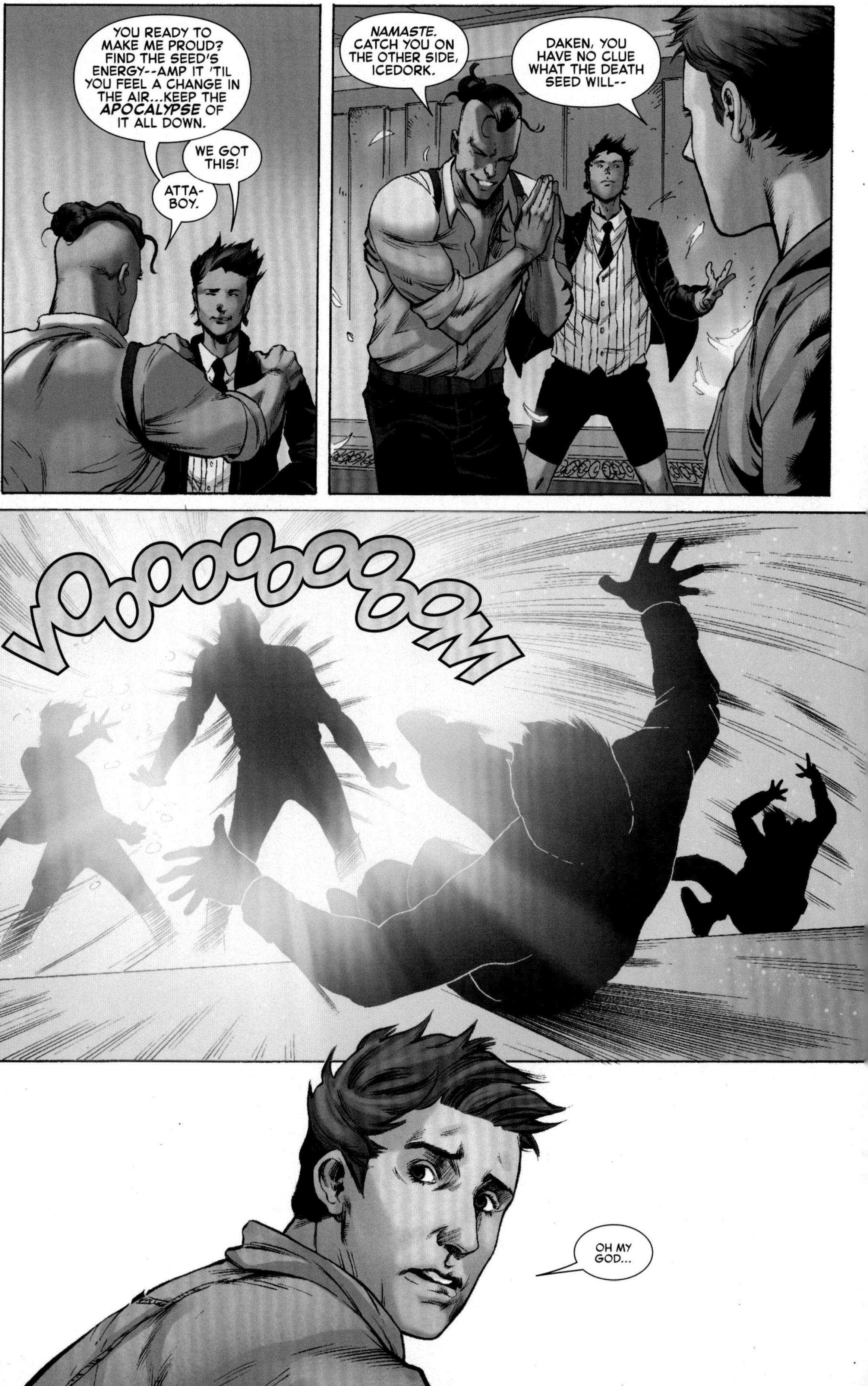
YOU READY TO MAKE ME PROUD? FIND THE SEED'S ENERGY--AMP IT 'TIL YOU FEEL A CHANGE IN THE AIR...KEEP THE *APOCALYPSE* OF IT ALL DOWN.
WE GOT THIS!
ATTA-BOY.
NAMASTE. CATCH YOU ON THE OTHER SIDE, ICEDORK.
DAKEN, YOU HAVE NO CLUE WHAT THE DEATH SEED WILL--
VOOOOOOOOOOM
OH MY GOD...

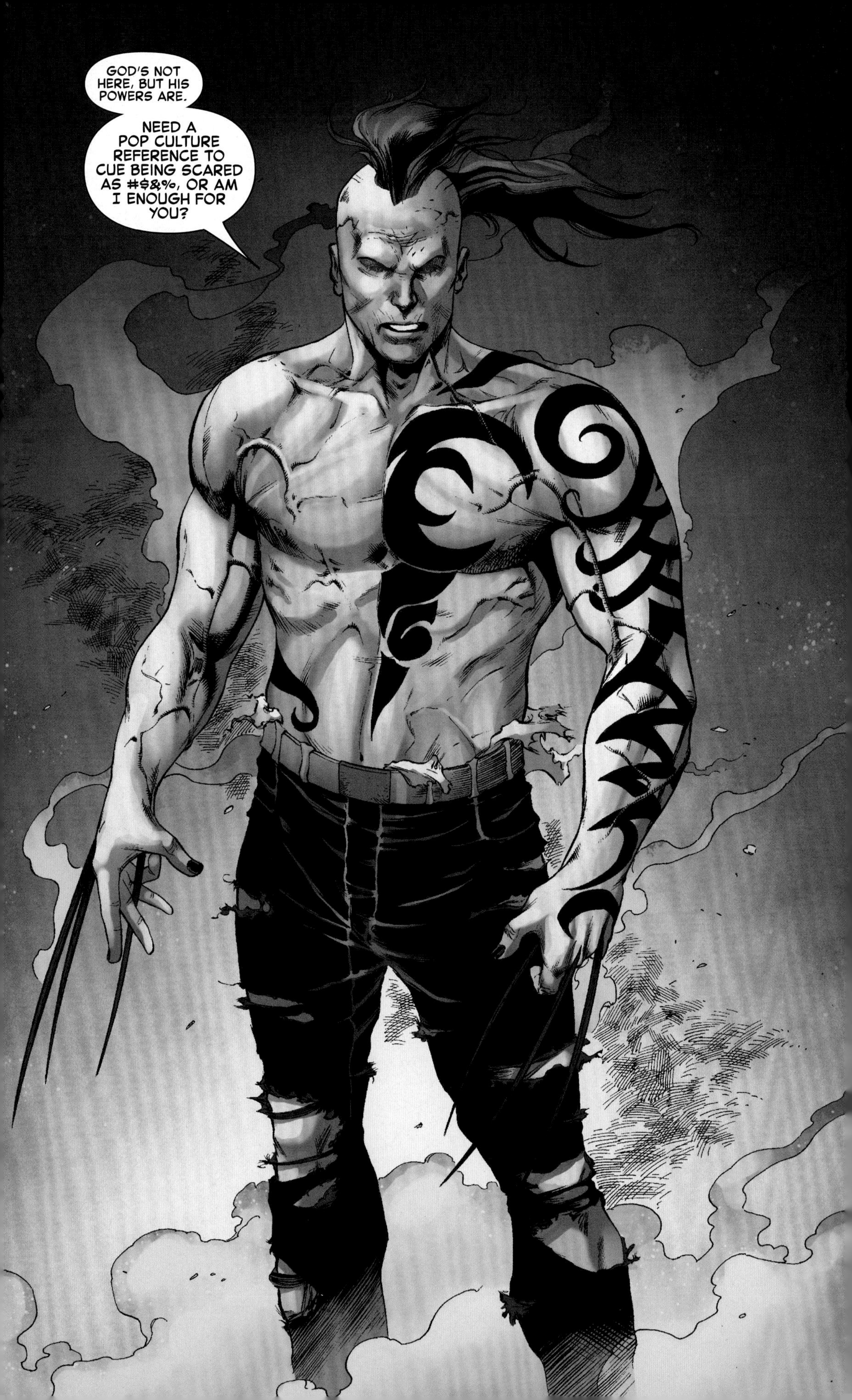
GOD'S NOT HERE, BUT HIS POWERS ARE.
NEED A POP CULTURE REFERENCE TO CUE BEING SCARED AS #$&%, OR AM I ENOUGH FOR YOU?

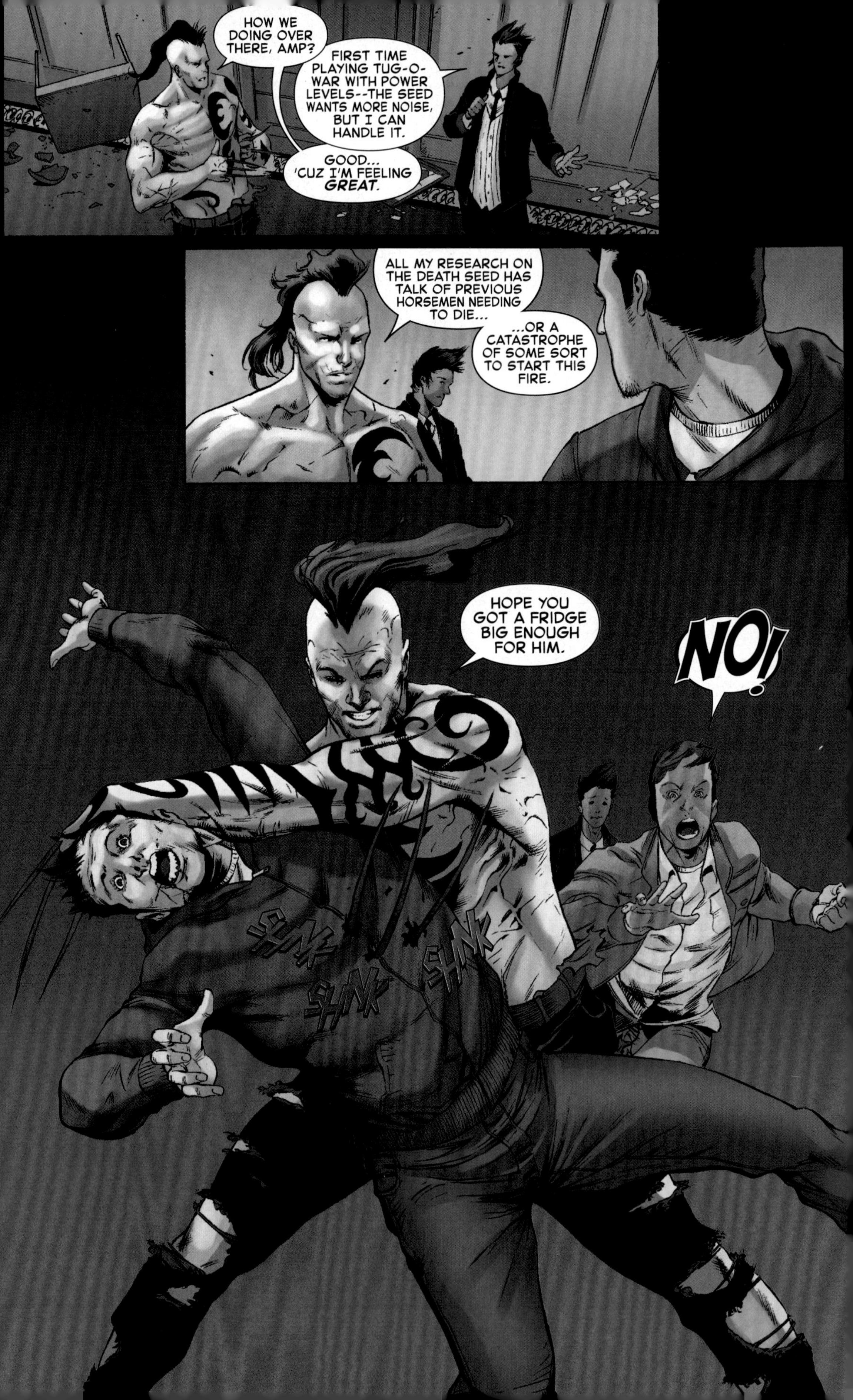
HOW WE DOING OVER THERE, AMP?
FIRST TIME PLAYING TUG-O-WAR WITH POWER LEVELS--THE SEED WANTS MORE NOISE, BUT I CAN HANDLE IT.
GOOD... 'CUZ I'M FEELING GREAT.
ALL MY RESEARCH ON THE DEATH SEED HAS TALK OF PREVIOUS HORSEMEN NEEDING TO DIE...
...OR A CATASTROPHE OF SOME SORT TO START THIS FIRE.
HOPE YOU GOT A FRIDGE BIG ENOUGH FOR HIM.
NO!
SHNK
SHNK
SHNK

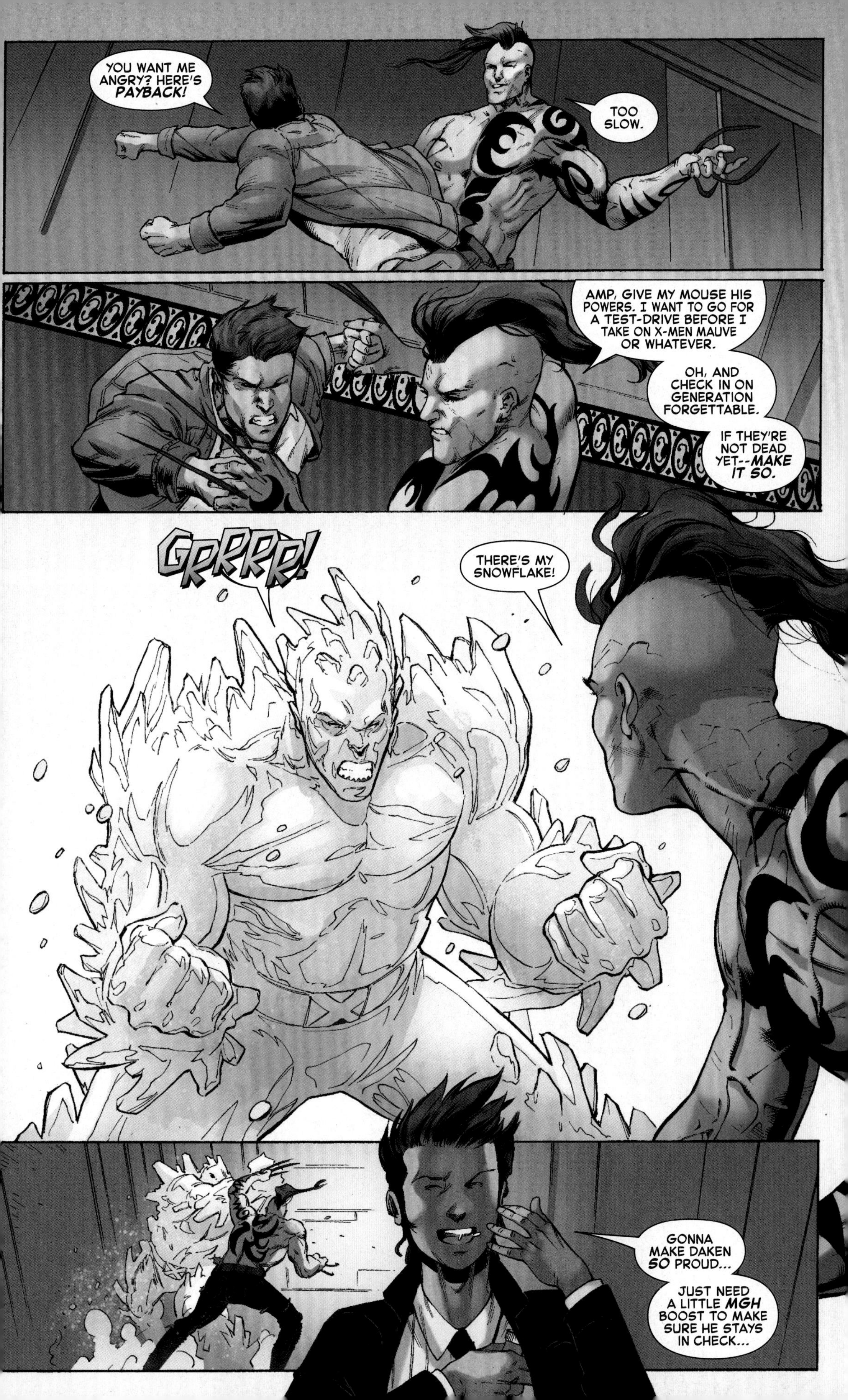

YOU WANT ME ANGRY? HERE'S PAYBACK!
TOO SLOW.
AMP, GIVE MY MOUSE HIS POWERS. I WANT TO GO FOR A TEST-DRIVE BEFORE I TAKE ON X-MEN MAUVE OR WHATEVER.
OH, AND CHECK IN ON GENERATION FORGETTABLE.
IF THEY'RE NOT DEAD YET--MAKE IT SO.
GRRRR!
THERE'S MY SNOWFLAKE!
GONNA MAKE DAKEN SO PROUD...
JUST NEED A LITTLE MGH BOOST TO MAKE SURE HE STAYS IN CHECK...

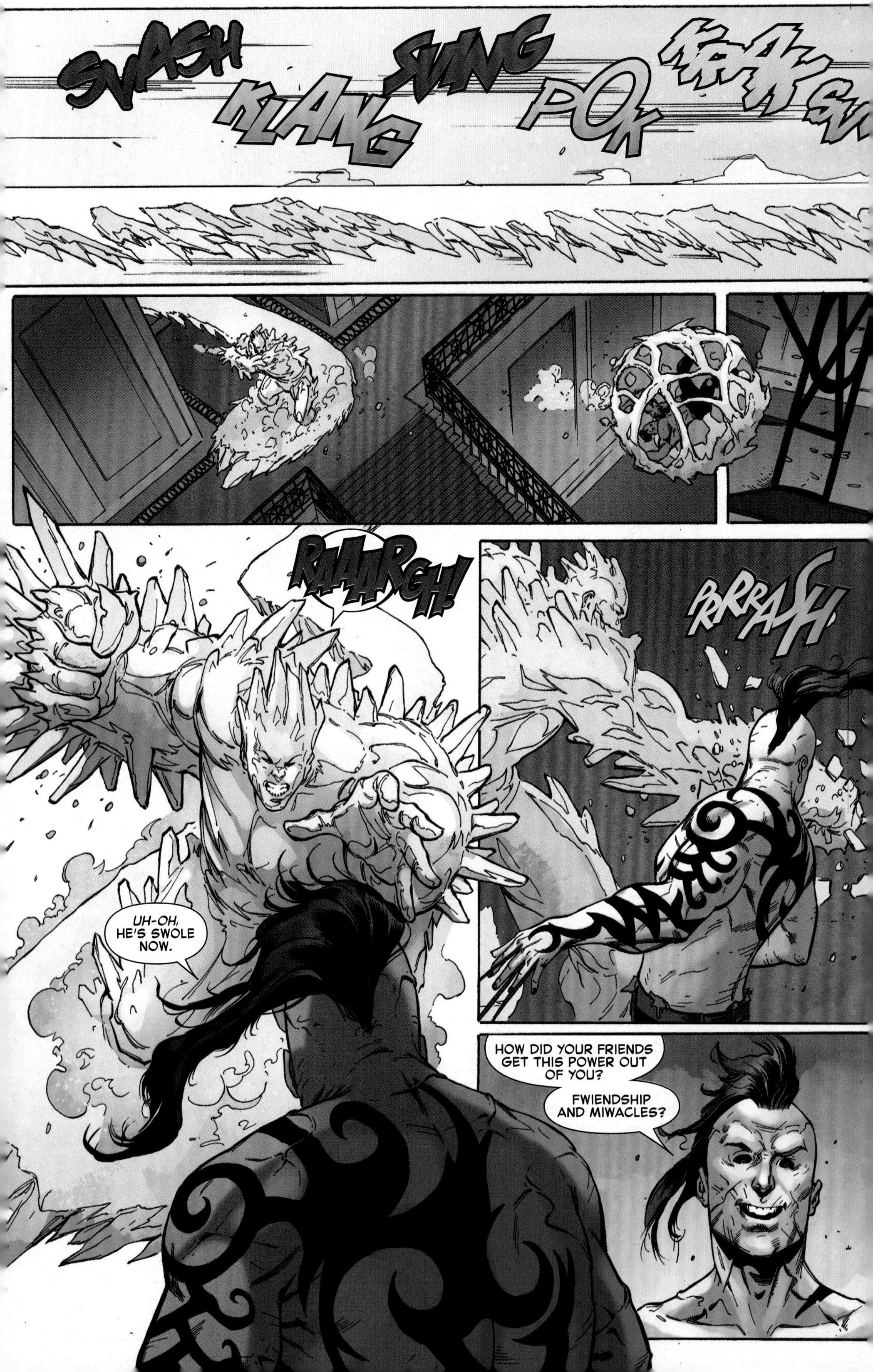
SWASH
KLANG
SWING
POK
KRAK
RAAARGH!
PRRRASH
UH-OH, HE'S SWOLE NOW.
HOW DID YOUR FRIENDS GET THIS POWER OUT OF YOU?
FWIENDSHIP AND MIWACLES?

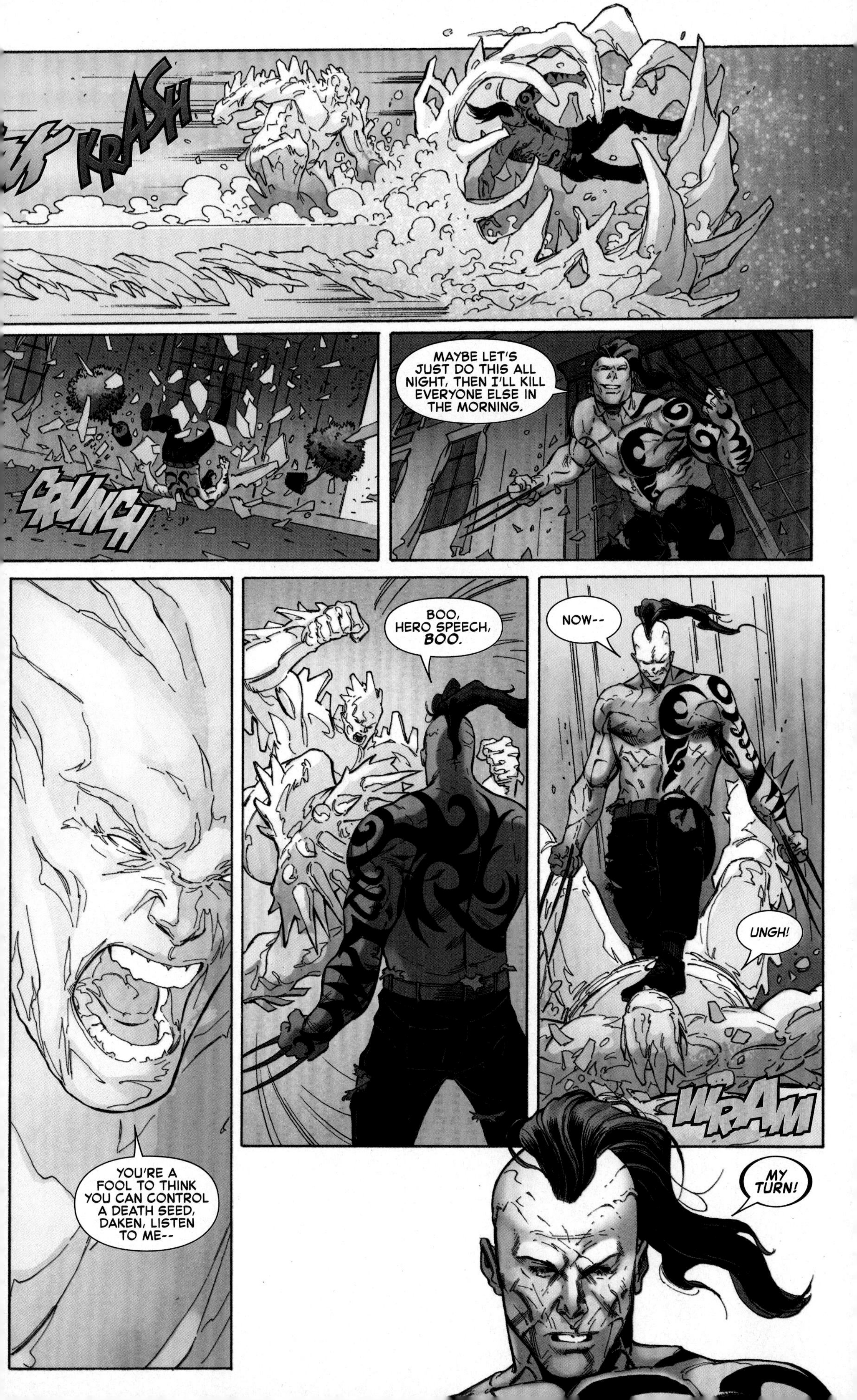
KRASH
CRUNCH
MAYBE LET'S JUST DO THIS ALL NIGHT, THEN I'LL KILL EVERYONE ELSE IN THE MORNING.
YOU'RE A FOOL TO THINK YOU CAN CONTROL A DEATH SEED, DAKEN, LISTEN TO ME--
BOO, HERO SPEECH, BOO.
NOW--
UNGH!
WRAM
MY TURN!

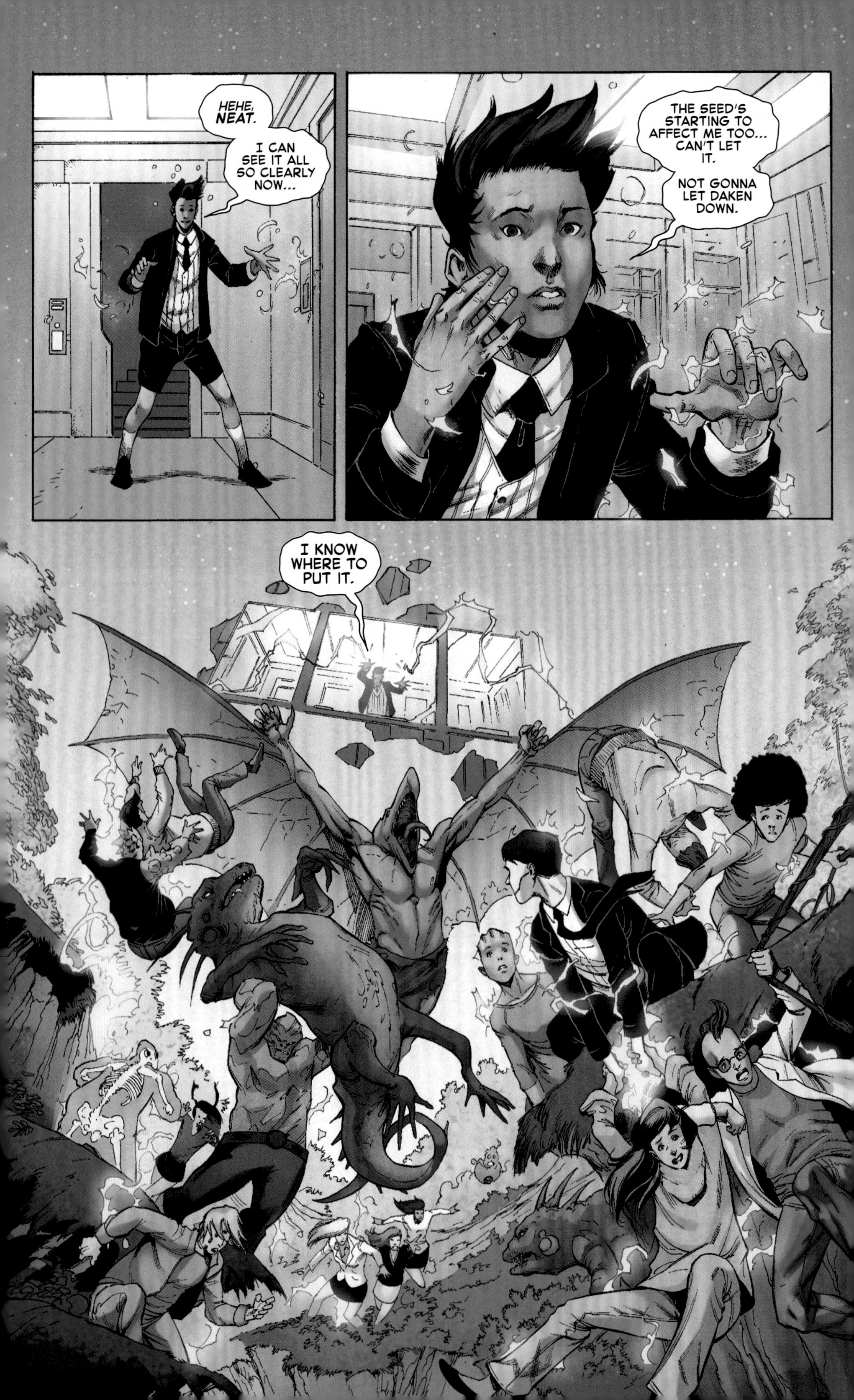
HEHE, NEAT.
I CAN SEE IT ALL SO CLEARLY NOW...
THE SEED'S STARTING TO AFFECT ME TOO... CAN'T LET IT.
NOT GONNA LET DAKEN DOWN.
I KNOW WHERE TO PUT IT.

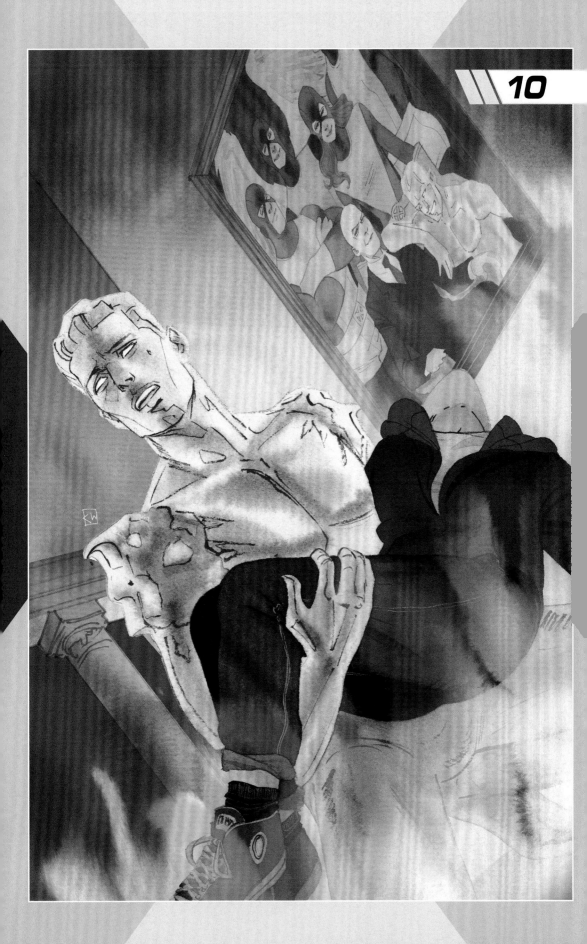

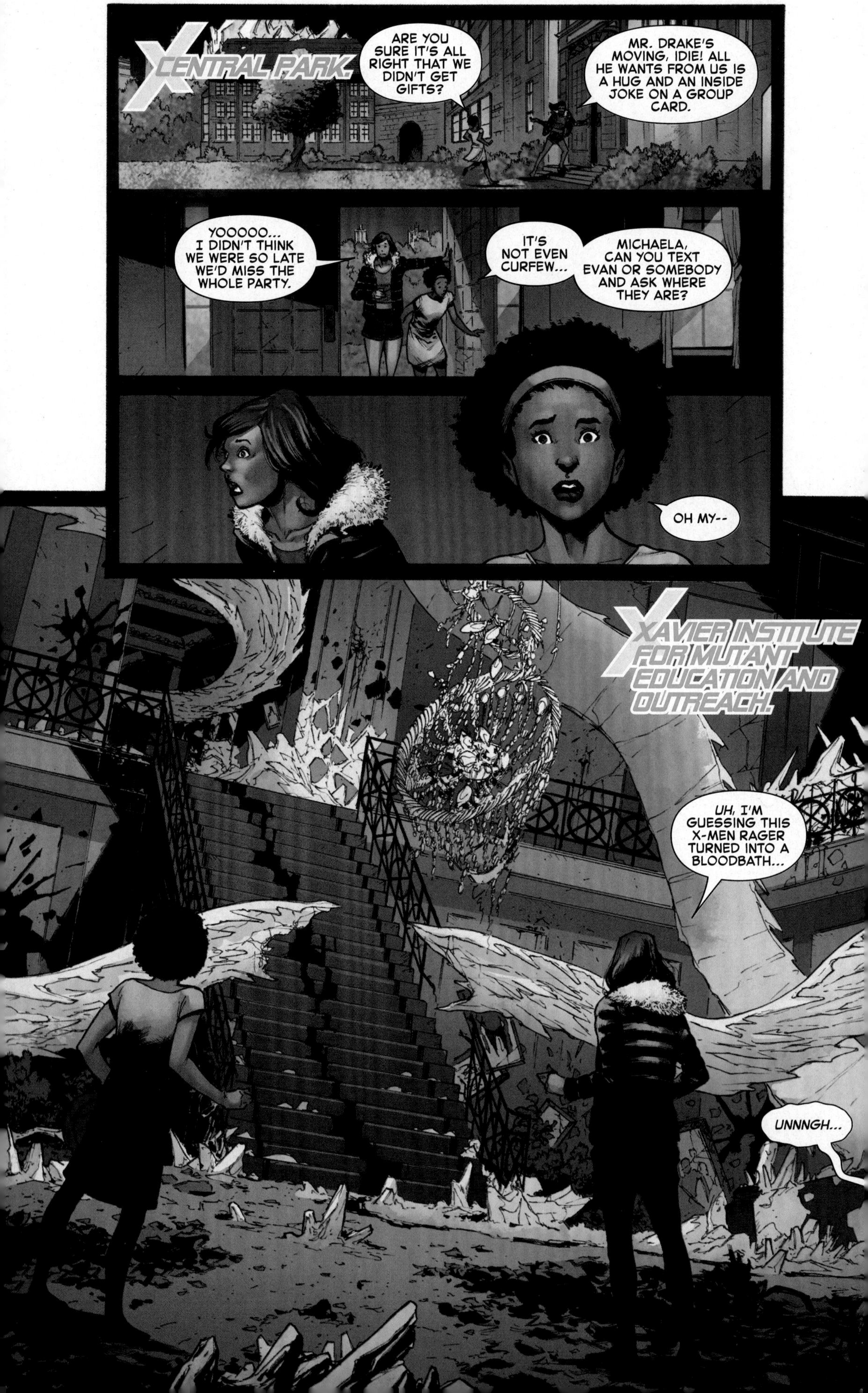
CENTRAL PARK.
ARE YOU SURE IT'S ALL RIGHT THAT WE DIDN'T GET GIFTS?
MR. DRAKE'S MOVING, IDIE! ALL HE WANTS FROM US IS A HUG AND AN INSIDE JOKE ON A GROUP CARD.
YOOOOO... I DIDN'T THINK WE WERE SO LATE WE'D MISS THE WHOLE PARTY.
IT'S NOT EVEN CURFEW...
MICHAELA, CAN YOU TEXT EVAN OR SOMEBODY AND ASK WHERE THEY ARE?
OH MY--
XAVIER INSTITUTE FOR MUTANT EDUCATION AND OUTREACH.
UH, I'M GUESSING THIS X-MEN RAGER TURNED INTO A BLOODBATH...
UNNNGH...

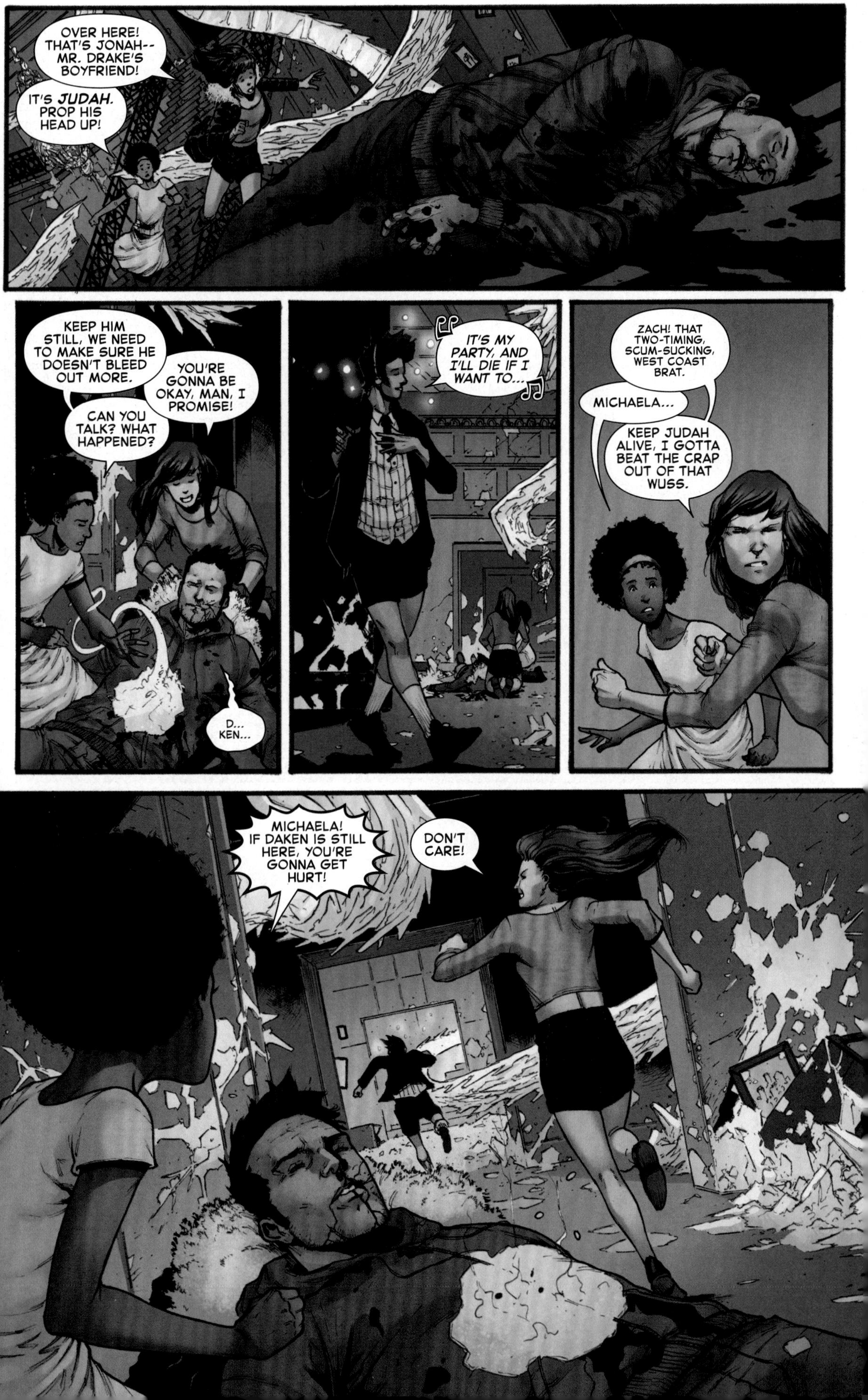
OVER HERE! THAT'S JONAH-- MR. DRAKE'S BOYFRIEND!
IT'S JUDAH. PROP HIS HEAD UP!
KEEP HIM STILL, WE NEED TO MAKE SURE HE DOESN'T BLEED OUT MORE.
CAN YOU TALK? WHAT HAPPENED?
YOU'RE GONNA BE OKAY, MAN, I PROMISE!
D... KEN...
IT'S MY PARTY, AND I'LL DIE IF I WANT TO...
ZACH! THAT TWO-TIMING, SCUM-SUCKING, WEST COAST BRAT.
MICHAELA...
KEEP JUDAH ALIVE, I GOTTA BEAT THE CRAP OUT OF THAT WUSS.
MICHAELA! IF DAKEN IS STILL HERE, YOU'RE GONNA GET HURT!
DON'T CARE!

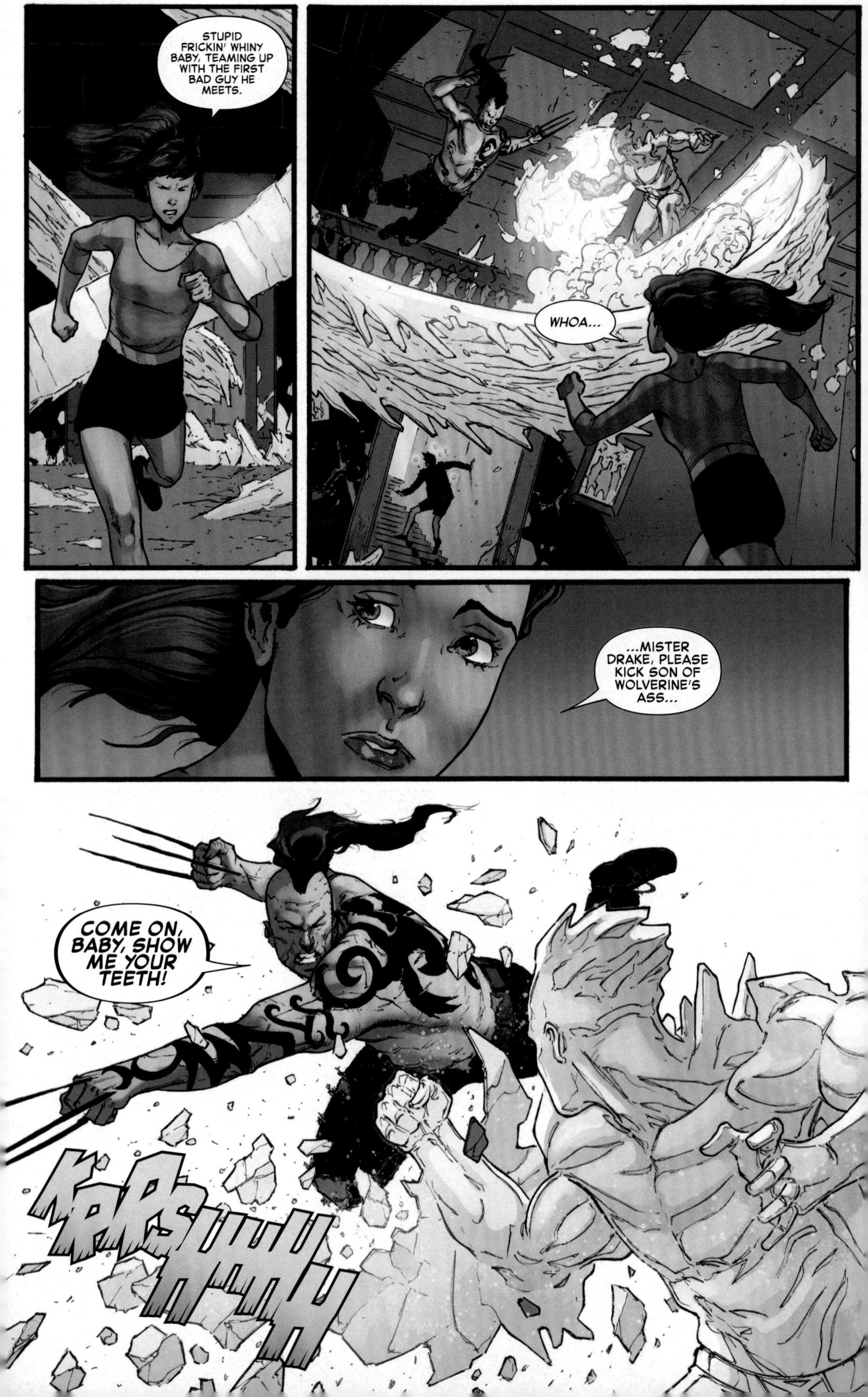
STUPID FRICKIN' WHINY BABY, TEAMING UP WITH THE FIRST BAD GUY HE MEETS.
WHOA...
...MISTER DRAKE, PLEASE KICK SON OF WOLVERINE'S ASS...
COME ON, BABY, SHOW ME YOUR TEETH!
KRASHHHHHH

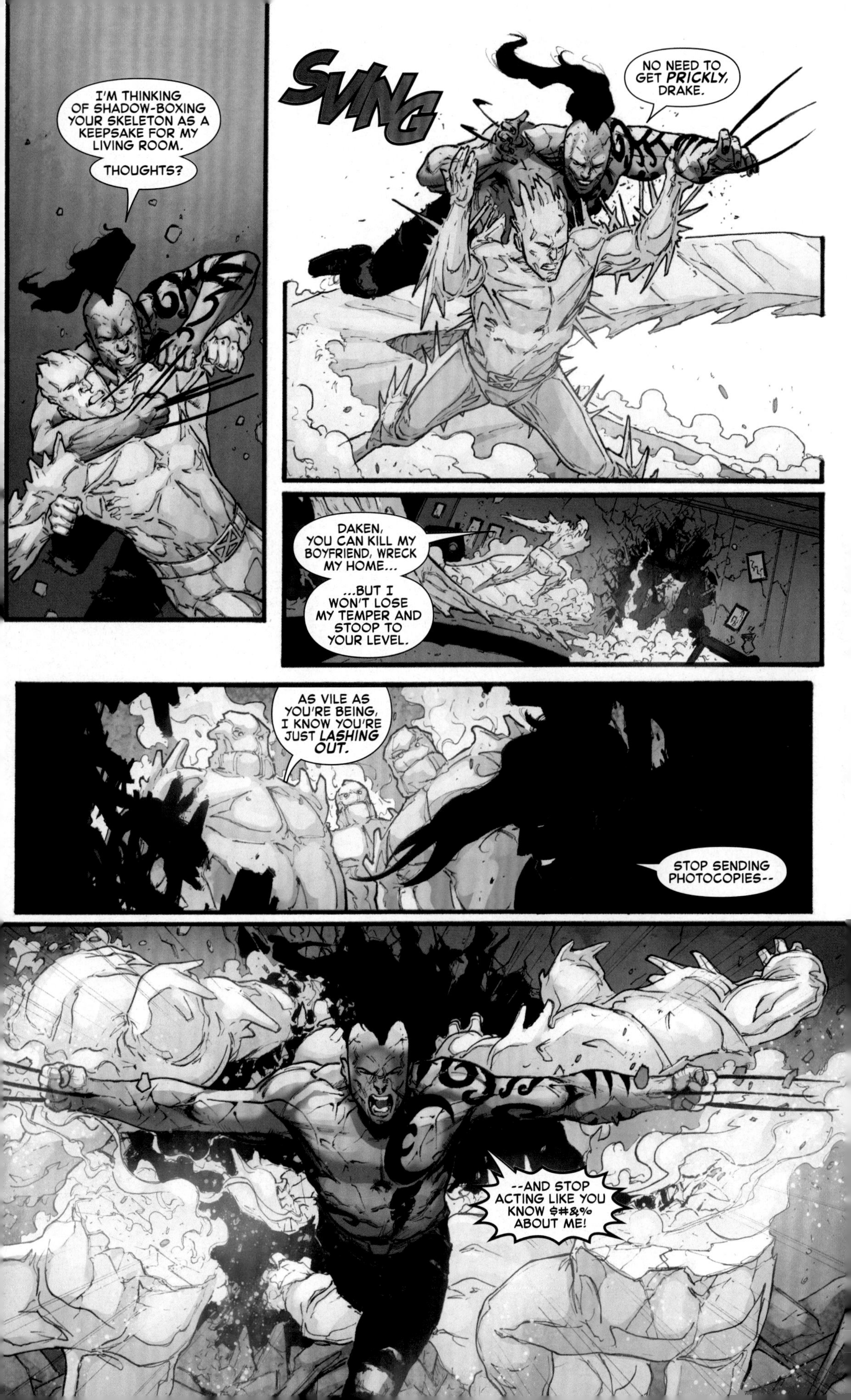
I'M THINKING OF SHADOW-BOXING YOUR SKELETON AS A KEEPSAKE FOR MY LIVING ROOM.
THOUGHTS?
SVING
NO NEED TO GET PRICKLY, DRAKE.
DAKEN, YOU CAN KILL MY BOYFRIEND, WRECK MY HOME...
...BUT I WON'T LOSE MY TEMPER AND STOOP TO YOUR LEVEL.
AS VILE AS YOU'RE BEING, I KNOW YOU'RE JUST LASHING OUT.
STOP SENDING PHOTOCOPIES--
--AND STOP ACTING LIKE YOU KNOW $#&% ABOUT ME!

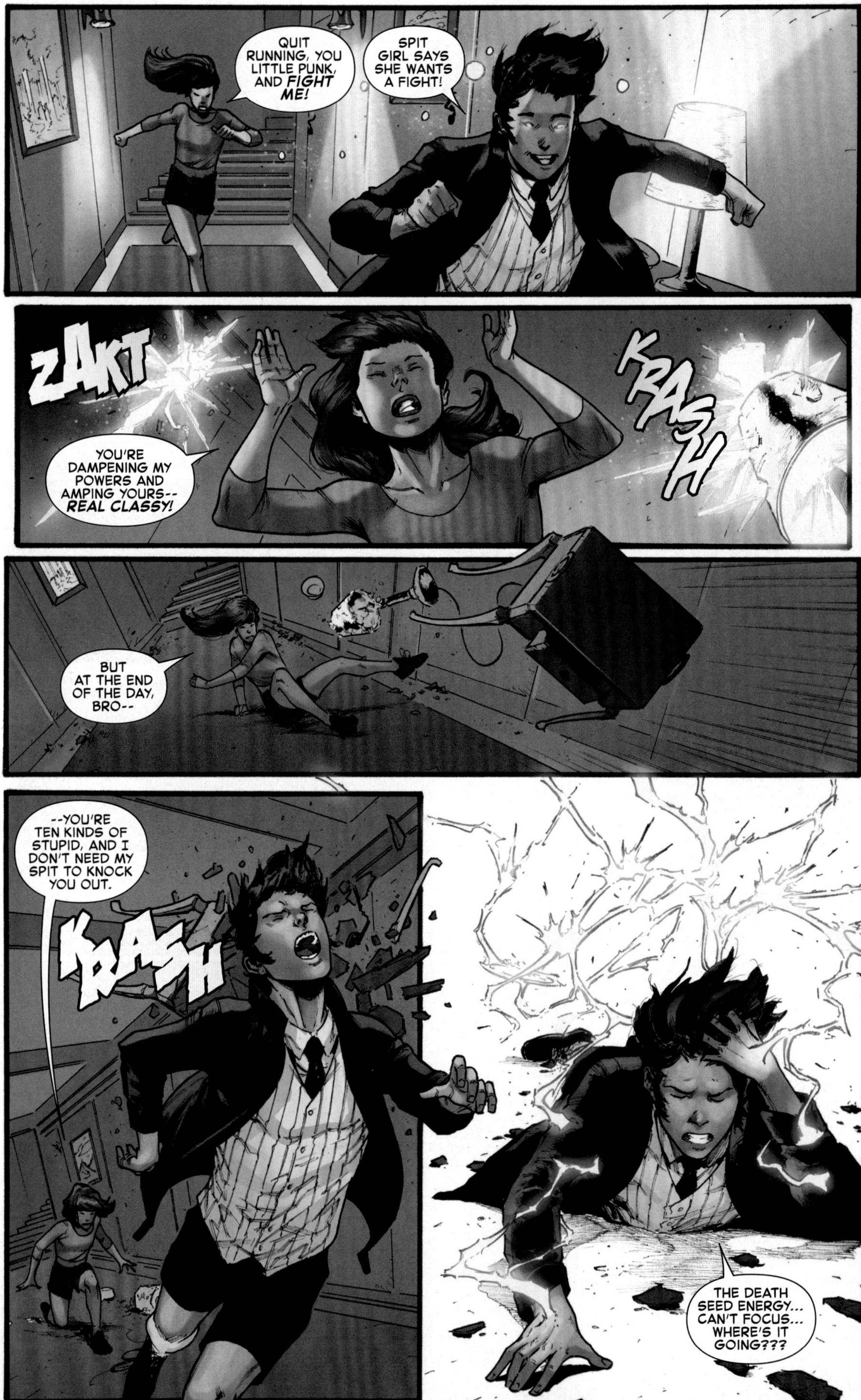
QUIT RUNNING, YOU LITTLE PUNK, AND FIGHT ME!
SPIT GIRL SAYS SHE WANTS A FIGHT!
ZAKT
KRASH
YOU'RE DAMPENING MY POWERS AND AMPING YOURS--REAL CLASSY!
BUT AT THE END OF THE DAY, BRO--
--YOU'RE TEN KINDS OF STUPID, AND I DON'T NEED MY SPIT TO KNOCK YOU OUT.
KRASH
THE DEATH SEED ENERGY... CAN'T FOCUS... WHERE'S IT GOING???

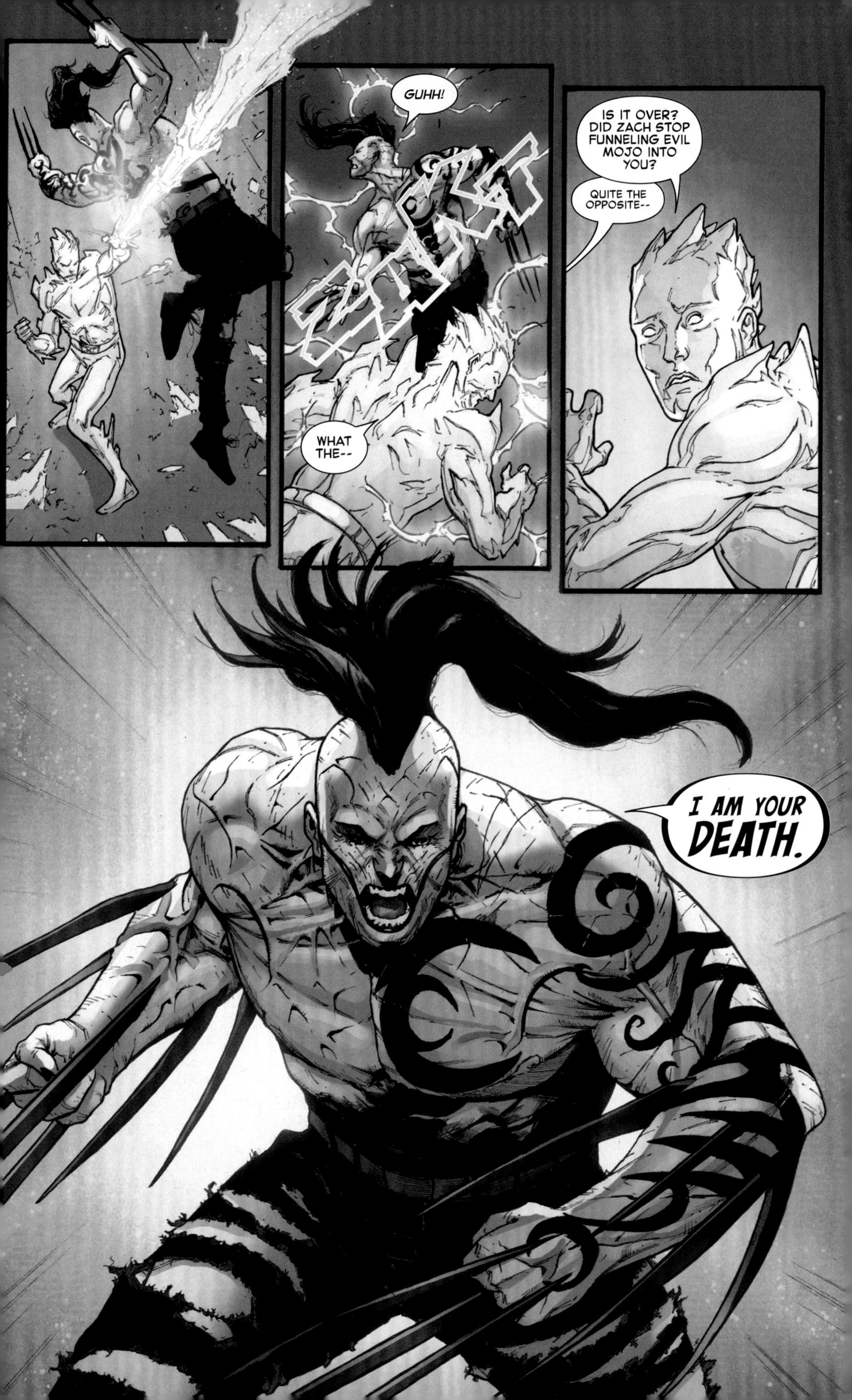
GUHH!
WHAT THE--
IS IT OVER? DID ZACH STOP FUNNELING EVIL MOJO INTO YOU?
QUITE THE OPPOSITE--
I AM YOUR DEATH.

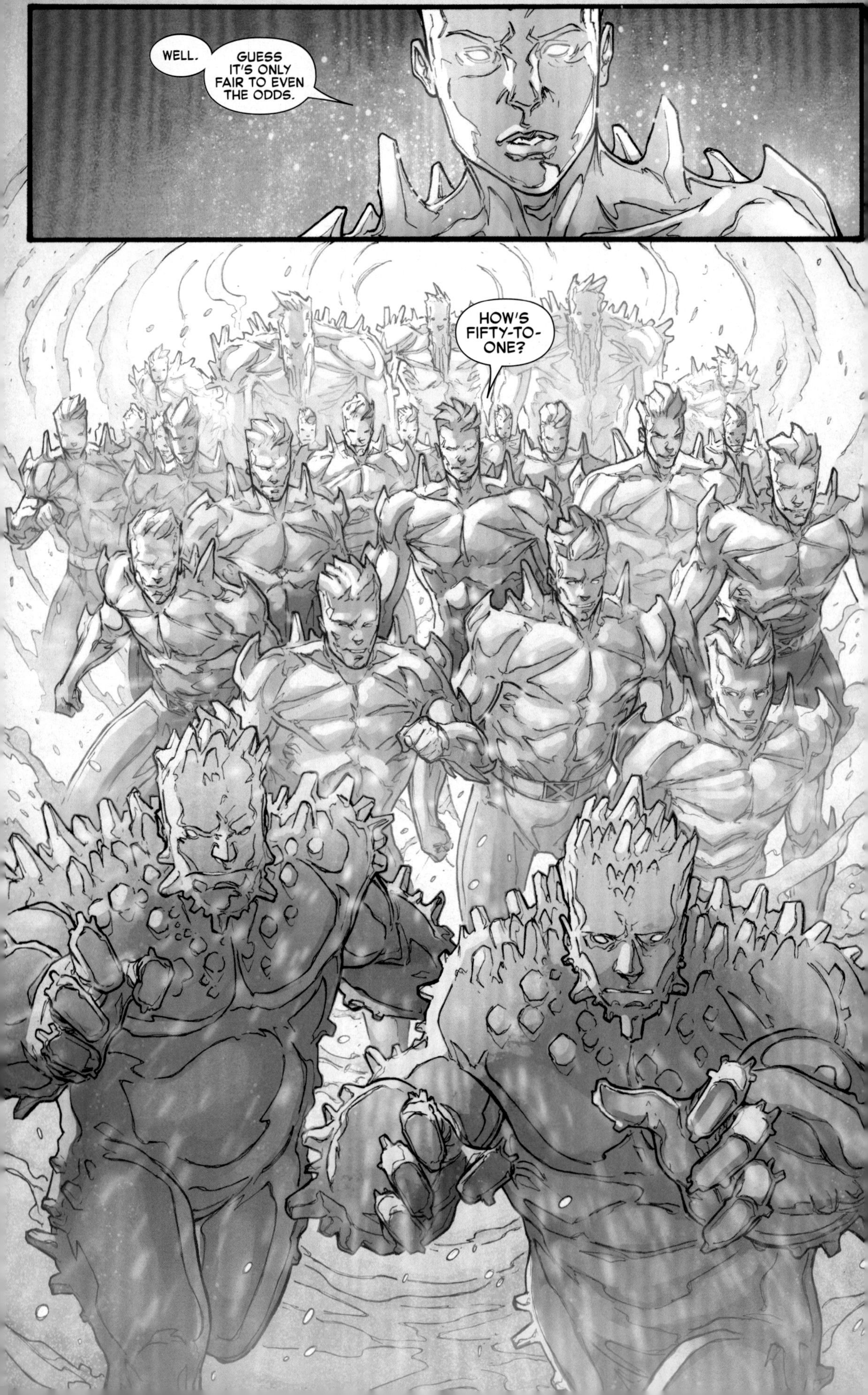
WELL.
GUESS IT'S ONLY FAIR TO EVEN THE ODDS.
HOW'S FIFTY-TO-ONE?

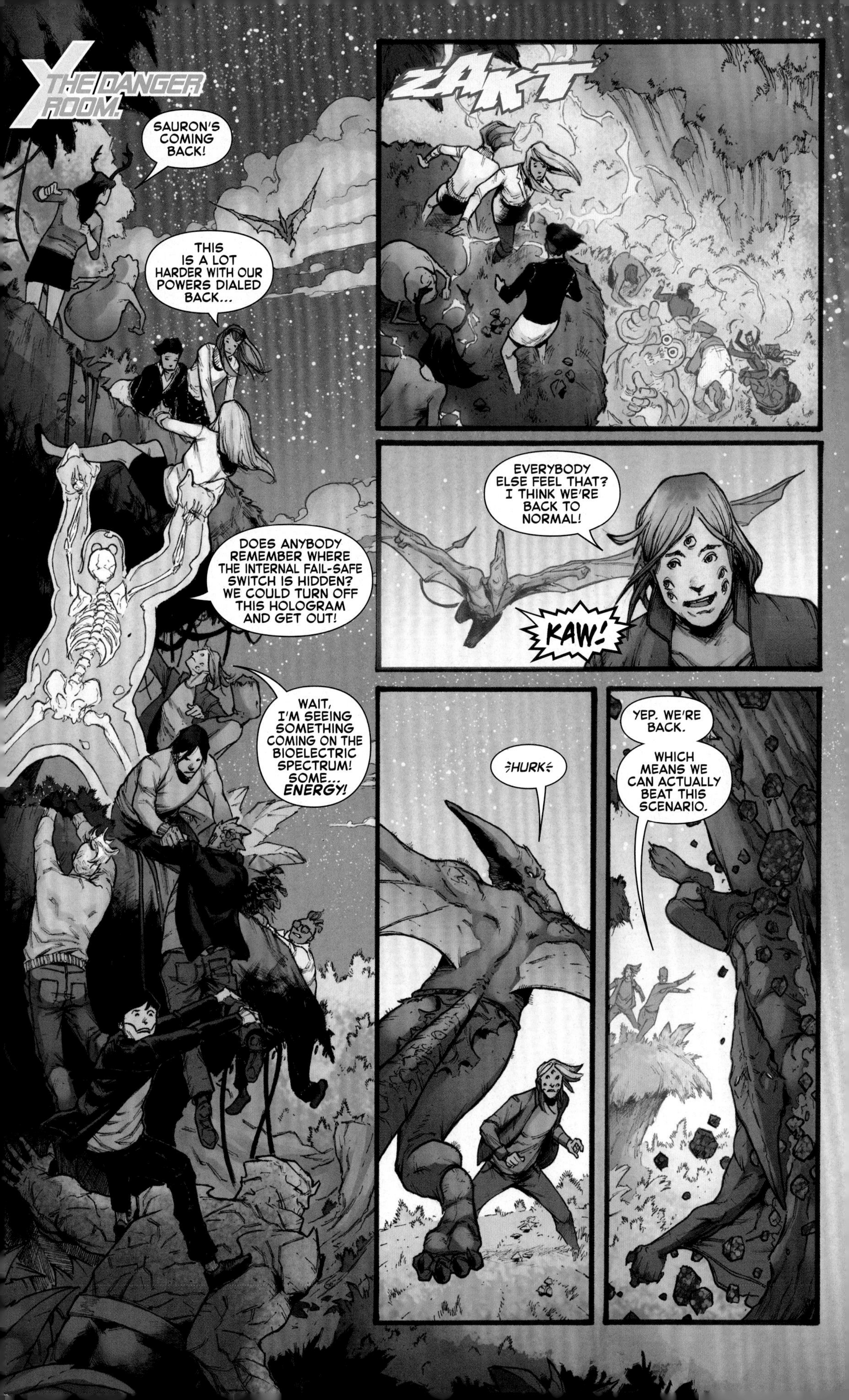
THE DANGER ROOM.
SAURON'S COMING BACK!
THIS IS A LOT HARDER WITH OUR POWERS DIALED BACK...
DOES ANYBODY REMEMBER WHERE THE INTERNAL FAIL-SAFE SWITCH IS HIDDEN? WE COULD TURN OFF THIS HOLOGRAM AND GET OUT!
WAIT, I'M SEEING SOMETHING COMING ON THE BIOELECTRIC SPECTRUM! SOME... ENERGY!
ZAKT
EVERYBODY ELSE FEEL THAT? I THINK WE'RE BACK TO NORMAL!
KAW!
HURK
YEP. WE'RE BACK.
WHICH MEANS WE CAN ACTUALLY BEAT THIS SCENARIO.

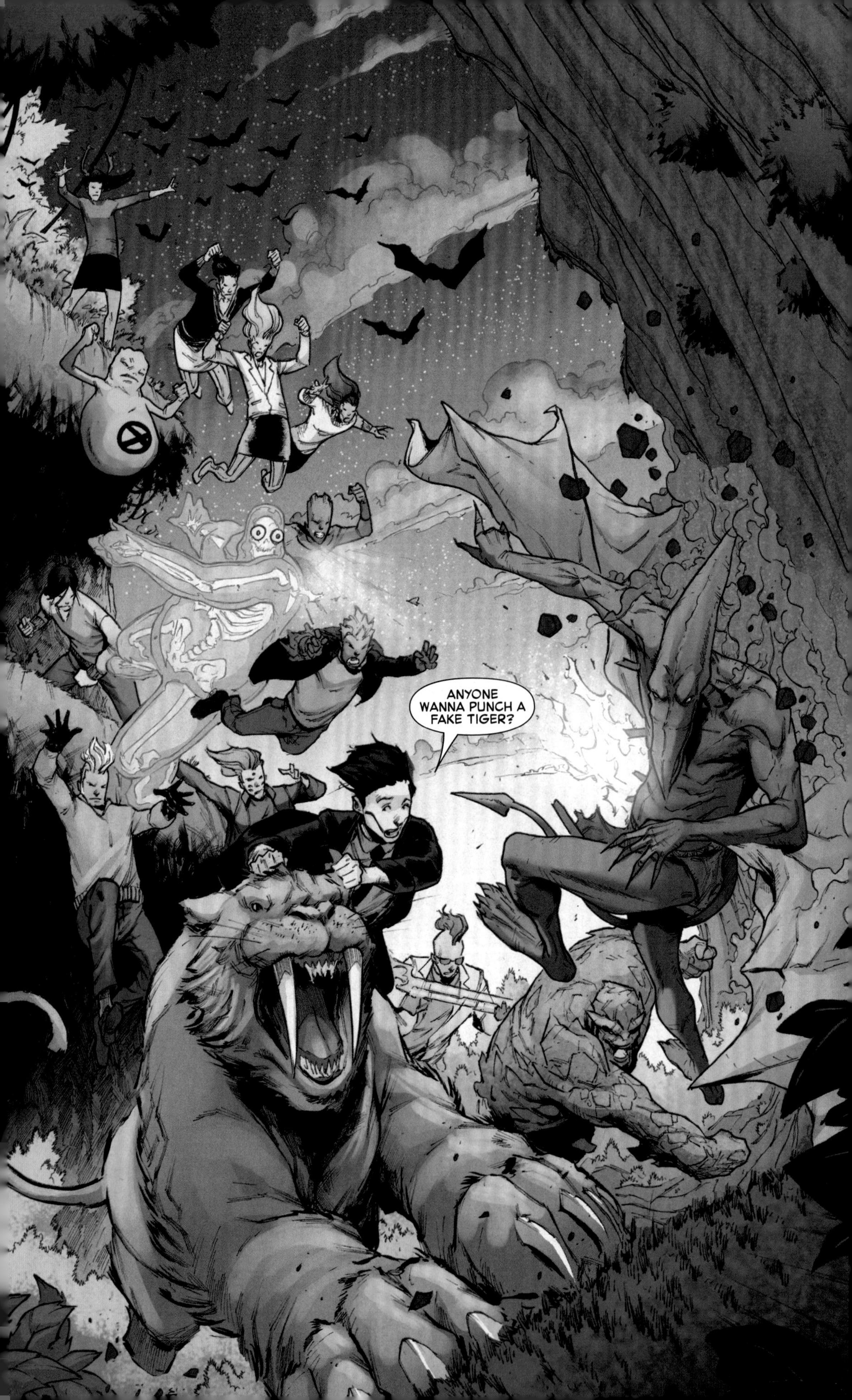
ANYONE WANNA PUNCH A FAKE TIGER?

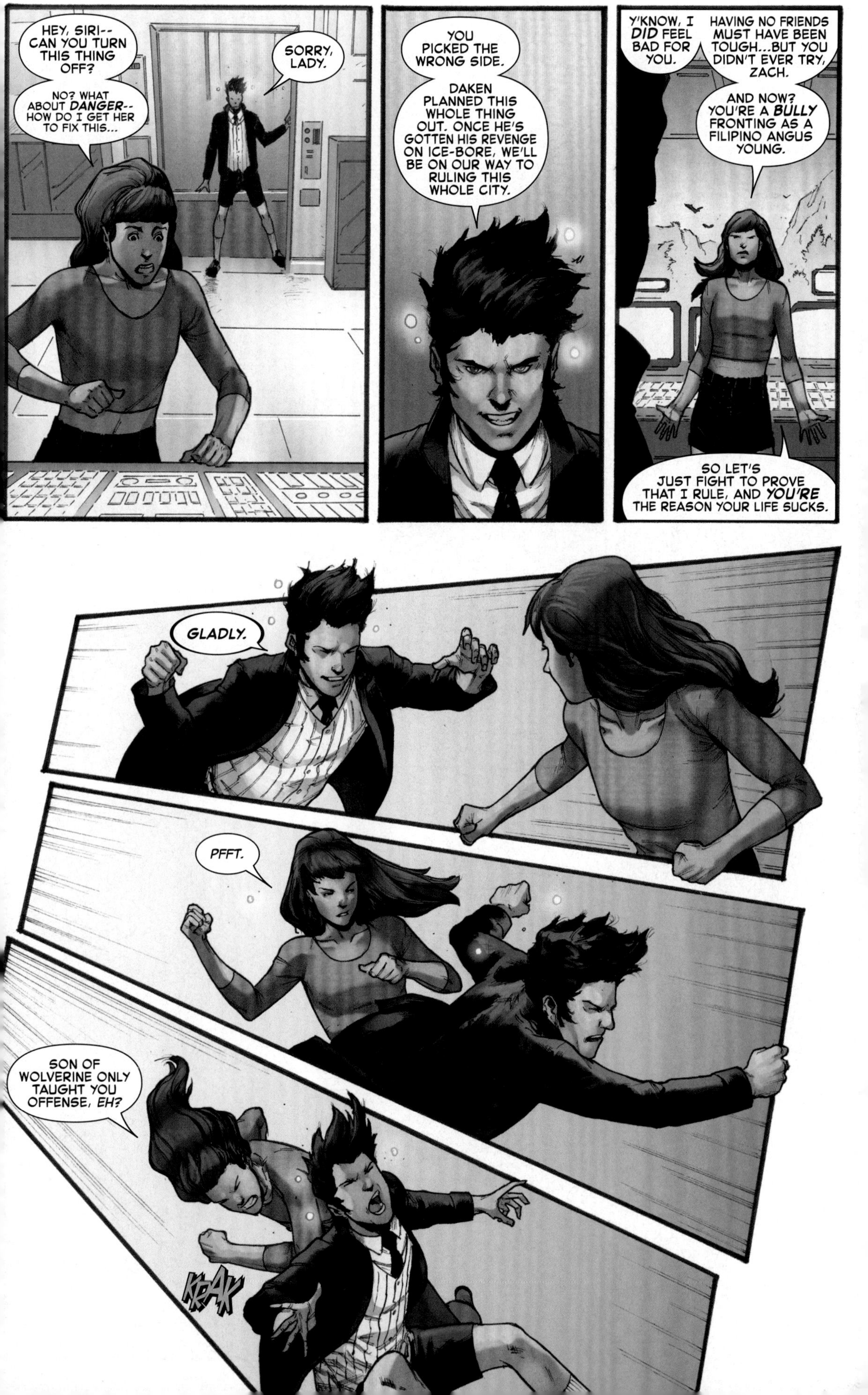
HEY, SIRI-- CAN YOU TURN THIS THING OFF?
NO? WHAT ABOUT DANGER-- HOW DO I GET HER TO FIX THIS...
SORRY, LADY.
YOU PICKED THE WRONG SIDE.
DAKEN PLANNED THIS WHOLE THING OUT. ONCE HE'S GOTTEN HIS REVENGE ON ICE-BORE, WE'LL BE ON OUR WAY TO RULING THIS WHOLE CITY.
Y'KNOW, I DID FEEL BAD FOR YOU.
HAVING NO FRIENDS MUST HAVE BEEN TOUGH...BUT YOU DIDN'T EVER TRY, ZACH.
AND NOW? YOU'RE A BULLY FRONTING AS A FILIPINO ANGUS YOUNG.
SO LET'S JUST FIGHT TO PROVE THAT I RULE, AND YOU'RE THE REASON YOUR LIFE SUCKS.
GLADLY.
PFFT.
SON OF WOLVERINE ONLY TAUGHT YOU OFFENSE, EH?
KRAK

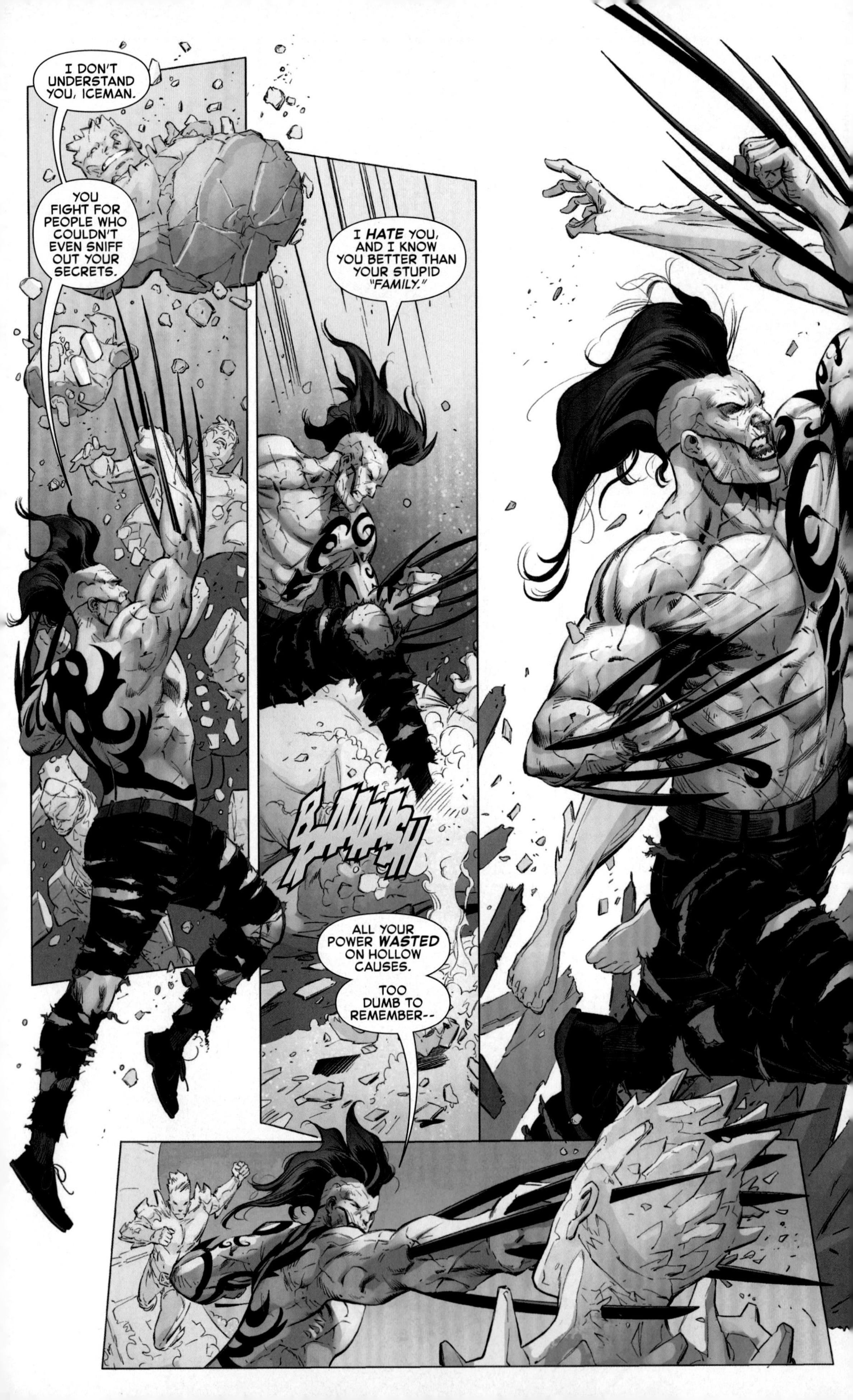
I DON'T UNDERSTAND YOU, ICEMAN.
YOU FIGHT FOR PEOPLE WHO COULDN'T EVEN SNIFF OUT YOUR SECRETS.
I HATE YOU, AND I KNOW YOU BETTER THAN YOUR STUPID "FAMILY."
BLAAASH
ALL YOUR POWER WASTED ON HOLLOW CAUSES.
TOO DUMB TO REMEMBER--

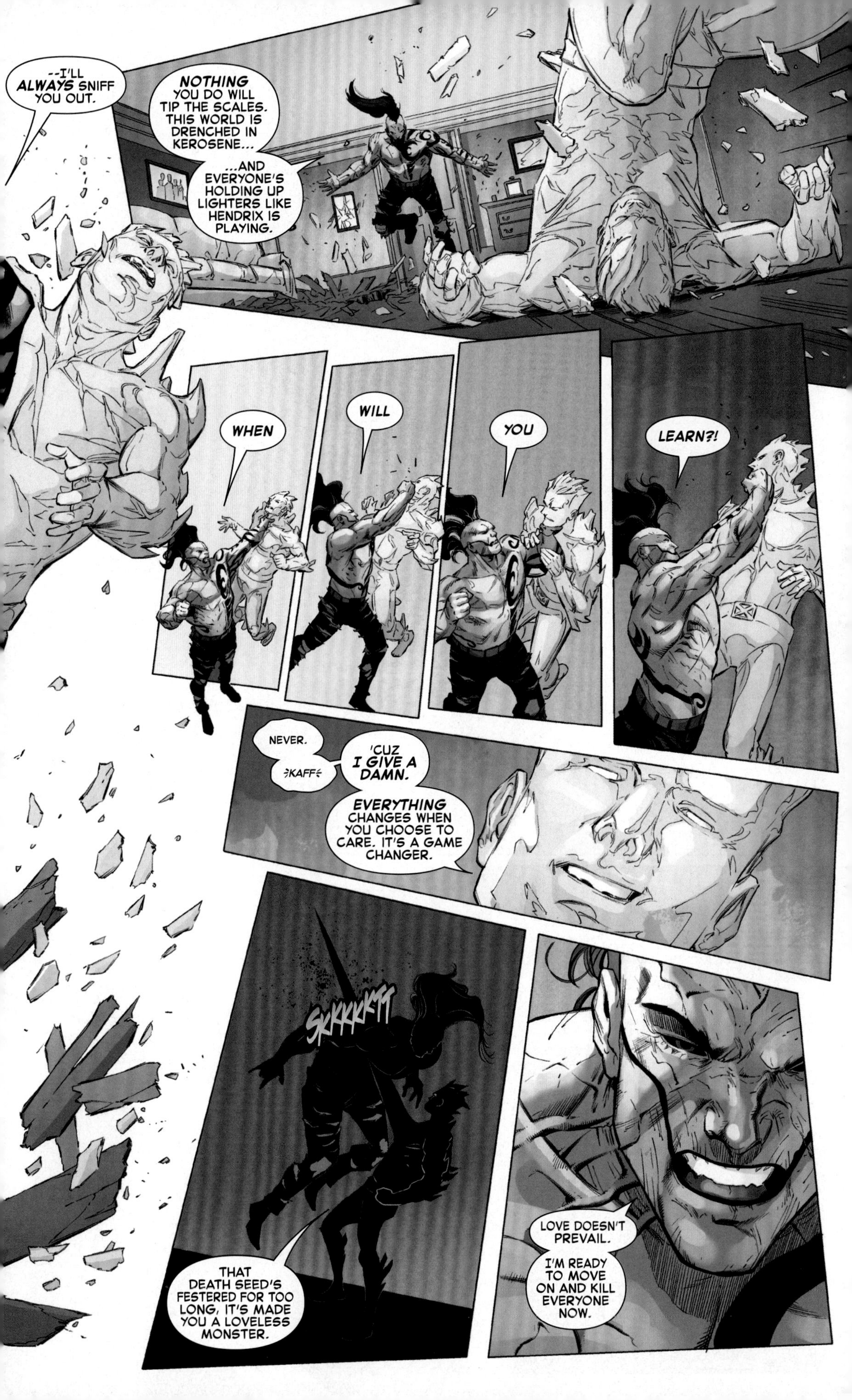
--I'LL ALWAYS SNIFF YOU OUT.
NOTHING YOU DO WILL TIP THE SCALES. THIS WORLD IS DRENCHED IN KEROSENE...
...AND EVERYONE'S HOLDING UP LIGHTERS LIKE HENDRIX IS PLAYING.
WHEN
WILL
YOU
LEARN?!
NEVER.
KAFF
'CUZ I GIVE A DAMN.
EVERYTHING CHANGES WHEN YOU CHOOSE TO CARE. IT'S A GAME CHANGER.
SKKKKKTT
THAT DEATH SEED'S FESTERED FOR TOO LONG, IT'S MADE YOU A LOVELESS MONSTER.
LOVE DOESN'T PREVAIL.
I'M READY TO MOVE ON AND KILL EVERYONE NOW.

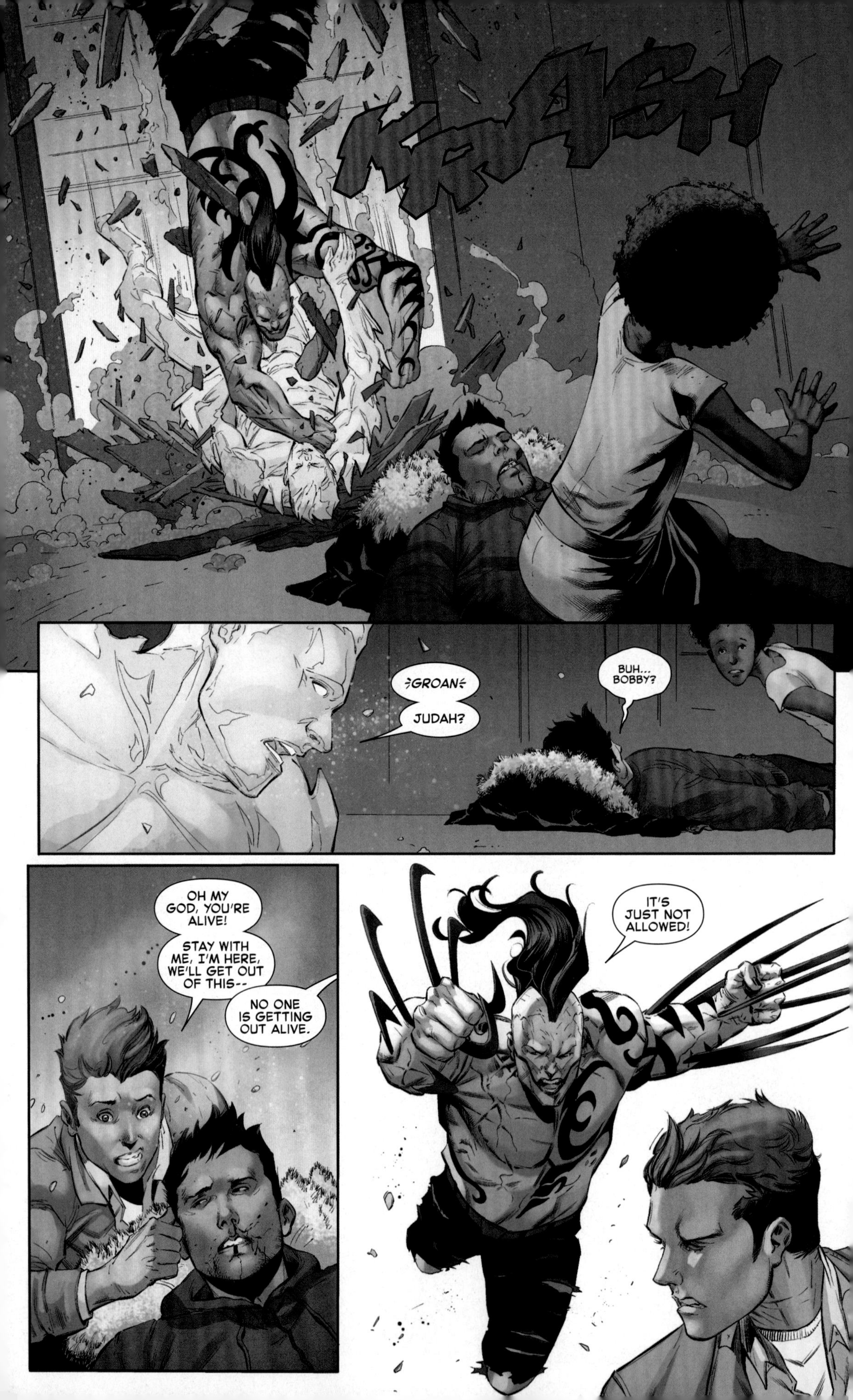
KRASH
≈GROAN≈
JUDAH?
BUH... BOBBY?
OH MY GOD, YOU'RE ALIVE!
STAY WITH ME, I'M HERE, WE'LL GET OUT OF THIS--
NO ONE IS GETTING OUT ALIVE.
IT'S JUST NOT ALLOWED!

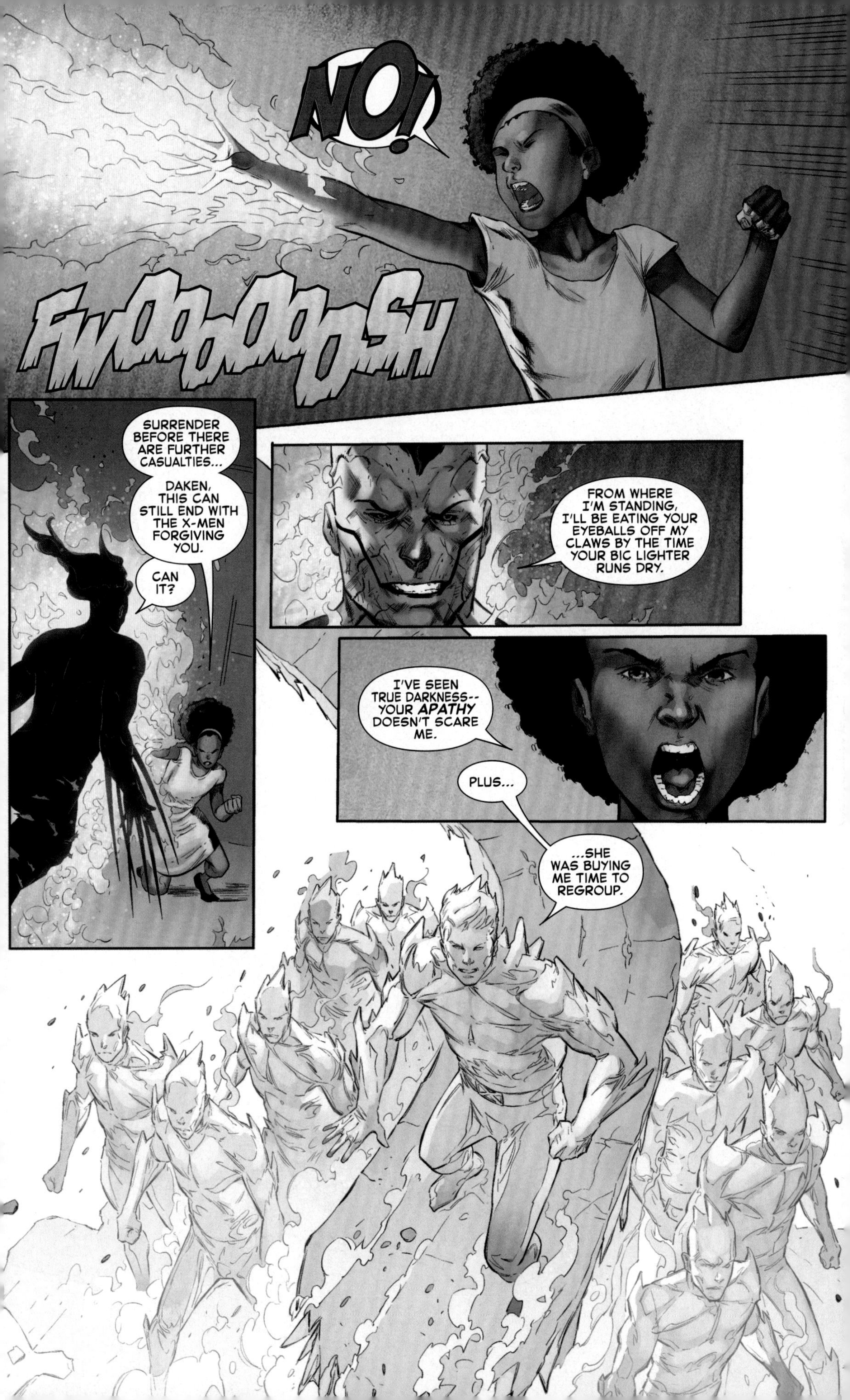
NO!
FWOOOOOOSH
SURRENDER BEFORE THERE ARE FURTHER CASUALTIES...
DAKEN, THIS CAN STILL END WITH THE X-MEN FORGIVING YOU.
CAN IT?
FROM WHERE I'M STANDING, I'LL BE EATING YOUR EYEBALLS OFF MY CLAWS BY THE TIME YOUR BIC LIGHTER RUNS DRY.
I'VE SEEN TRUE DARKNESS-- YOUR APATHY DOESN'T SCARE ME.
PLUS...
...SHE WAS BUYING ME TIME TO REGROUP.

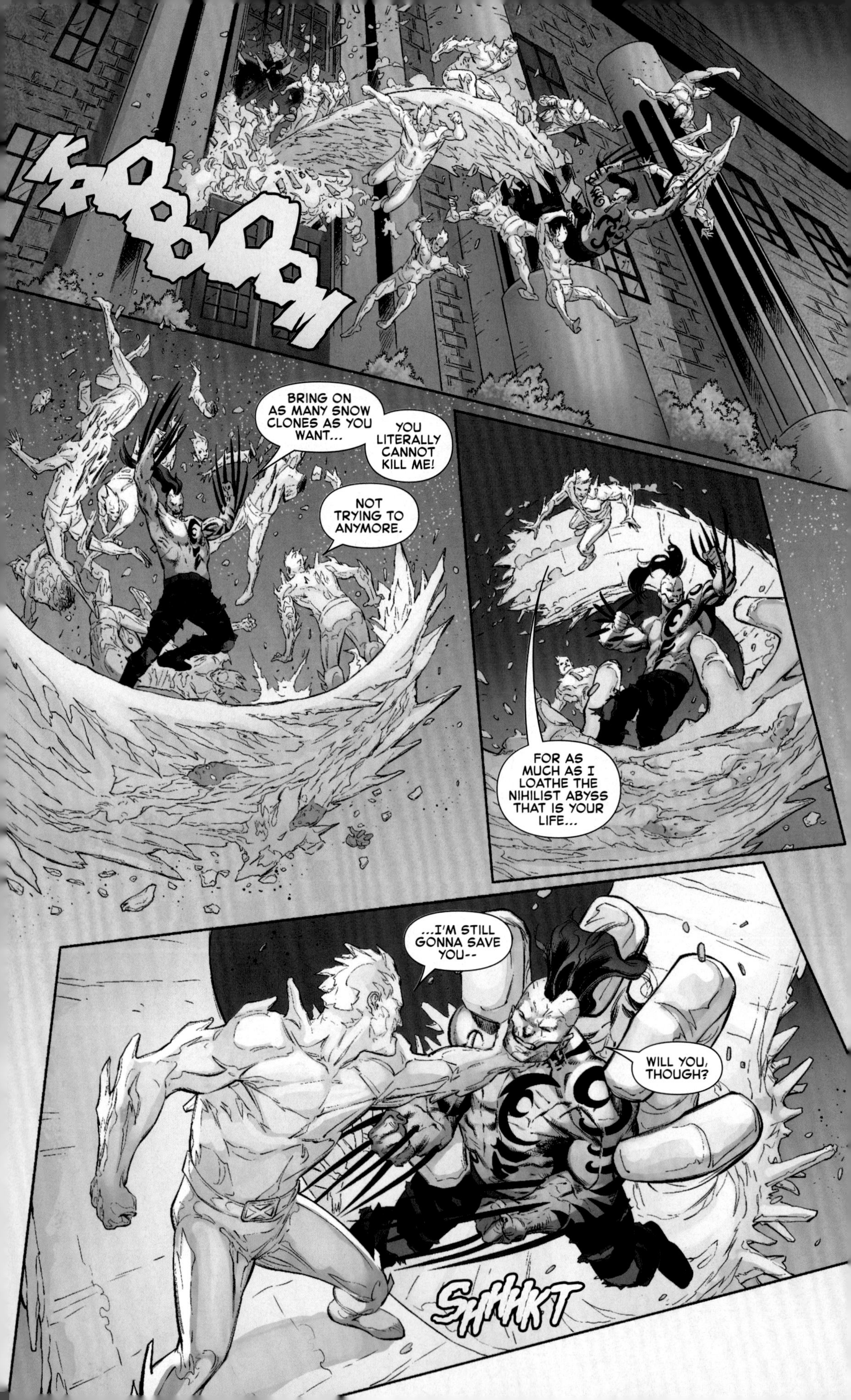
KRAKOOOOOM
BRING ON AS MANY SNOW CLONES AS YOU WANT...
YOU LITERALLY CANNOT KILL ME!
NOT TRYING TO ANYMORE.
FOR AS MUCH AS I LOATHE THE NIHILIST ABYSS THAT IS YOUR LIFE...
...I'M STILL GONNA SAVE YOU--
WILL YOU, THOUGH?
SHHHKT

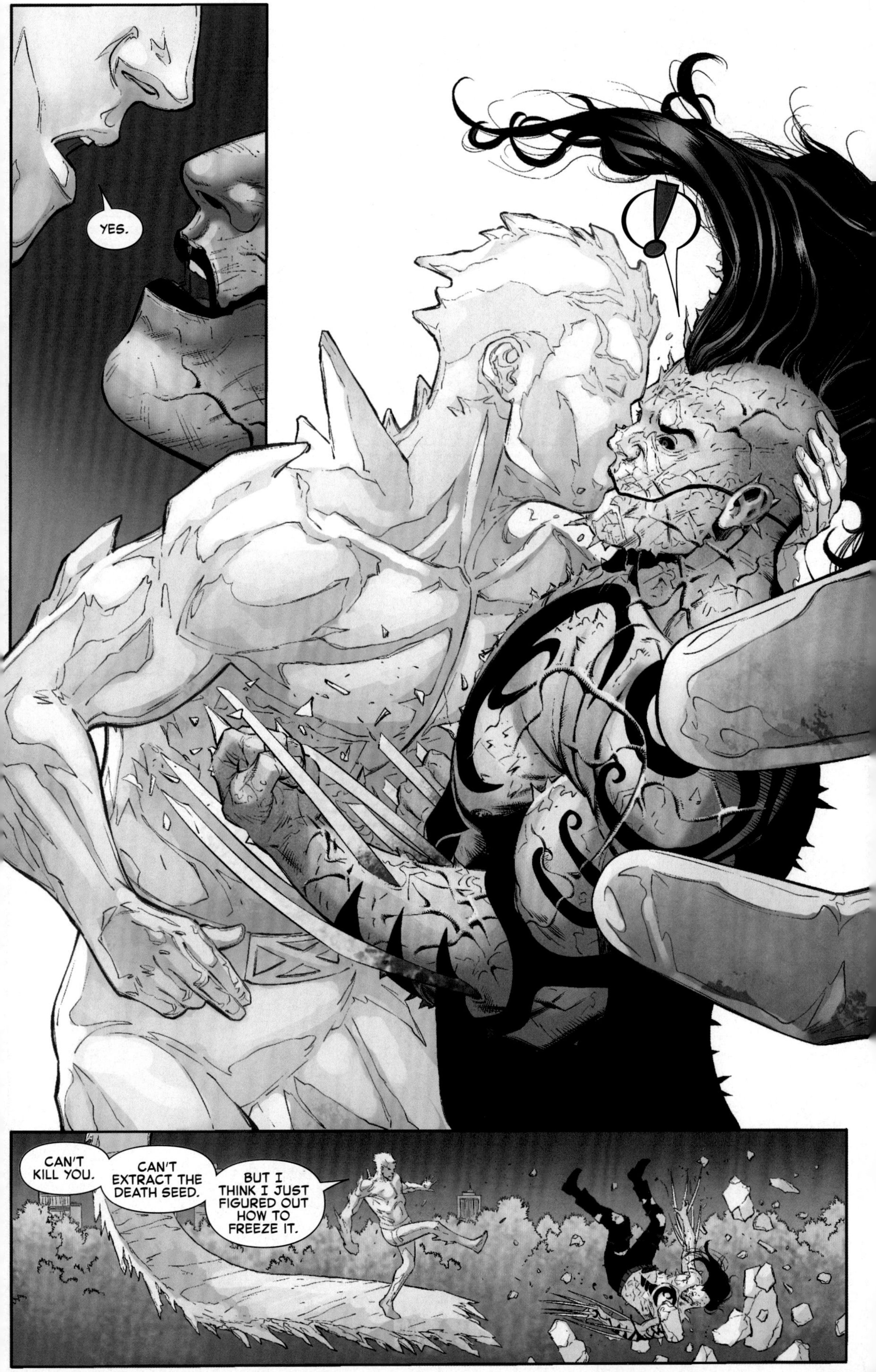
YES.
!
CAN'T KILL YOU.
CAN'T EXTRACT THE DEATH SEED.
BUT I THINK I JUST FIGURED OUT HOW TO FREEZE IT.

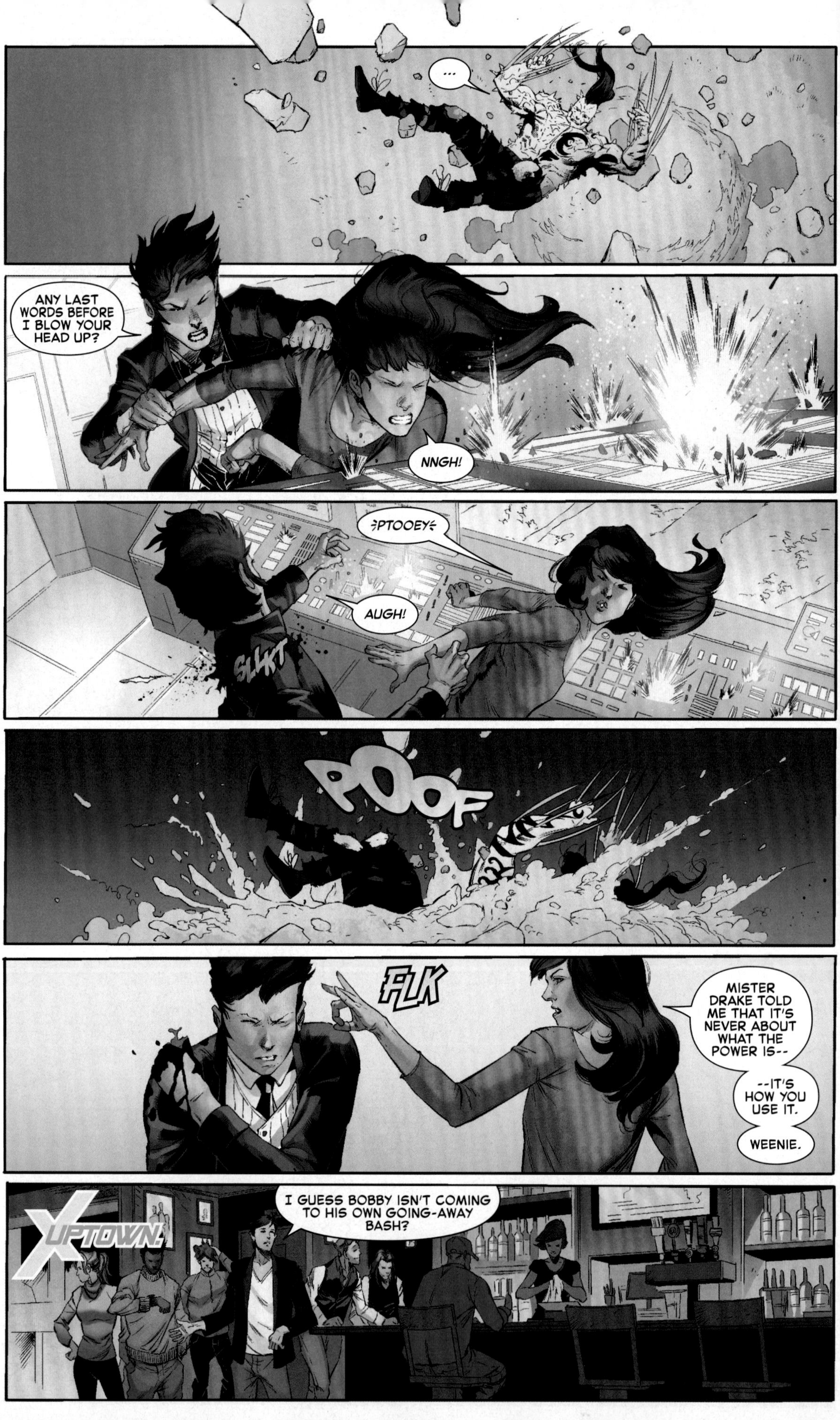
...
ANY LAST WORDS BEFORE I BLOW YOUR HEAD UP?
NNGH!
PTOOEY
AUGH!
SLIKT
POOF
FLIK
MISTER DRAKE TOLD ME THAT IT'S NEVER ABOUT WHAT THE POWER IS--
--IT'S HOW YOU USE IT.
WEENIE.
X UPTOWN.
I GUESS BOBBY ISN'T COMING TO HIS OWN GOING-AWAY BASH?

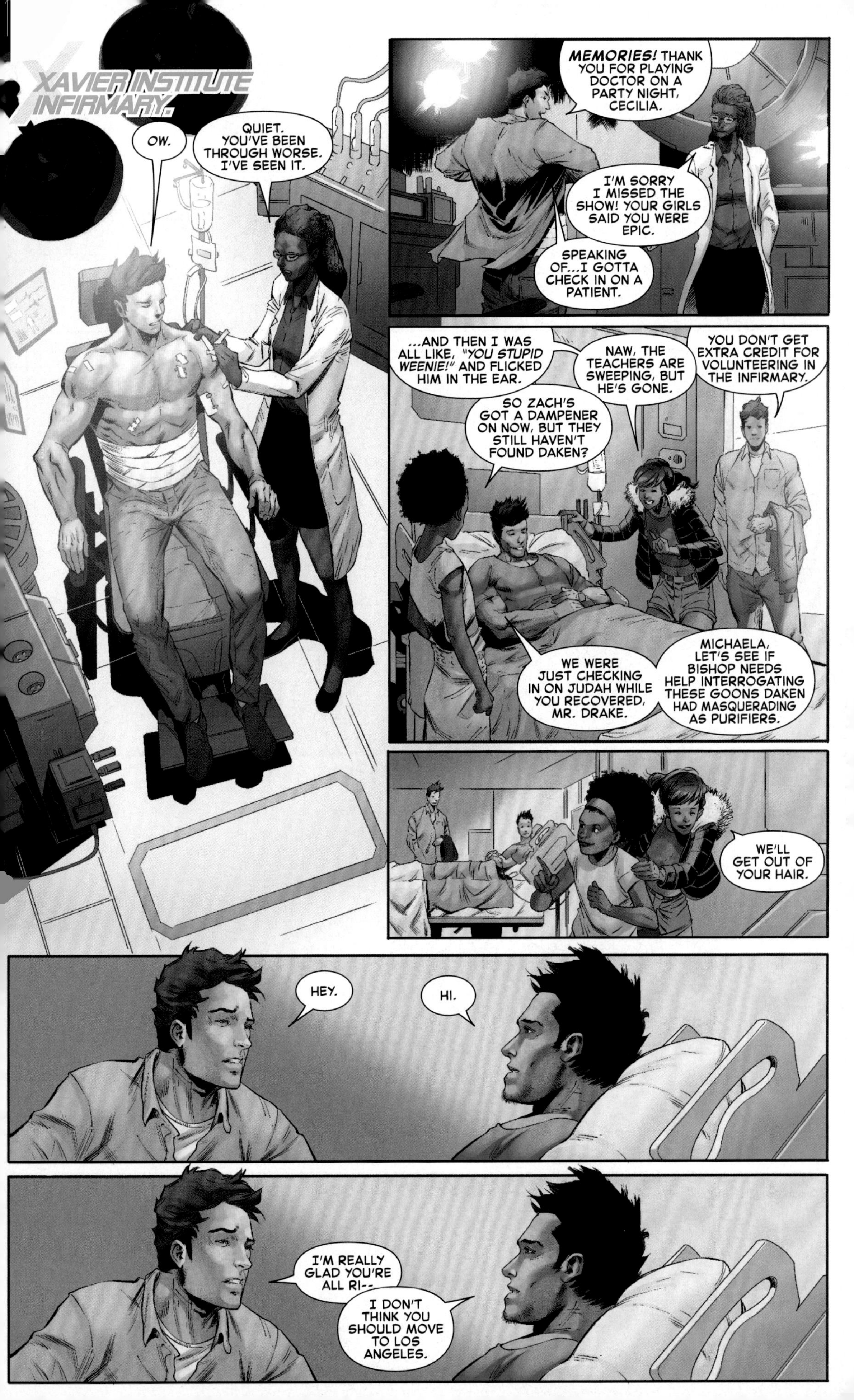

XAVIER INSTITUTE INFIRMARY.
OW.
QUIET. YOU'VE BEEN THROUGH WORSE. I'VE SEEN IT.
MEMORIES! THANK YOU FOR PLAYING DOCTOR ON A PARTY NIGHT, CECILIA.
I'M SORRY I MISSED THE SHOW! YOUR GIRLS SAID YOU WERE EPIC.
SPEAKING OF...I GOTTA CHECK IN ON A PATIENT.
...AND THEN I WAS ALL LIKE, "YOU STUPID WEENIE!" AND FLICKED HIM IN THE EAR.
SO ZACH'S GOT A DAMPENER ON NOW, BUT THEY STILL HAVEN'T FOUND DAKEN?
NAW, THE TEACHERS ARE SWEEPING, BUT HE'S GONE.
YOU DON'T GET EXTRA CREDIT FOR VOLUNTEERING IN THE INFIRMARY.
WE WERE JUST CHECKING IN ON JUDAH WHILE YOU RECOVERED, MR. DRAKE.
MICHAELA, LET'S SEE IF BISHOP NEEDS HELP INTERROGATING THESE GOONS DAKEN HAD MASQUERADING AS PURIFIERS.
WE'LL GET OUT OF YOUR HAIR.
HEY.
HI.
I'M REALLY GLAD YOU'RE ALL RI--
I DON'T THINK YOU SHOULD MOVE TO LOS ANGELES.

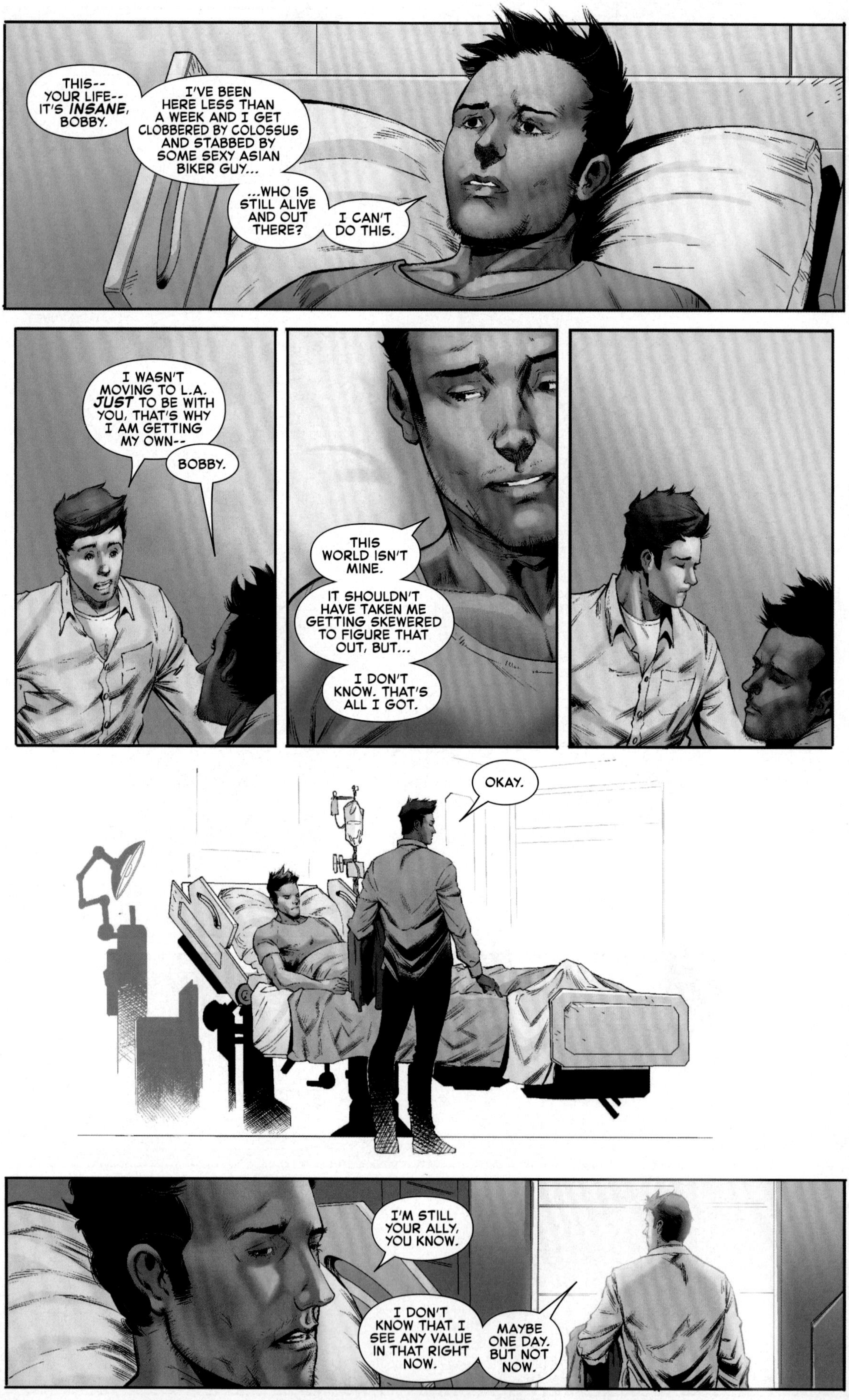

THIS-- YOUR LIFE-- IT'S INSANE, BOBBY.
I'VE BEEN HERE LESS THAN A WEEK AND I GET CLOBBERED BY COLOSSUS AND STABBED BY SOME SEXY ASIAN BIKER GUY...
...WHO IS STILL ALIVE AND OUT THERE?
I CAN'T DO THIS.
I WASN'T MOVING TO L.A. JUST TO BE WITH YOU, THAT'S WHY I AM GETTING MY OWN--
BOBBY.
THIS WORLD ISN'T MINE.
IT SHOULDN'T HAVE TAKEN ME GETTING SKEWERED TO FIGURE THAT OUT, BUT...
I DON'T KNOW. THAT'S ALL I GOT.
OKAY.
I'M STILL YOUR ALLY, YOU KNOW.
I DON'T KNOW THAT I SEE ANY VALUE IN THAT RIGHT NOW.
MAYBE ONE DAY. BUT NOT NOW.

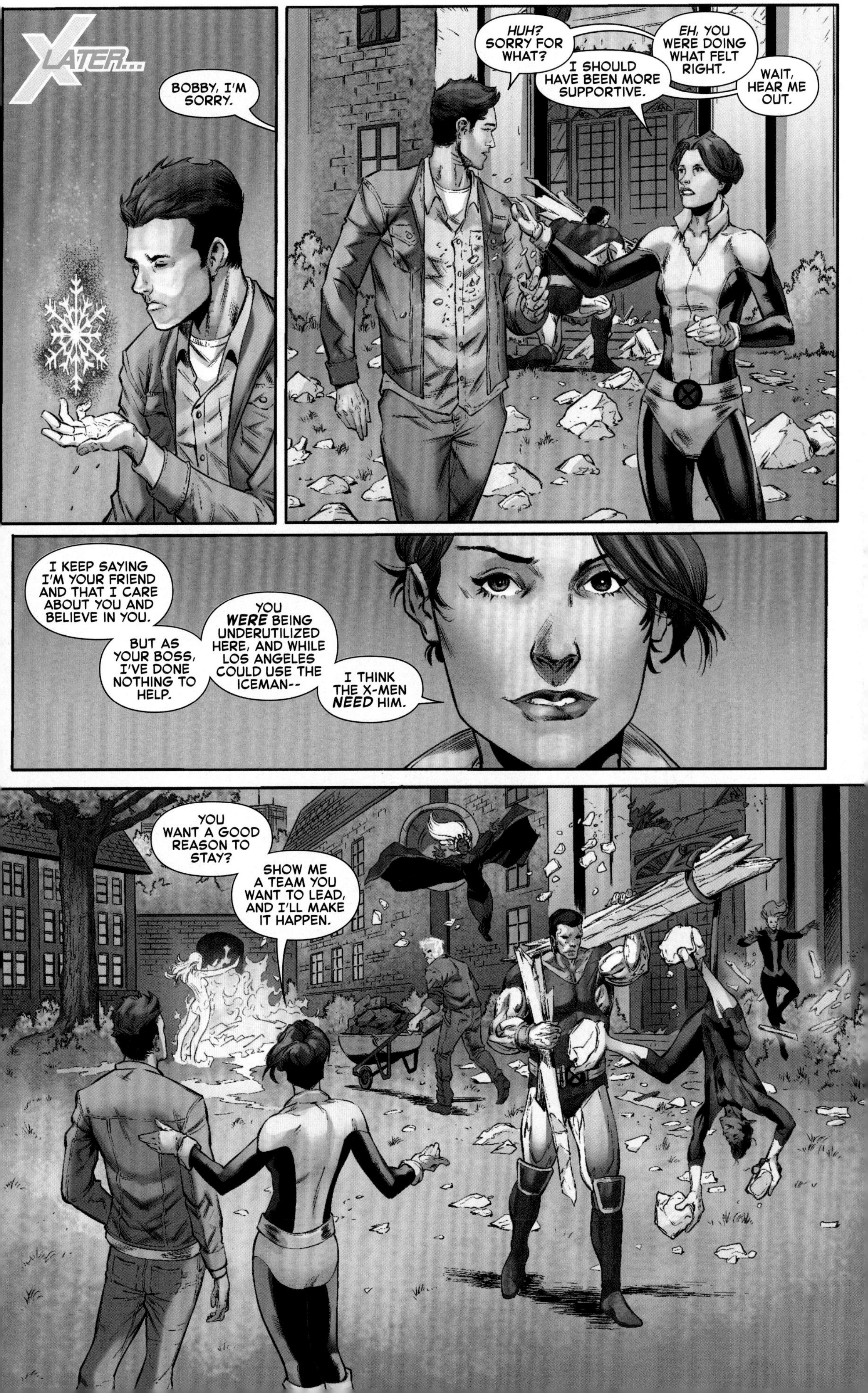

X-LATER...
BOBBY, I'M SORRY.
HUH? SORRY FOR WHAT?
I SHOULD HAVE BEEN MORE SUPPORTIVE.
EH, YOU WERE DOING WHAT FELT RIGHT.
WAIT, HEAR ME OUT.
I KEEP SAYING I'M YOUR FRIEND AND THAT I CARE ABOUT YOU AND BELIEVE IN YOU.
BUT AS YOUR BOSS, I'VE DONE NOTHING TO HELP.
YOU WERE BEING UNDERUTILIZED HERE, AND WHILE LOS ANGELES COULD USE THE ICEMAN--
I THINK THE X-MEN NEED HIM.
YOU WANT A GOOD REASON TO STAY?
SHOW ME A TEAM YOU WANT TO LEAD, AND I'LL MAKE IT HAPPEN.

11

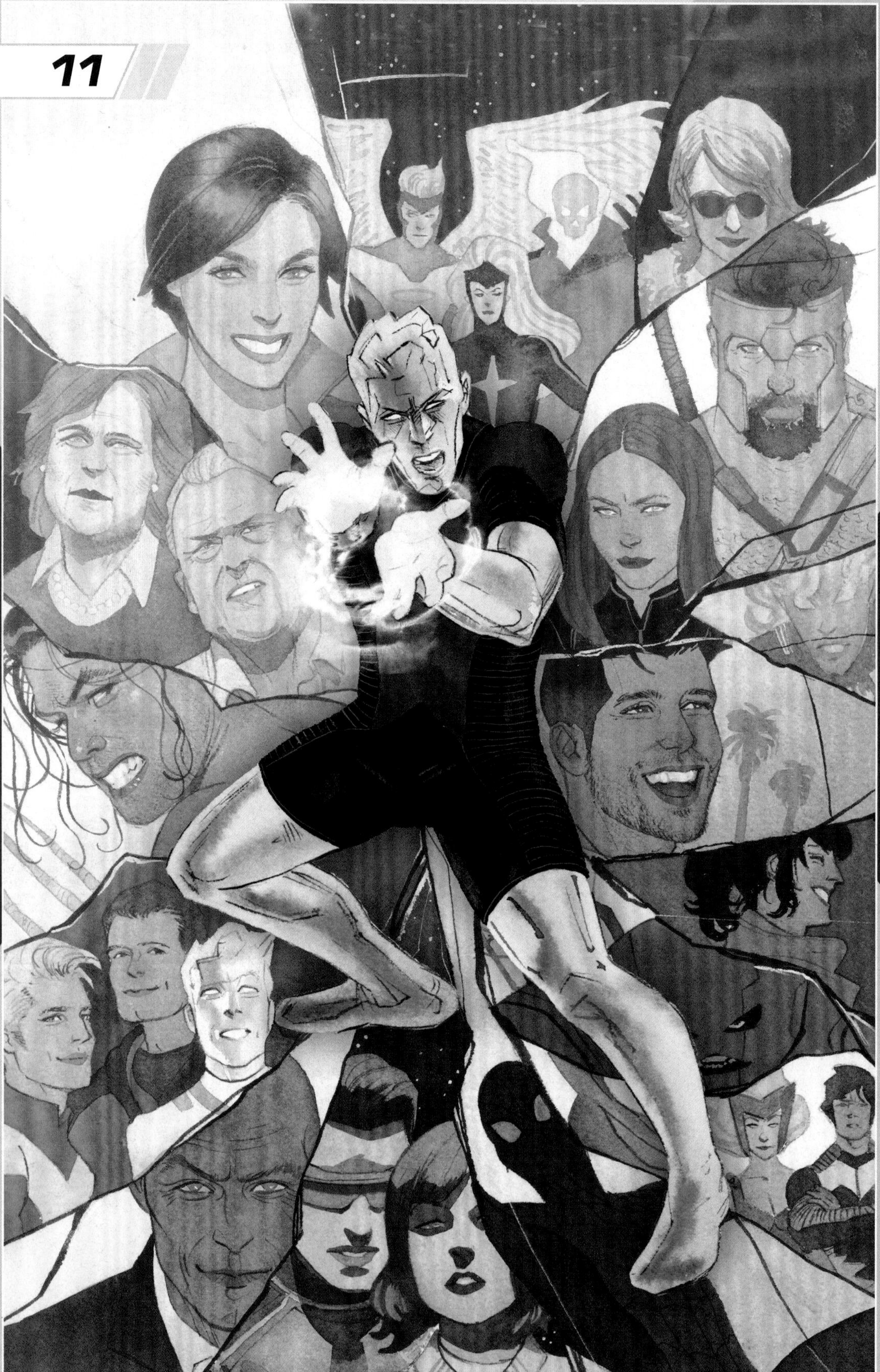

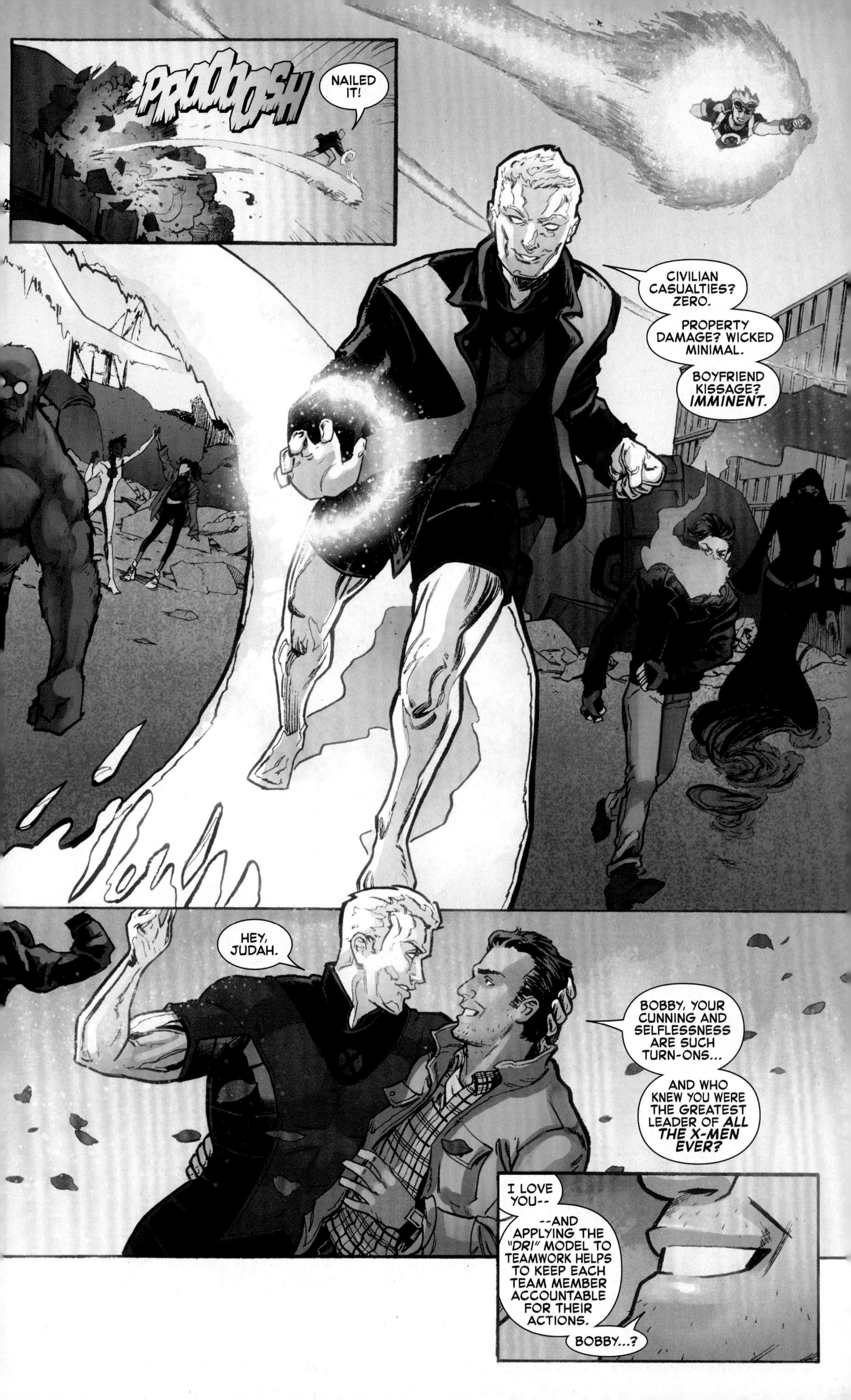
PROOOOSH
NAILED IT!
CIVILIAN CASUALTIES? ZERO.
PROPERTY DAMAGE? WICKED MINIMAL.
BOYFRIEND KISSAGE? *IMMINENT.*
HEY, JUDAH.
BOBBY, YOUR CUNNING AND SELFLESSNESS ARE SUCH TURN-ONS...
AND WHO KNEW YOU WERE THE GREATEST LEADER OF *ALL THE X-MEN EVER?*
I LOVE YOU--
--AND APPLYING THE "*DRI*" MODEL TO TEAMWORK HELPS TO KEEP EACH TEAM MEMBER ACCOUNTABLE FOR THEIR ACTIONS.
BOBBY...?

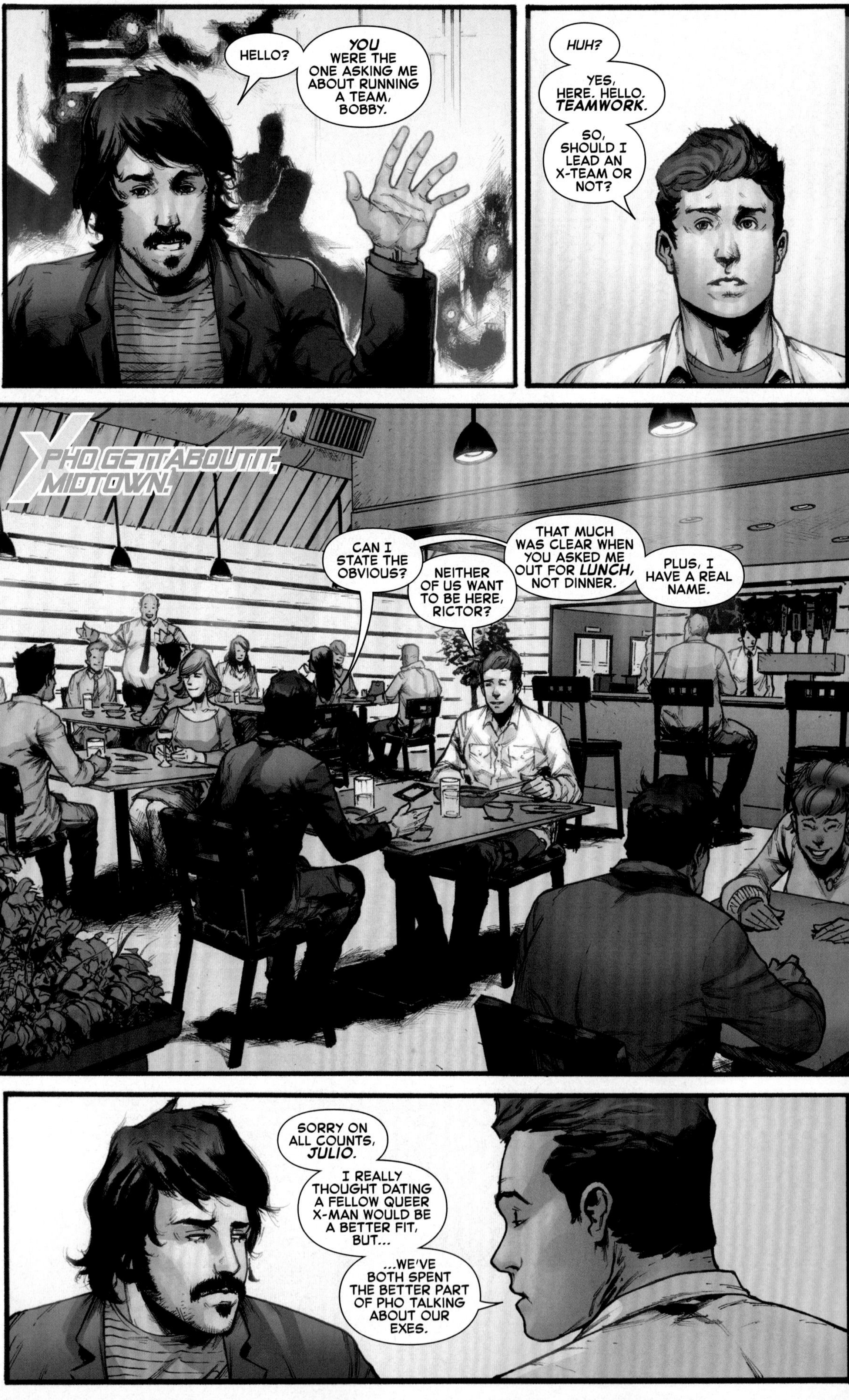
HELLO?
YOU WERE THE ONE ASKING ME ABOUT RUNNING A TEAM, BOBBY.
HUH?
YES, HERE. HELLO. TEAMWORK.
SO, SHOULD I LEAD AN X-TEAM OR NOT?
PHO GETTABOUTIT, MIDTOWN.
CAN I STATE THE OBVIOUS?
NEITHER OF US WANT TO BE HERE, RICTOR?
THAT MUCH WAS CLEAR WHEN YOU ASKED ME OUT FOR LUNCH, NOT DINNER.
PLUS, I HAVE A REAL NAME.
SORRY ON ALL COUNTS, JULIO.
I REALLY THOUGHT DATING A FELLOW QUEER X-MAN WOULD BE A BETTER FIT, BUT...
...WE'VE BOTH SPENT THE BETTER PART OF PHO TALKING ABOUT OUR EXES.

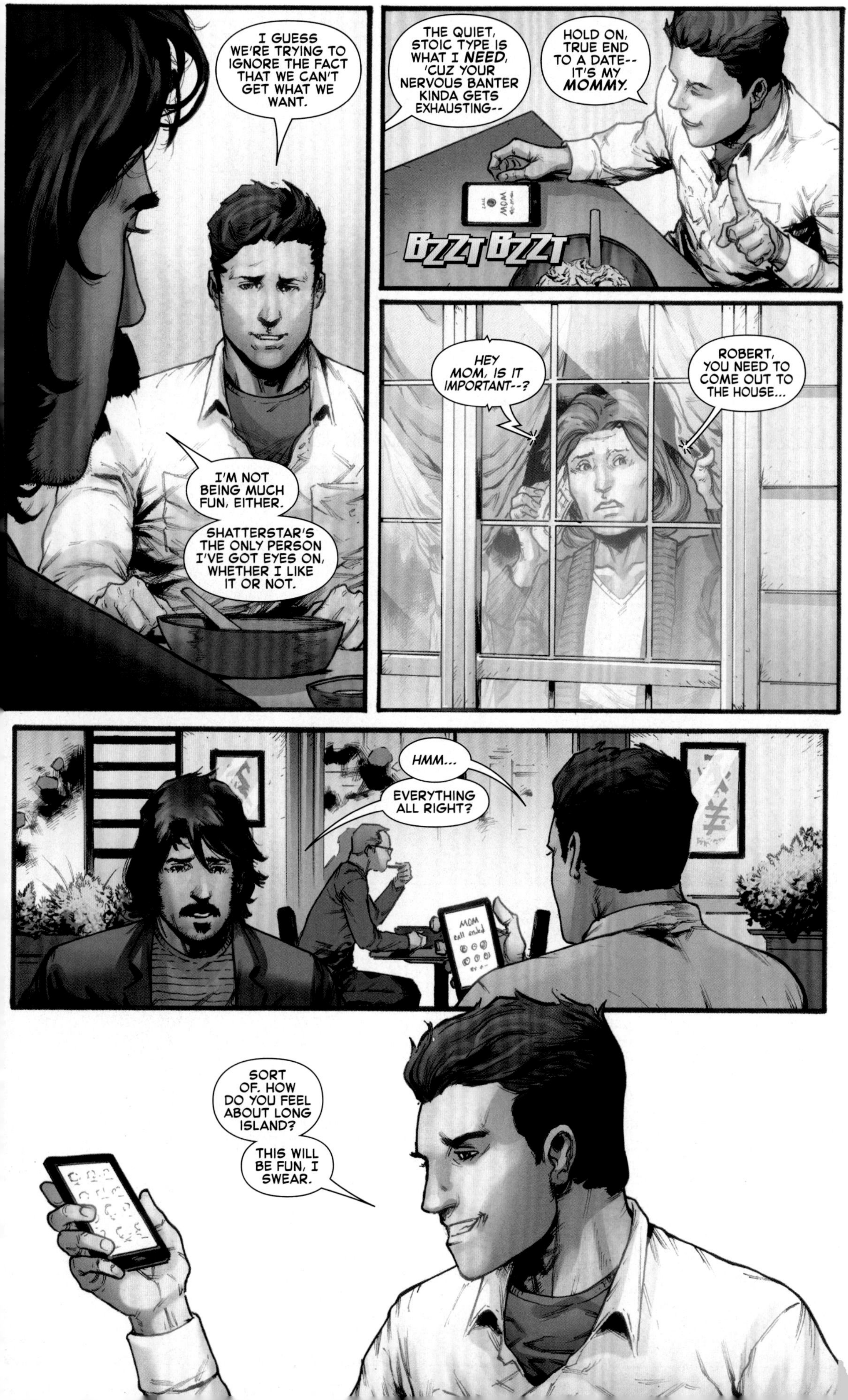
I GUESS WE'RE TRYING TO IGNORE THE FACT THAT WE CAN'T GET WHAT WE WANT.
I'M NOT BEING MUCH FUN, EITHER.
SHATTERSTAR'S THE ONLY PERSON I'VE GOT EYES ON, WHETHER I LIKE IT OR NOT.
THE QUIET, STOIC TYPE IS WHAT I *NEED*, 'CUZ YOUR NERVOUS BANTER KINDA GETS EXHAUSTING--
HOLD ON, TRUE END TO A DATE-- IT'S MY *MOMMY*.
MOM
BZZT BZZT
HEY MOM, IS IT IMPORTANT--?
ROBERT, YOU NEED TO COME OUT TO THE HOUSE...
HMM...
EVERYTHING ALL RIGHT?
MOM
call ended
SORT OF. HOW DO YOU FEEL ABOUT LONG ISLAND?
THIS WILL BE FUN, I SWEAR.

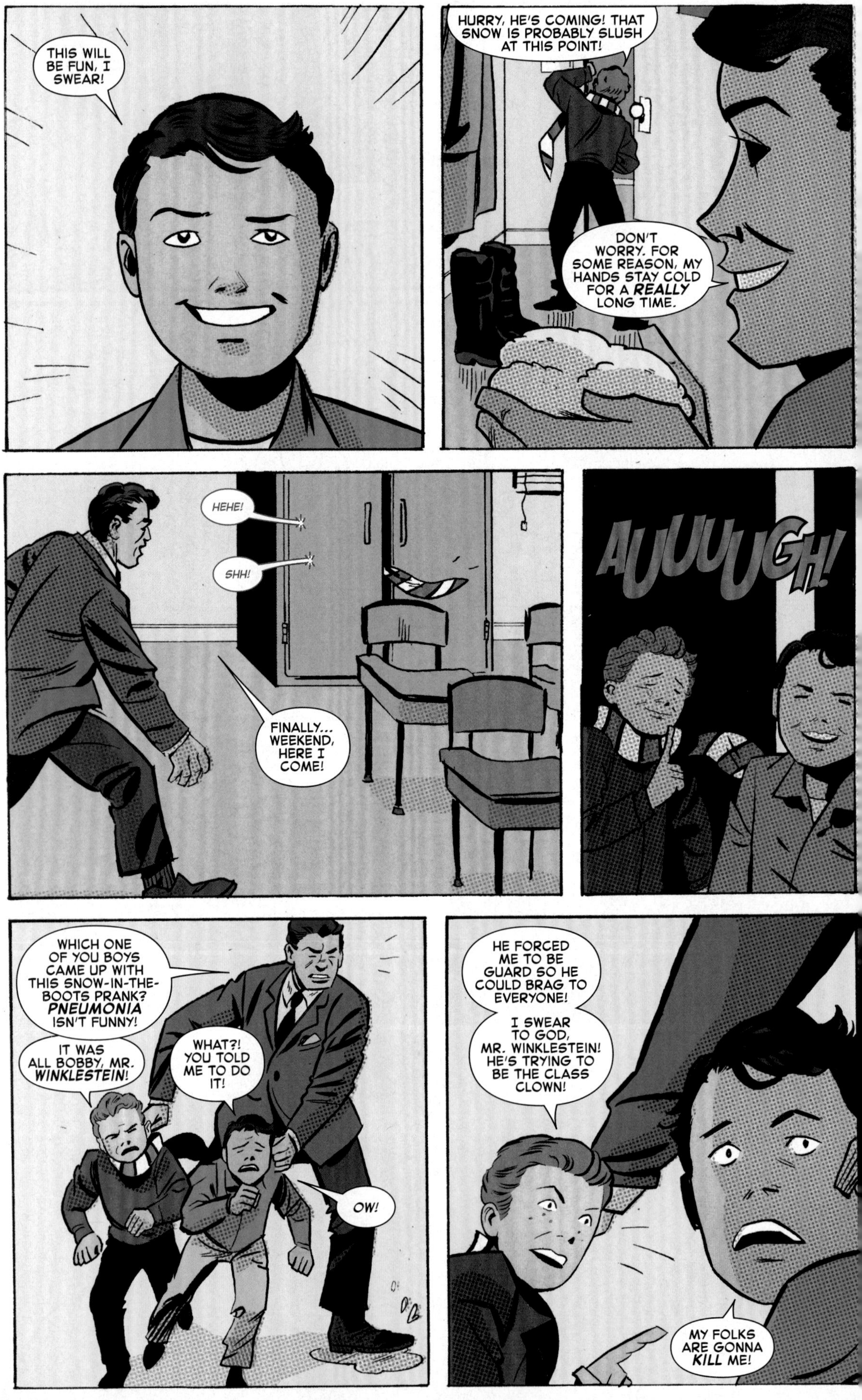
THIS WILL BE FUN, I SWEAR!
HURRY, HE'S COMING! THAT SNOW IS PROBABLY SLUSH AT THIS POINT!
DON'T WORRY. FOR SOME REASON, MY HANDS STAY COLD FOR A *REALLY* LONG TIME.
HEHE!
SHH!
FINALLY... WEEKEND, HERE I COME!
AUUUUGH!
WHICH ONE OF YOU BOYS CAME UP WITH THIS SNOW-IN-THE-BOOTS PRANK? *PNEUMONIA* ISN'T FUNNY!
IT WAS ALL BOBBY, MR. *WINKLESTEIN*!
WHAT?! YOU TOLD ME TO DO IT!
OW!
HE FORCED ME TO BE GUARD SO HE COULD BRAG TO EVERYONE!
I SWEAR TO GOD, MR. WINKLESTEIN! HE'S TRYING TO BE THE CLASS CLOWN!
MY FOLKS ARE GONNA *KILL* ME!

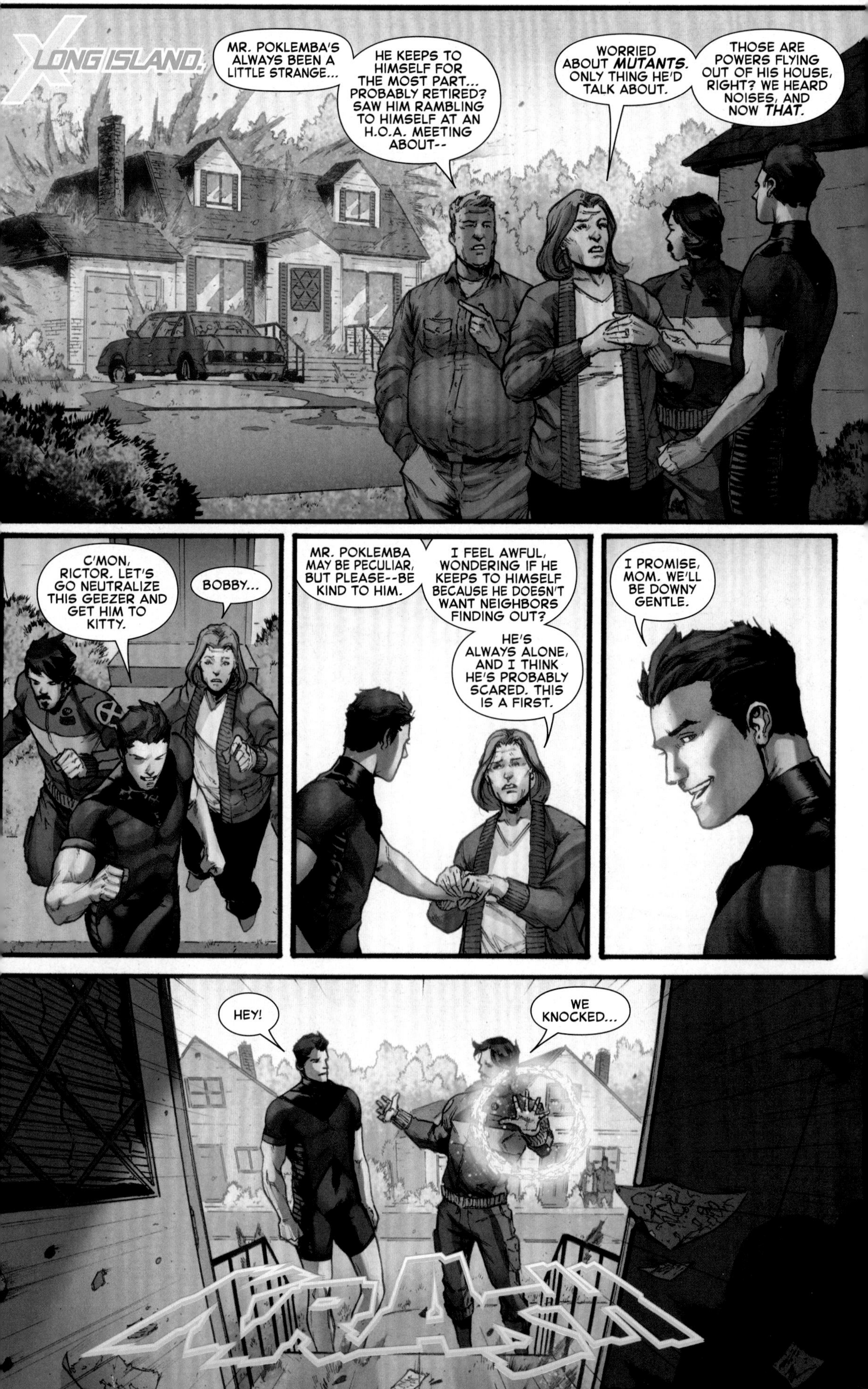
LONG ISLAND.
MR. POKLEMBA'S ALWAYS BEEN A LITTLE STRANGE...
HE KEEPS TO HIMSELF FOR THE MOST PART... PROBABLY RETIRED? SAW HIM RAMBLING TO HIMSELF AT AN H.O.A. MEETING ABOUT--
WORRIED ABOUT MUTANTS. ONLY THING HE'D TALK ABOUT.
THOSE ARE POWERS FLYING OUT OF HIS HOUSE, RIGHT? WE HEARD NOISES, AND NOW THAT.
C'MON, RICTOR. LET'S GO NEUTRALIZE THIS GEEZER AND GET HIM TO KITTY.
BOBBY...
MR. POKLEMBA MAY BE PECULIAR, BUT PLEASE--BE KIND TO HIM.
I FEEL AWFUL, WONDERING IF HE KEEPS TO HIMSELF BECAUSE HE DOESN'T WANT NEIGHBORS FINDING OUT?
HE'S ALWAYS ALONE, AND I THINK HE'S PROBABLY SCARED. THIS IS A FIRST.
I PROMISE, MOM. WE'LL BE DOWNY GENTLE.
HEY!
WE KNOCKED...

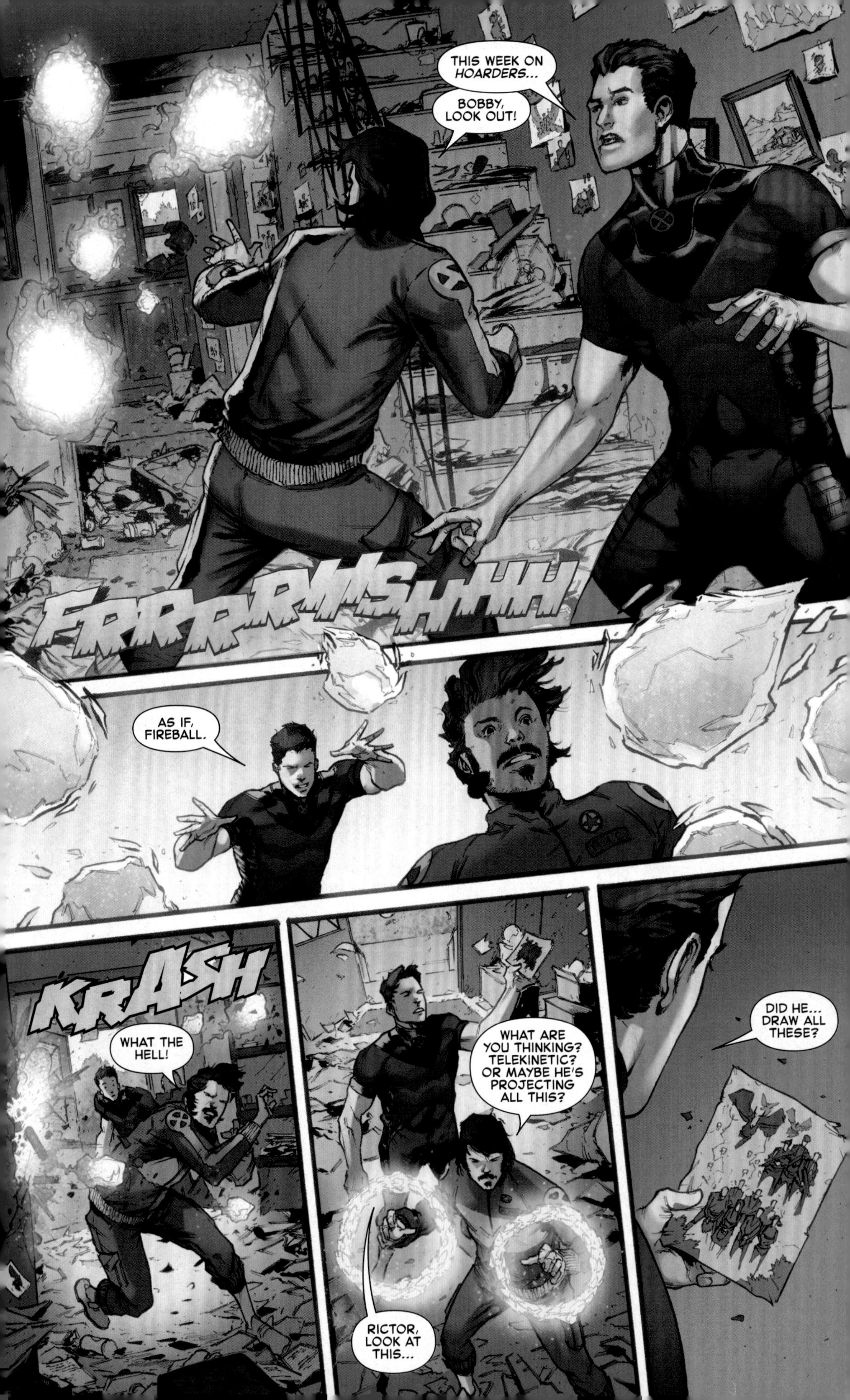
THIS WEEK ON *HOARDERS*...
BOBBY, LOOK OUT!
FRRRMSHHHH
AS IF, FIREBALL.
KRASH
WHAT THE HELL!
WHAT ARE YOU THINKING? TELEKINETIC? OR MAYBE HE'S PROJECTING ALL THIS?
RICTOR, LOOK AT THIS...
DID HE... DRAW ALL THESE?

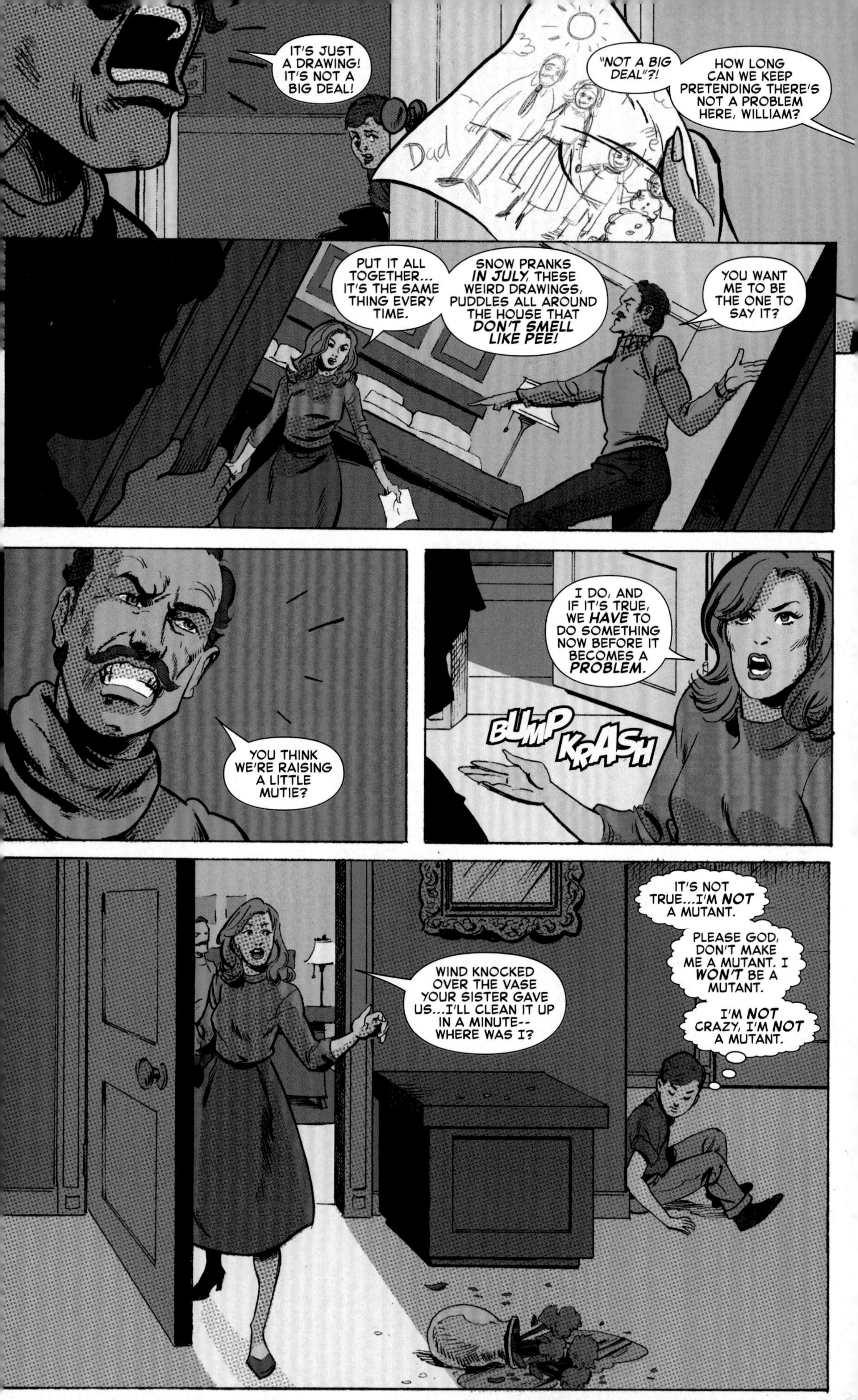
IT'S JUST A DRAWING! IT'S NOT A BIG DEAL!
"NOT A BIG DEAL"?!
HOW LONG CAN WE KEEP PRETENDING THERE'S NOT A PROBLEM HERE, WILLIAM?
Dad
PUT IT ALL TOGETHER... IT'S THE SAME THING EVERY TIME.
SNOW PRANKS IN JULY, THESE WEIRD DRAWINGS, PUDDLES ALL AROUND THE HOUSE THAT DON'T SMELL LIKE PEE!
YOU WANT ME TO BE THE ONE TO SAY IT?
YOU THINK WE'RE RAISING A LITTLE MUTIE?
I DO, AND IF IT'S TRUE, WE HAVE TO DO SOMETHING NOW BEFORE IT BECOMES A PROBLEM.
BUMP
KRASH
WIND KNOCKED OVER THE VASE YOUR SISTER GAVE US...I'LL CLEAN IT UP IN A MINUTE-- WHERE WAS I?
IT'S NOT TRUE...I'M NOT A MUTANT.
PLEASE GOD, DON'T MAKE ME A MUTANT. I WON'T BE A MUTANT.
I'M NOT CRAZY, I'M NOT A MUTANT.

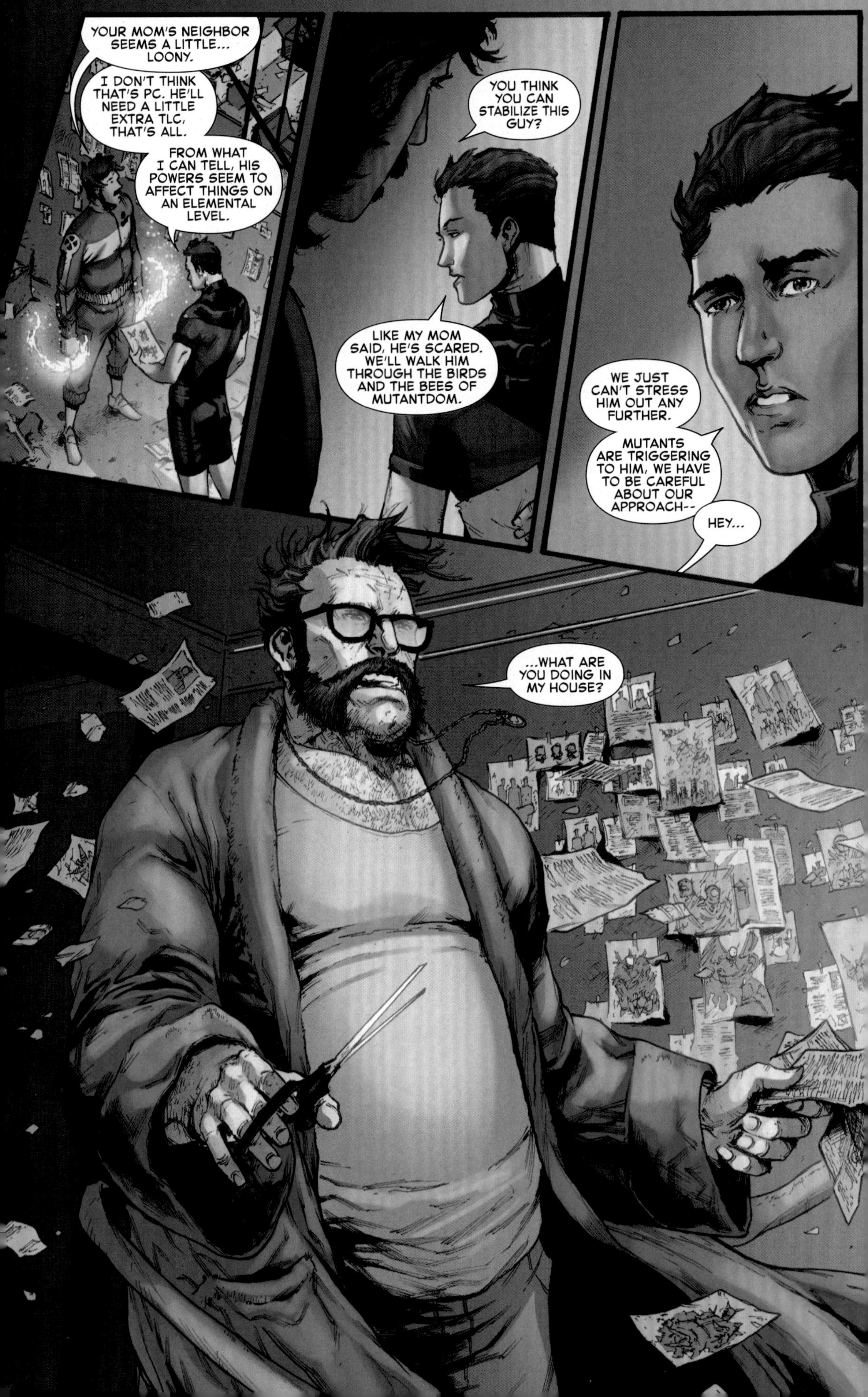
YOUR MOM'S NEIGHBOR SEEMS A LITTLE... LOONY.
I DON'T THINK THAT'S PC. HE'LL NEED A LITTLE EXTRA TLC, THAT'S ALL.
FROM WHAT I CAN TELL, HIS POWERS SEEM TO AFFECT THINGS ON AN ELEMENTAL LEVEL.
YOU THINK YOU CAN STABILIZE THIS GUY?
LIKE MY MOM SAID, HE'S SCARED. WE'LL WALK HIM THROUGH THE BIRDS AND THE BEES OF MUTANTDOM.
WE JUST CAN'T STRESS HIM OUT ANY FURTHER.
MUTANTS ARE TRIGGERING TO HIM, WE HAVE TO BE CAREFUL ABOUT OUR APPROACH--
HEY...
...WHAT ARE YOU DOING IN MY HOUSE?

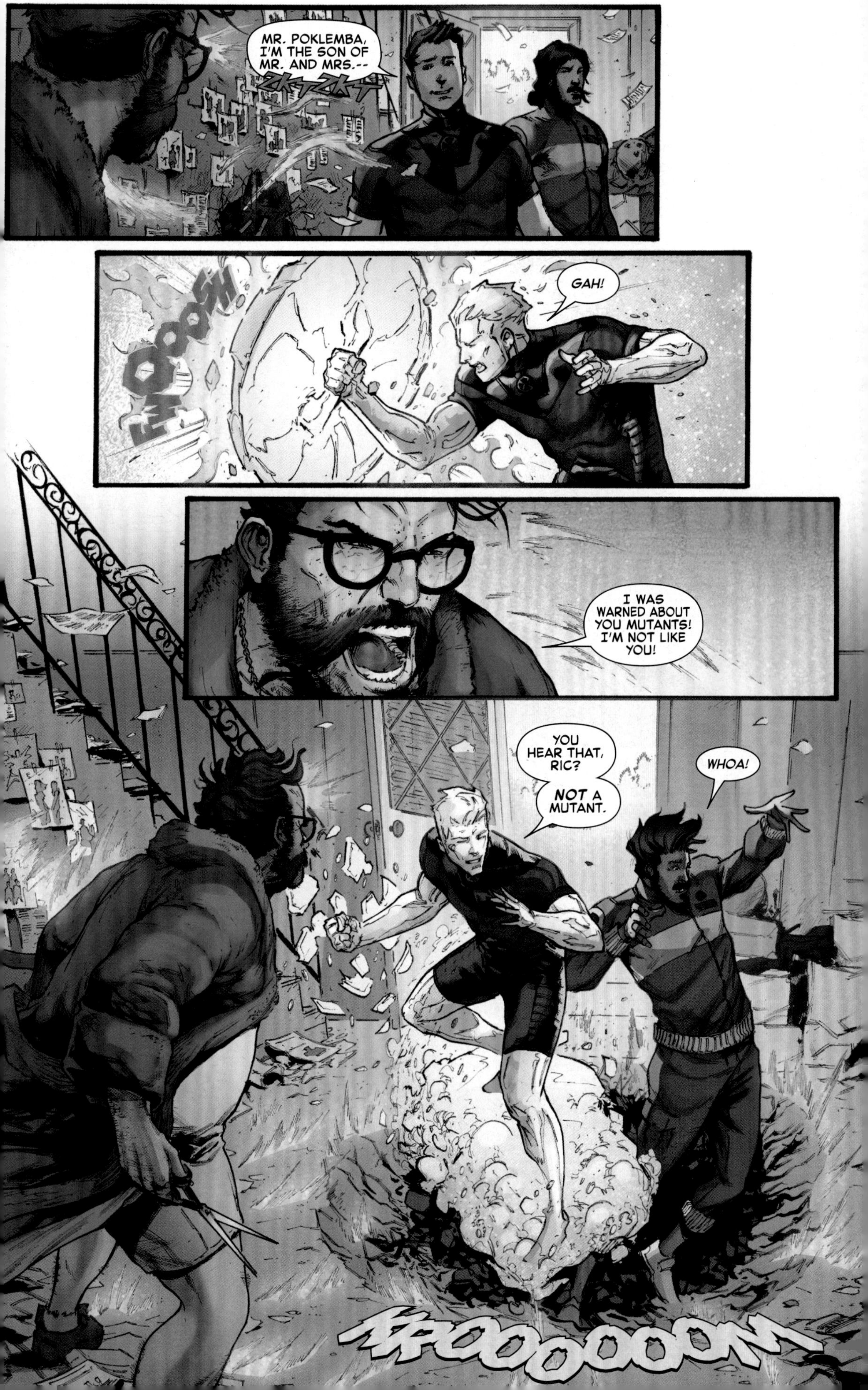

MR. POKLEMBA, I'M THE SON OF MR. AND MRS.--
ZKTZKT
FWOOOSH
GAH!
I WAS WARNED ABOUT YOU MUTANTS! I'M NOT LIKE YOU!
YOU HEAR THAT, RIC?
NOT A MUTANT.
WHOA!
KROOOOOOOM

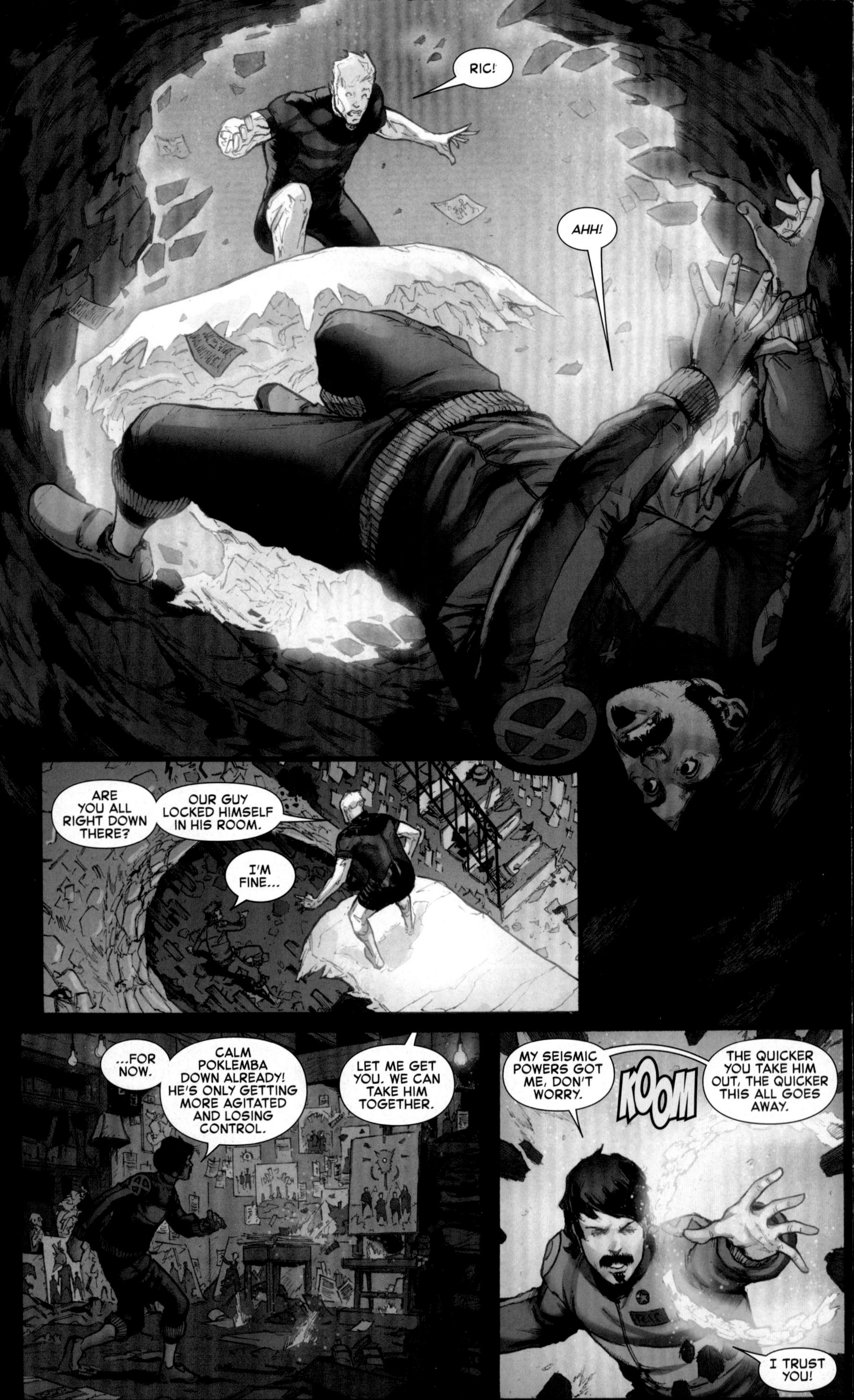
RIC!
AHH!
ARE YOU ALL RIGHT DOWN THERE?
OUR GUY LOCKED HIMSELF IN HIS ROOM.
I'M FINE...
...FOR NOW.
CALM POKLEMBA DOWN ALREADY! HE'S ONLY GETTING MORE AGITATED AND LOSING CONTROL.
LET ME GET YOU. WE CAN TAKE HIM TOGETHER.
MY SEISMIC POWERS GOT ME, DON'T WORRY.
KOOM
THE QUICKER YOU TAKE HIM OUT, THE QUICKER THIS ALL GOES AWAY.
I TRUST YOU!

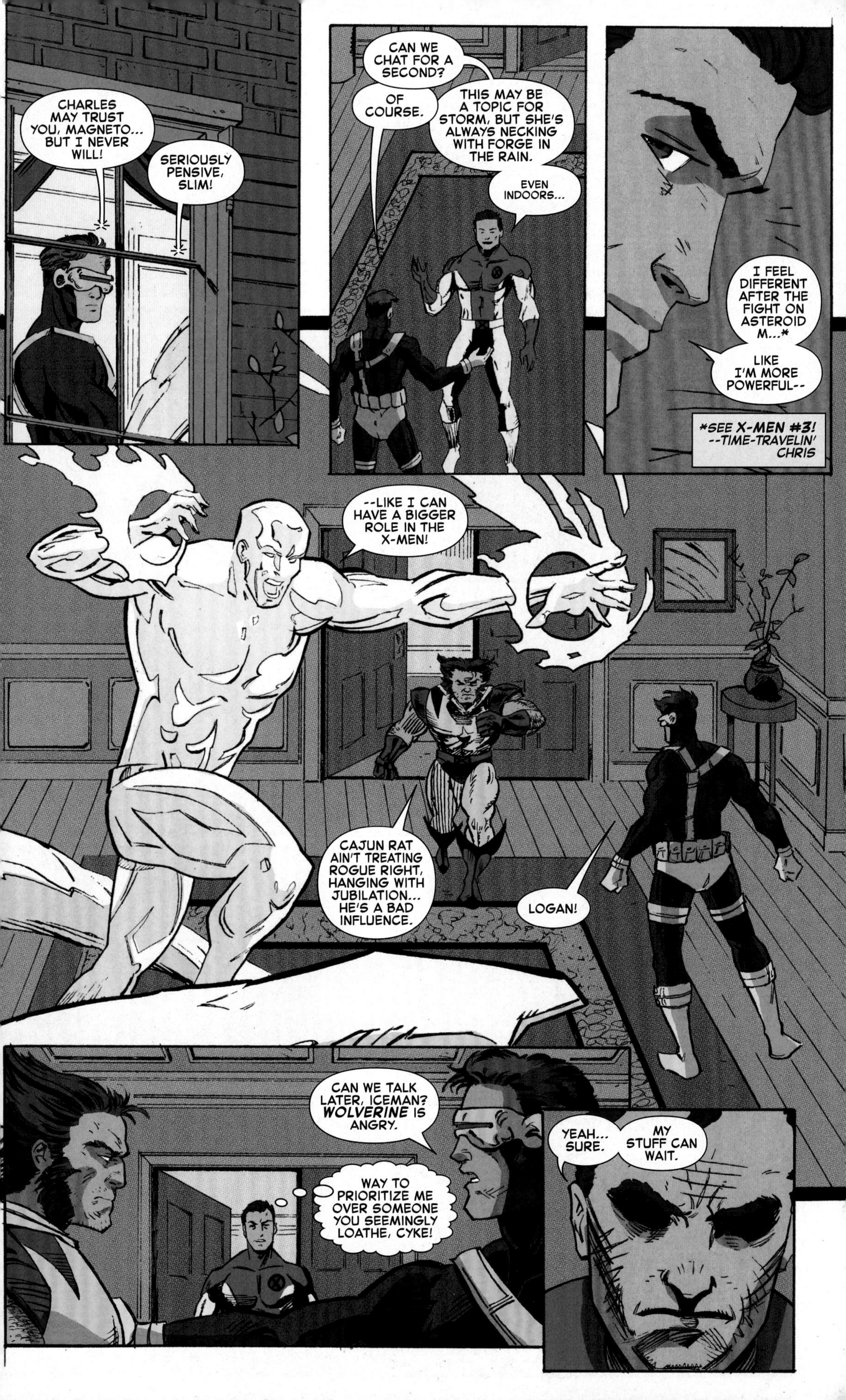

CHARLES MAY TRUST YOU, MAGNETO... BUT I NEVER WILL!
SERIOUSLY PENSIVE, SLIM!
CAN WE CHAT FOR A SECOND?
OF COURSE.
THIS MAY BE A TOPIC FOR STORM, BUT SHE'S ALWAYS NECKING WITH FORGE IN THE RAIN.
EVEN INDOORS...
I FEEL DIFFERENT AFTER THE FIGHT ON ASTEROID M...*
LIKE I'M MORE POWERFUL--
*SEE X-MEN #3! --TIME-TRAVELIN' CHRIS
--LIKE I CAN HAVE A BIGGER ROLE IN THE X-MEN!
CAJUN RAT AIN'T TREATING ROGUE RIGHT, HANGING WITH JUBILATION... HE'S A BAD INFLUENCE.
LOGAN!
CAN WE TALK LATER, ICEMAN? WOLVERINE IS ANGRY.
WAY TO PRIORITIZE ME OVER SOMEONE YOU SEEMINGLY LOATHE, CYKE!
YEAH... SURE.
MY STUFF CAN WAIT.

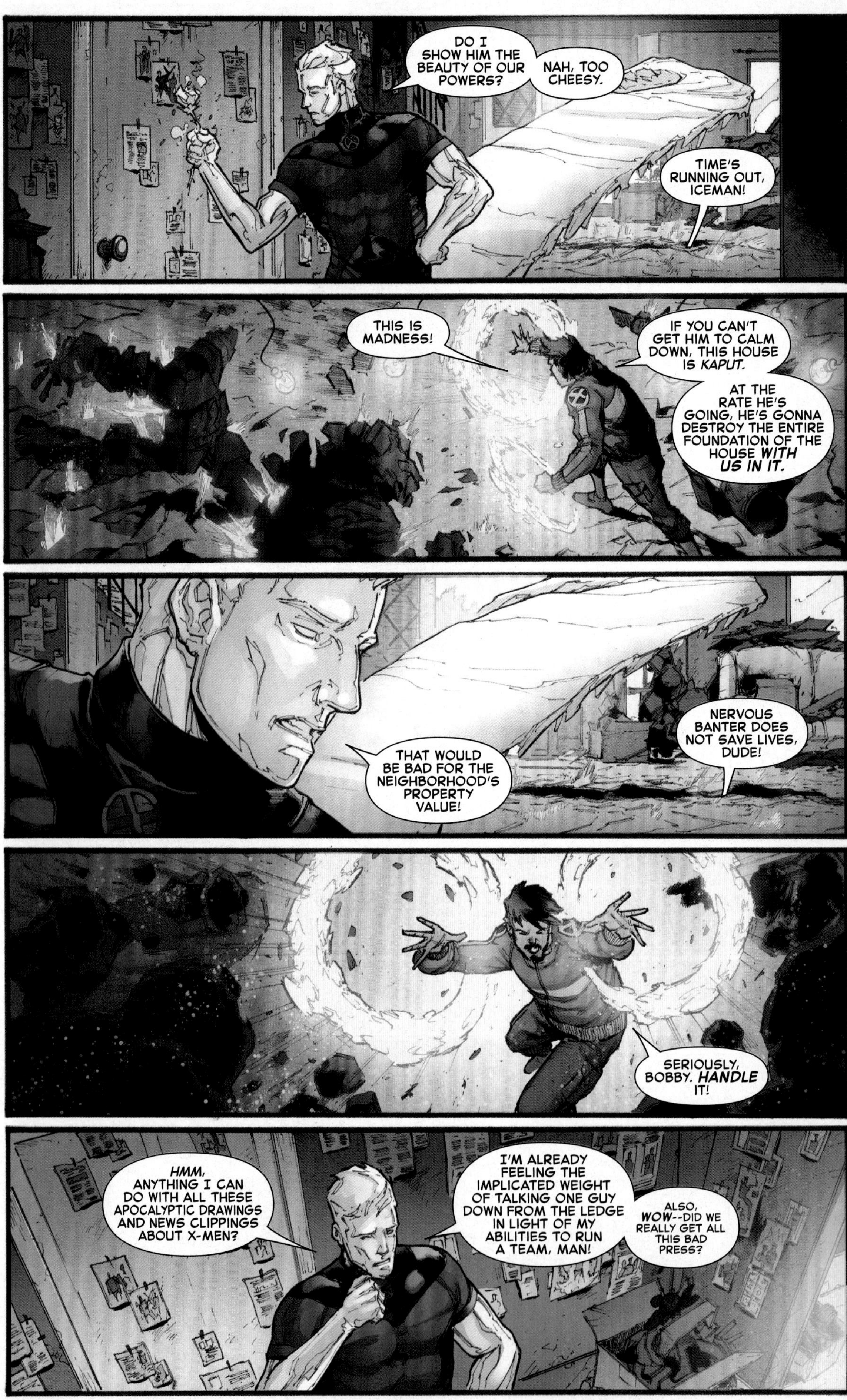
DO I SHOW HIM THE BEAUTY OF OUR POWERS?
NAH, TOO CHEESY.
TIME'S RUNNING OUT, ICEMAN!
THIS IS MADNESS!
IF YOU CAN'T GET HIM TO CALM DOWN, THIS HOUSE IS *KAPUT.*
AT THE RATE HE'S GOING, HE'S GONNA DESTROY THE ENTIRE FOUNDATION OF THE HOUSE ***WITH US IN IT.***
THAT WOULD BE BAD FOR THE NEIGHBORHOOD'S PROPERTY VALUE!
NERVOUS BANTER DOES NOT SAVE LIVES, DUDE!
SERIOUSLY, BOBBY. ***HANDLE*** IT!
HMM, ANYTHING I CAN DO WITH ALL THESE APOCALYPTIC DRAWINGS AND NEWS CLIPPINGS ABOUT X-MEN?
I'M ALREADY FEELING THE IMPLICATED WEIGHT OF TALKING ONE GUY DOWN FROM THE LEDGE IN LIGHT OF MY ABILITIES TO RUN A TEAM, MAN!
ALSO, ***WOW***--DID WE REALLY GET ALL THIS BAD PRESS?

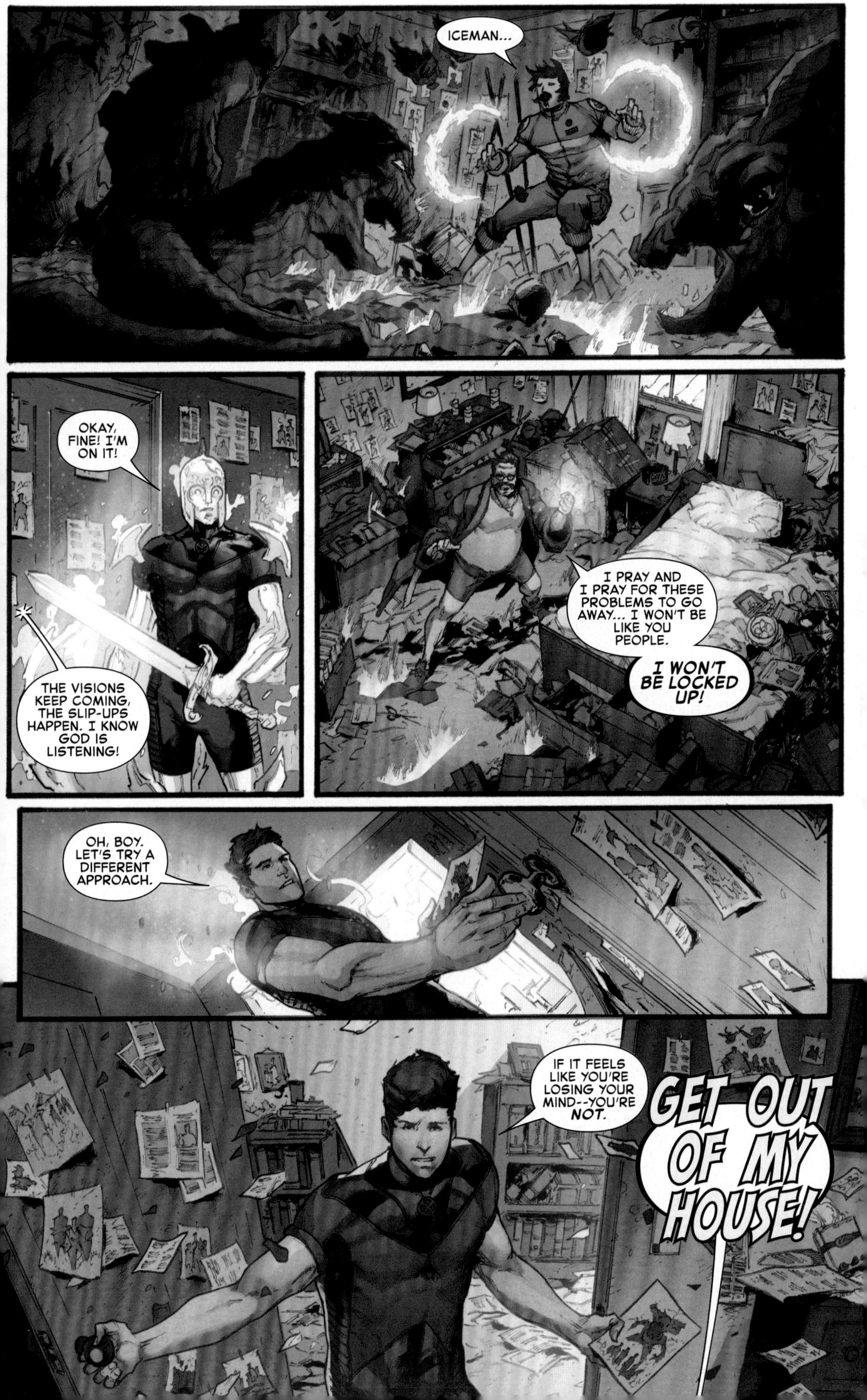
ICEMAN...
OKAY, FINE! I'M ON IT!
THE VISIONS KEEP COMING, THE SLIP-UPS HAPPEN. I KNOW GOD IS LISTENING!
I PRAY AND I PRAY FOR THESE PROBLEMS TO GO AWAY... I WON'T BE LIKE YOU PEOPLE.
I WON'T BE LOCKED UP!
OH, BOY. LET'S TRY A DIFFERENT APPROACH.
IF IT FEELS LIKE YOU'RE LOSING YOUR MIND--YOU'RE NOT.
GET OUT OF MY HOUSE!

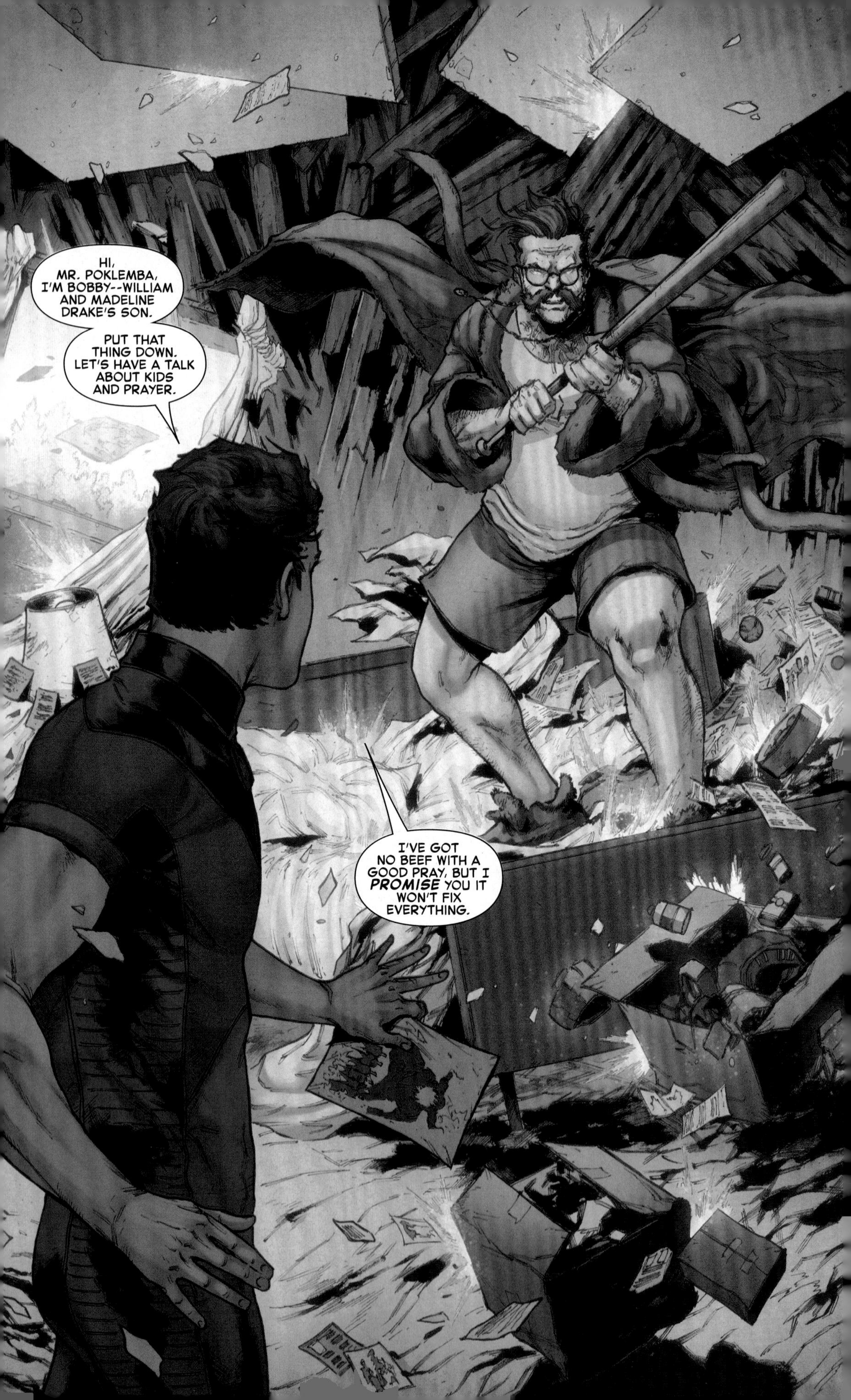
HI, MR. POKLEMBA, I'M BOBBY--WILLIAM AND MADELINE DRAKE'S SON.
PUT THAT THING DOWN. LET'S HAVE A TALK ABOUT KIDS AND PRAYER.
I'VE GOT NO BEEF WITH A GOOD PRAY, BUT I *PROMISE* YOU IT WON'T FIX EVERYTHING.

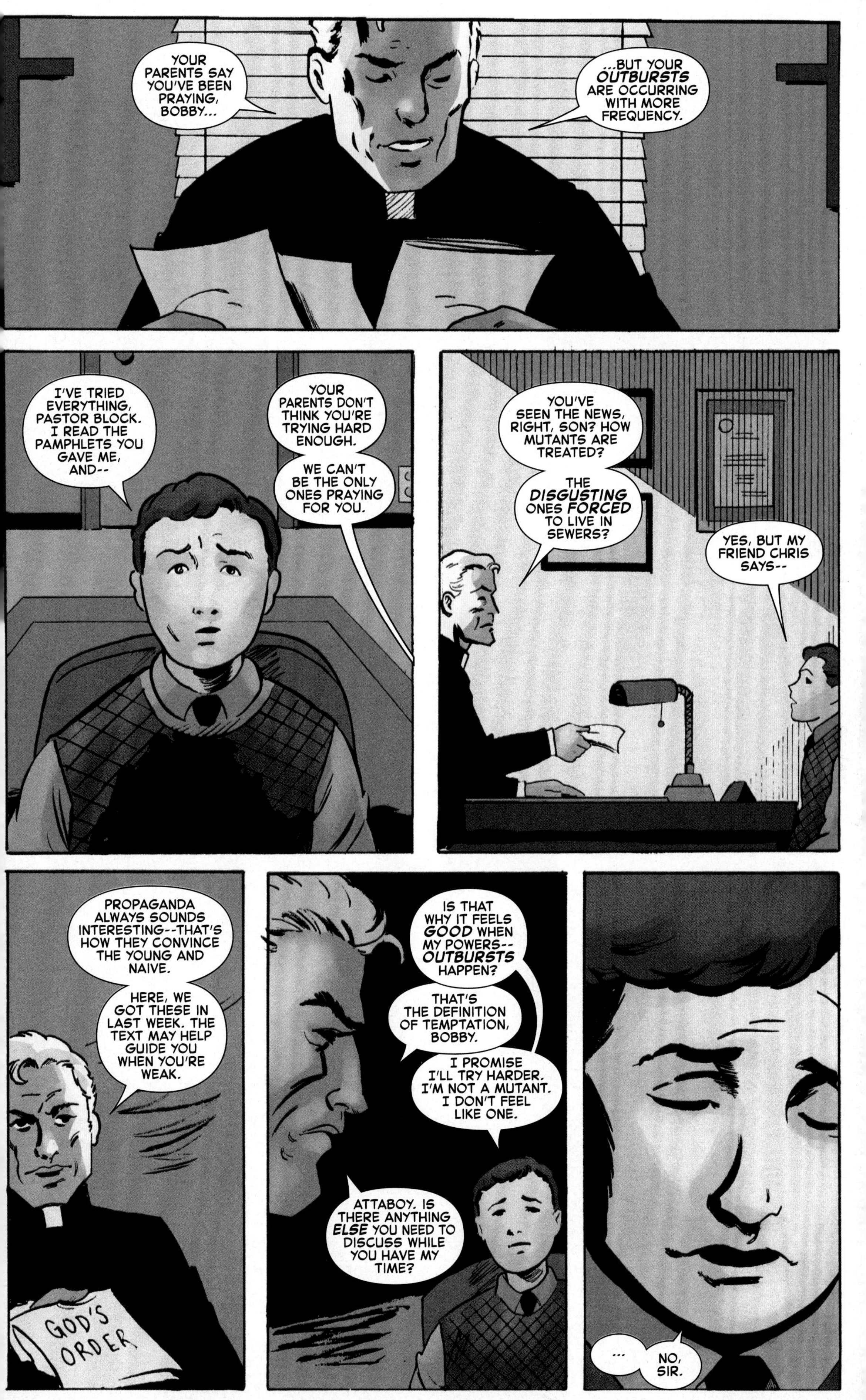

YOUR PARENTS SAY YOU'VE BEEN PRAYING, BOBBY...
...BUT YOUR OUTBURSTS ARE OCCURRING WITH MORE FREQUENCY.
I'VE TRIED EVERYTHING, PASTOR BLOCK. I READ THE PAMPHLETS YOU GAVE ME, AND--
YOUR PARENTS DON'T THINK YOU'RE TRYING HARD ENOUGH.
WE CAN'T BE THE ONLY ONES PRAYING FOR YOU.
YOU'VE SEEN THE NEWS, RIGHT, SON? HOW MUTANTS ARE TREATED?
THE DISGUSTING ONES FORCED TO LIVE IN SEWERS?
YES, BUT MY FRIEND CHRIS SAYS--
PROPAGANDA ALWAYS SOUNDS INTERESTING--THAT'S HOW THEY CONVINCE THE YOUNG AND NAIVE.
HERE, WE GOT THESE IN LAST WEEK. THE TEXT MAY HELP GUIDE YOU WHEN YOU'RE WEAK.
GOD'S ORDER
IS THAT WHY IT FEELS GOOD WHEN MY POWERS--OUTBURSTS HAPPEN?
THAT'S THE DEFINITION OF TEMPTATION, BOBBY.
I PROMISE I'LL TRY HARDER. I'M NOT A MUTANT. I DON'T FEEL LIKE ONE.
ATTABOY. IS THERE ANYTHING ELSE YOU NEED TO DISCUSS WHILE YOU HAVE MY TIME?
...
NO, SIR.

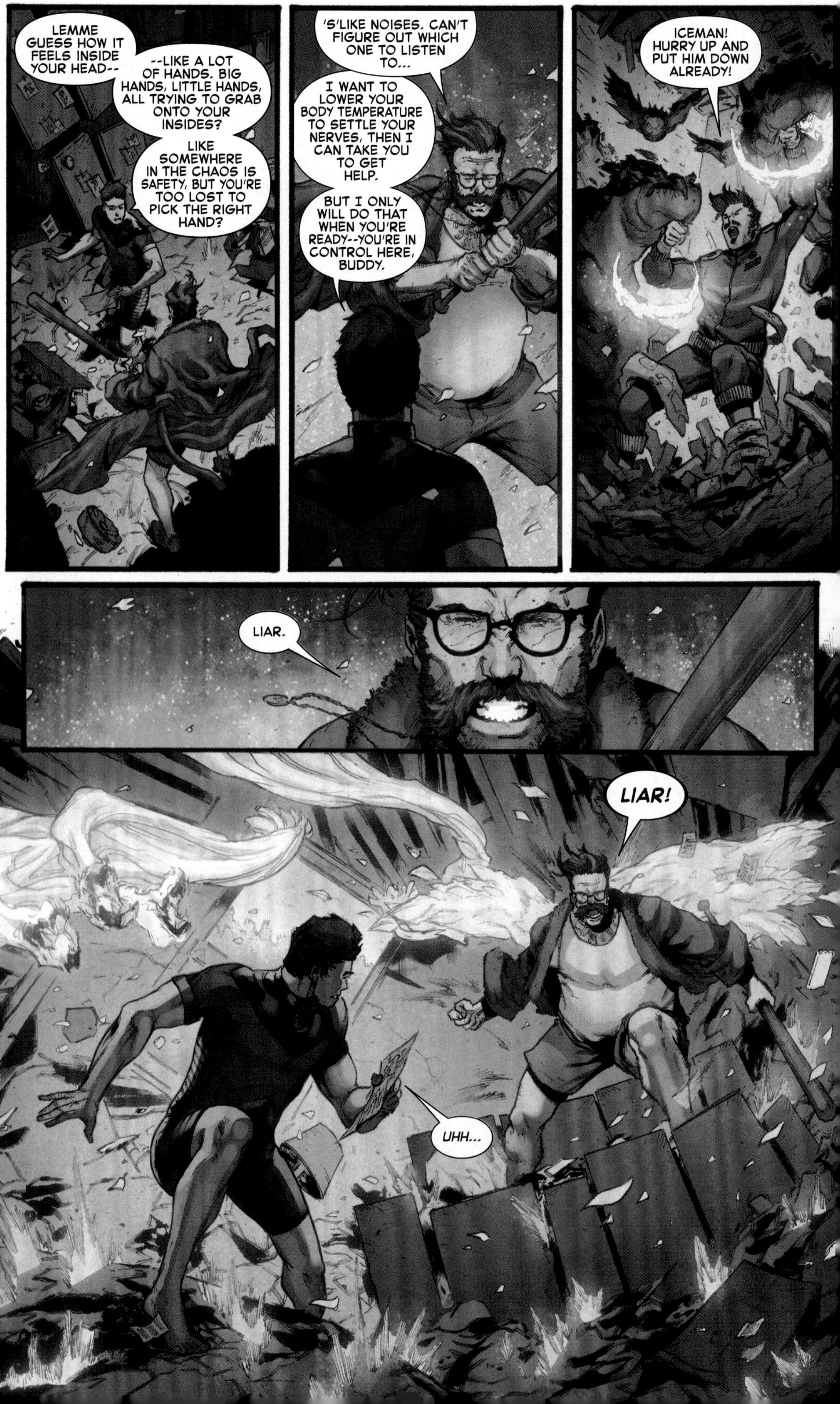

LEMME GUESS HOW IT FEELS INSIDE YOUR HEAD--
--LIKE A LOT OF HANDS. BIG HANDS, LITTLE HANDS, ALL TRYING TO GRAB ONTO YOUR INSIDES?
LIKE SOMEWHERE IN THE CHAOS IS SAFETY, BUT YOU'RE TOO LOST TO PICK THE RIGHT HAND?
'S'LIKE NOISES. CAN'T FIGURE OUT WHICH ONE TO LISTEN TO...
I WANT TO LOWER YOUR BODY TEMPERATURE TO SETTLE YOUR NERVES, THEN I CAN TAKE YOU TO GET HELP.
BUT I ONLY WILL DO THAT WHEN YOU'RE READY--YOU'RE IN CONTROL HERE, BUDDY.
ICEMAN! HURRY UP AND PUT HIM DOWN ALREADY!
LIAR.
LIAR!
UHH...

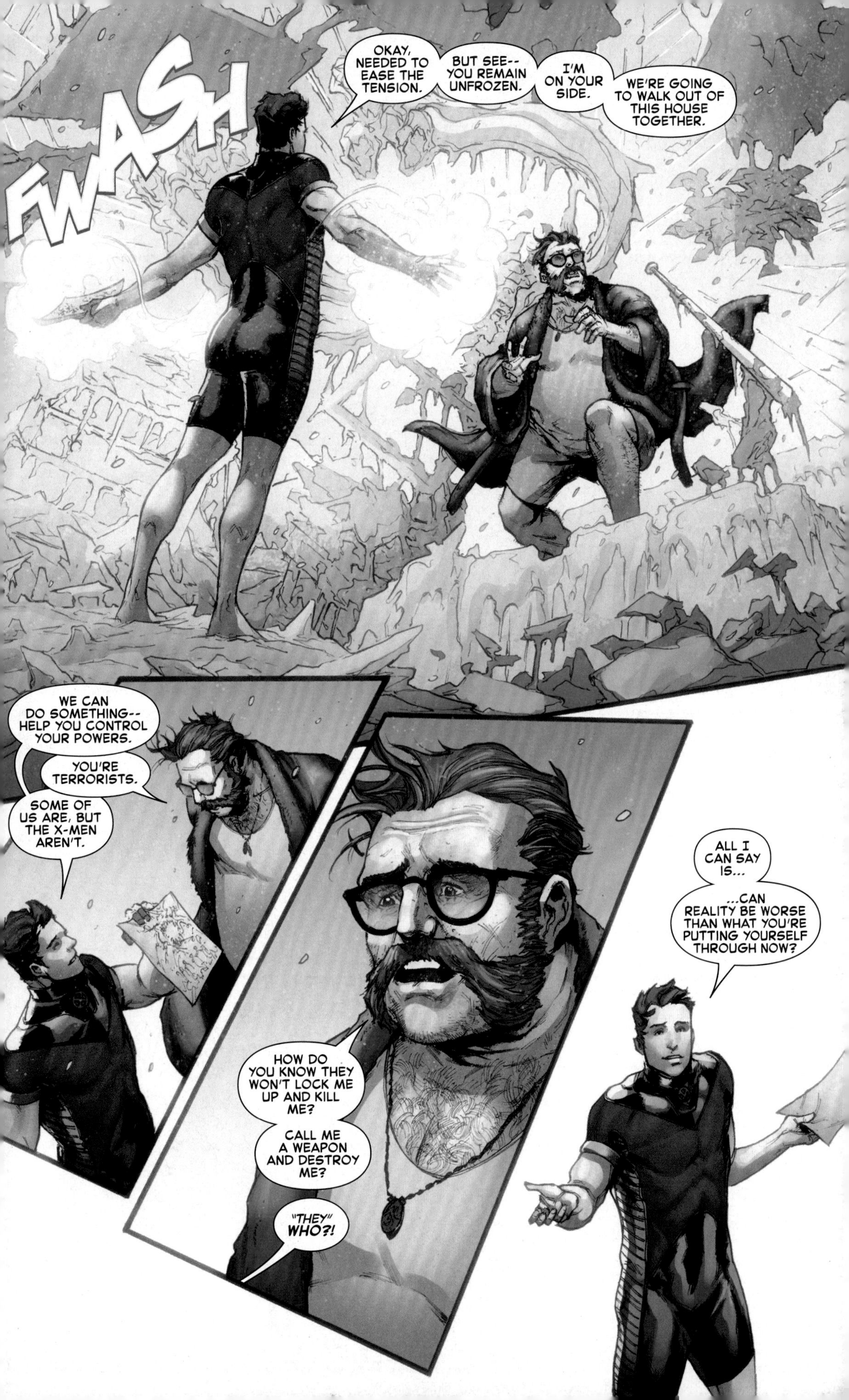
FWASH
OKAY, NEEDED TO EASE THE TENSION.
BUT SEE-- YOU REMAIN UNFROZEN.
I'M ON YOUR SIDE.
WE'RE GOING TO WALK OUT OF THIS HOUSE TOGETHER.
WE CAN DO SOMETHING-- HELP YOU CONTROL YOUR POWERS.
YOU'RE TERRORISTS.
SOME OF US ARE, BUT THE X-MEN AREN'T.
HOW DO YOU KNOW THEY WON'T LOCK ME UP AND KILL ME?
CALL ME A WEAPON AND DESTROY ME?
"THEY" WHO?!
ALL I CAN SAY IS...
...CAN REALITY BE WORSE THAN WHAT YOU'RE PUTTING YOURSELF THROUGH NOW?

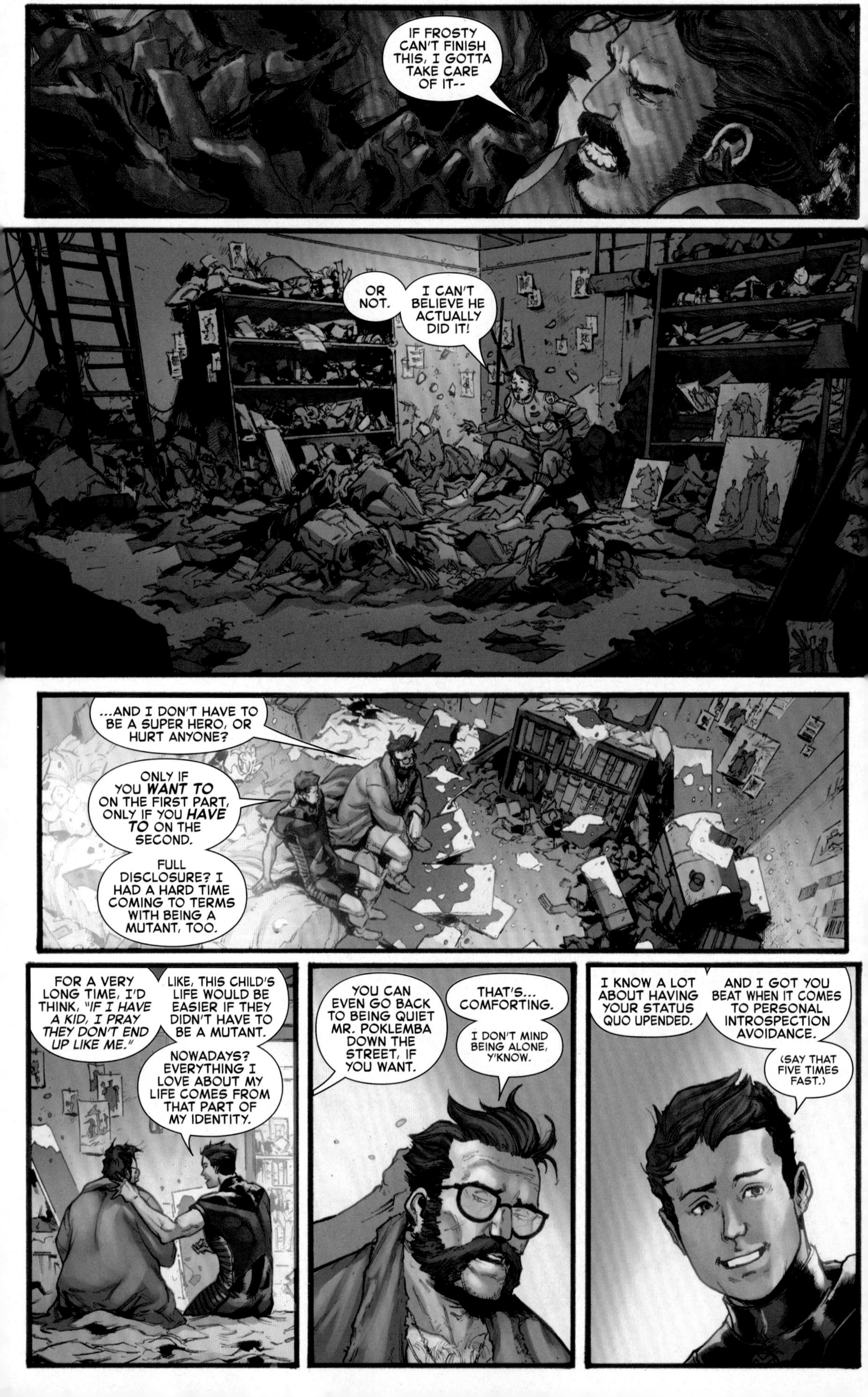
IF FROSTY CAN'T FINISH THIS, I GOTTA TAKE CARE OF IT--
OR NOT.
I CAN'T BELIEVE HE ACTUALLY DID IT!
...AND I DON'T HAVE TO BE A SUPER HERO, OR HURT ANYONE?
ONLY IF YOU *WANT TO* ON THE FIRST PART, ONLY IF YOU *HAVE TO* ON THE SECOND.
FULL DISCLOSURE? I HAD A HARD TIME COMING TO TERMS WITH BEING A MUTANT, TOO.
FOR A VERY LONG TIME, I'D THINK, *"IF I HAVE A KID, I PRAY THEY DON'T END UP LIKE ME."*
LIKE, THIS CHILD'S LIFE WOULD BE EASIER IF THEY DIDN'T HAVE TO BE A MUTANT.
NOWADAYS? EVERYTHING I LOVE ABOUT MY LIFE COMES FROM THAT PART OF MY IDENTITY.
YOU CAN EVEN GO BACK TO BEING QUIET MR. POKLEMBA DOWN THE STREET, IF YOU WANT.
THAT'S... COMFORTING.
I DON'T MIND BEING ALONE, Y'KNOW.
I KNOW A LOT ABOUT HAVING YOUR STATUS QUO UPENDED.
AND I GOT YOU BEAT WHEN IT COMES TO PERSONAL INTROSPECTION AVOIDANCE.
(SAY THAT FIVE TIMES FAST.)

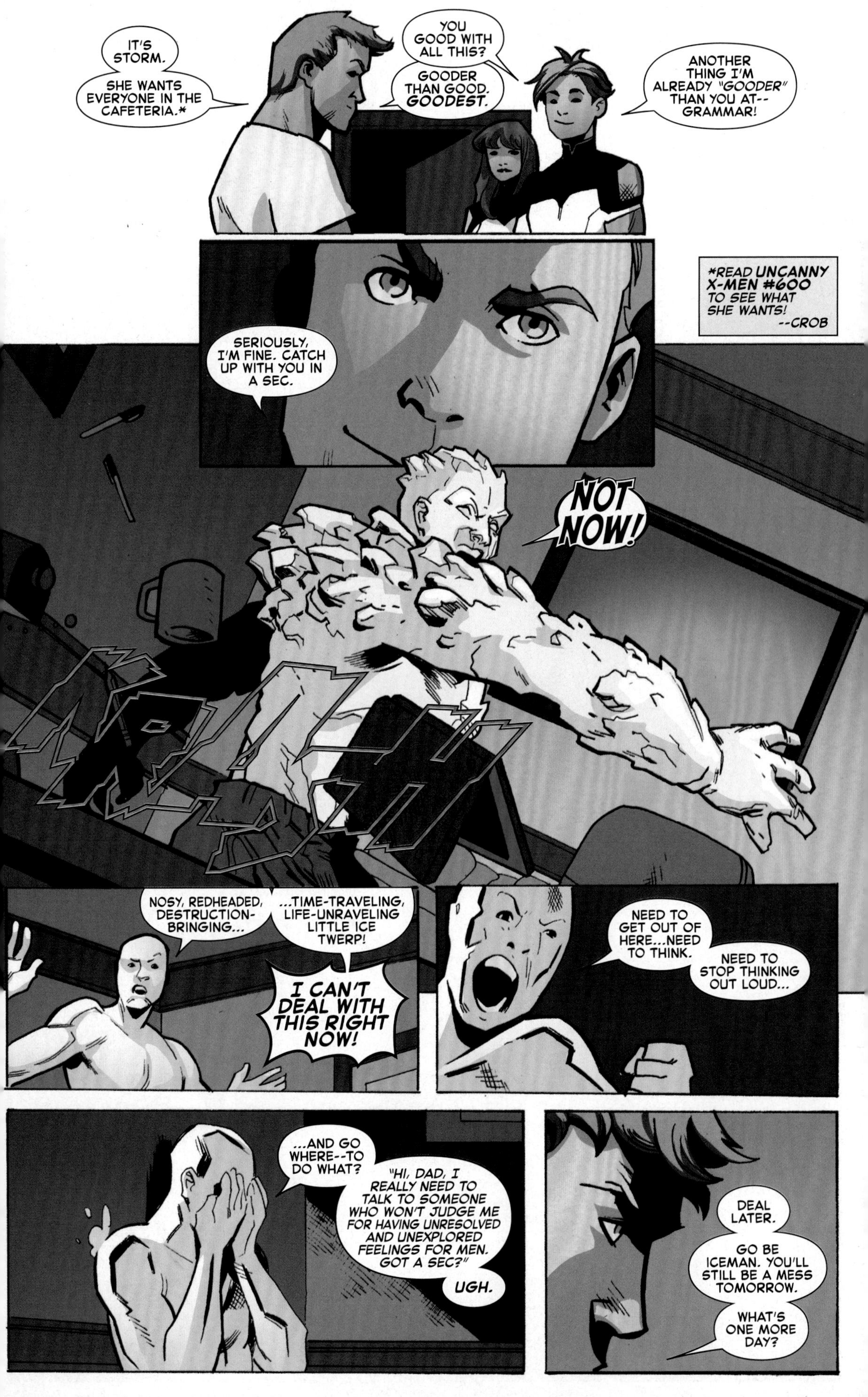

IT'S STORM.
SHE WANTS EVERYONE IN THE CAFETERIA.*
YOU GOOD WITH ALL THIS?
GOODER THAN GOOD. GOODEST.
ANOTHER THING I'M ALREADY "GOODER" THAN YOU AT-- GRAMMAR!
*READ UNCANNY X-MEN #600 TO SEE WHAT SHE WANTS! --CROB
SERIOUSLY, I'M FINE. CATCH UP WITH YOU IN A SEC.
NOT NOW!
NOSY, REDHEADED, DESTRUCTION-BRINGING...
...TIME-TRAVELING, LIFE-UNRAVELING LITTLE ICE TWERP!
I CAN'T DEAL WITH THIS RIGHT NOW!
NEED TO GET OUT OF HERE...NEED TO THINK.
NEED TO STOP THINKING OUT LOUD...
...AND GO WHERE--TO DO WHAT?
"HI, DAD, I REALLY NEED TO TALK TO SOMEONE WHO WON'T JUDGE ME FOR HAVING UNRESOLVED AND UNEXPLORED FEELINGS FOR MEN. GOT A SEC?"
UGH.
DEAL LATER.
GO BE ICEMAN. YOU'LL STILL BE A MESS TOMORROW.
WHAT'S ONE MORE DAY?

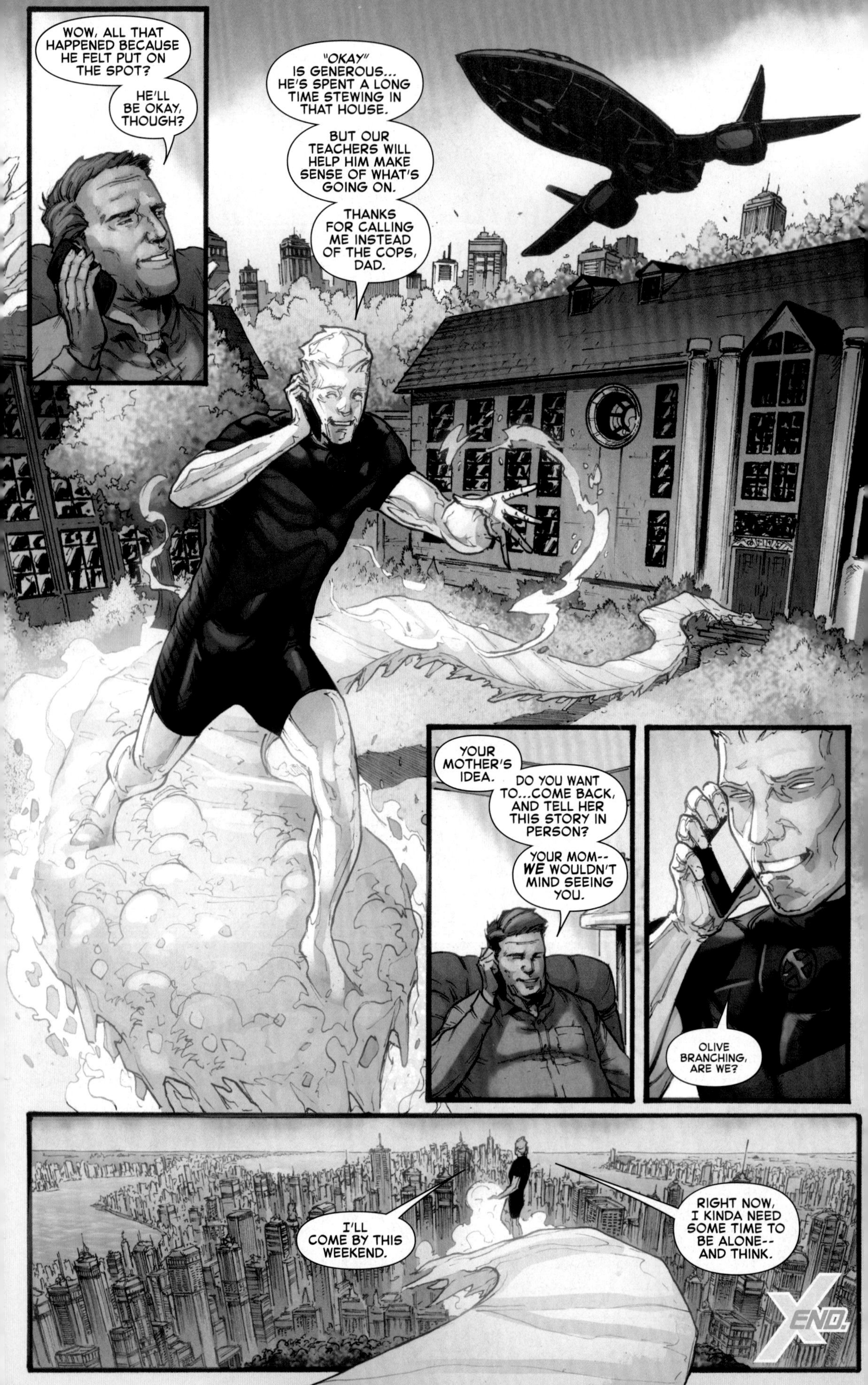

WOW, ALL THAT HAPPENED BECAUSE HE FELT PUT ON THE SPOT?
HE'LL BE OKAY, THOUGH?
"OKAY" IS GENEROUS... HE'S SPENT A LONG TIME STEWING IN THAT HOUSE.
BUT OUR TEACHERS WILL HELP HIM MAKE SENSE OF WHAT'S GOING ON.
THANKS FOR CALLING ME INSTEAD OF THE COPS, DAD.
YOUR MOTHER'S IDEA.
DO YOU WANT TO...COME BACK, AND TELL HER THIS STORY IN PERSON?
YOUR MOM-- WE WOULDN'T MIND SEEING YOU.
OLIVE BRANCHING, ARE WE?
I'LL COME BY THIS WEEKEND.
RIGHT NOW, I KINDA NEED SOME TIME TO BE ALONE-- AND THINK.
END.

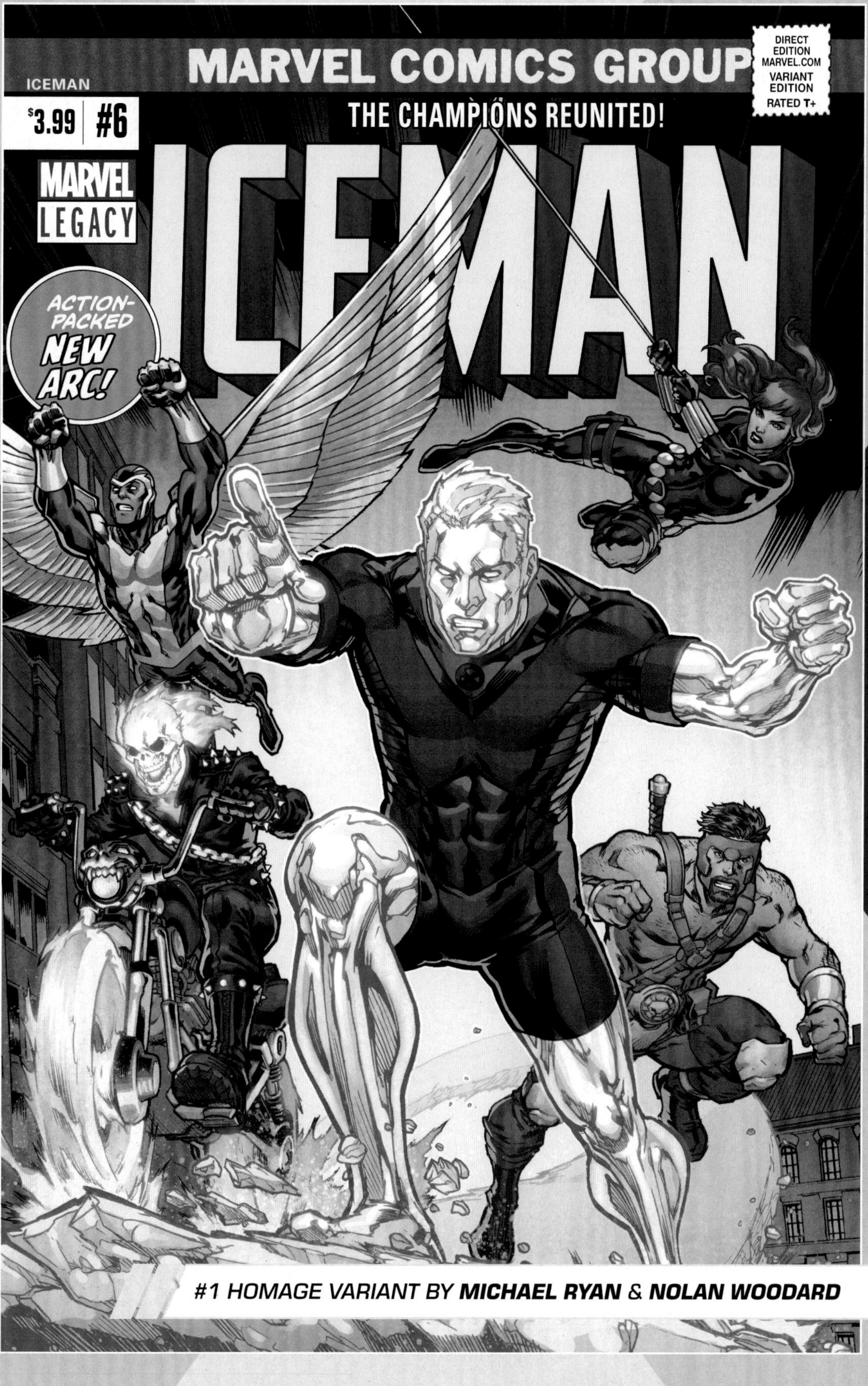
MARVEL COMICS GROUP
DIRECT EDITION MARVEL.COM
VARIANT EDITION
RATED T+
ICEMAN
$3.99 #6
THE CHAMPIONS REUNITED!
MARVEL LEGACY
ICEMAN
ACTION-PACKED NEW ARC!
#1 HOMAGE VARIANT BY **MICHAEL RYAN** & **NOLAN WOODARD**

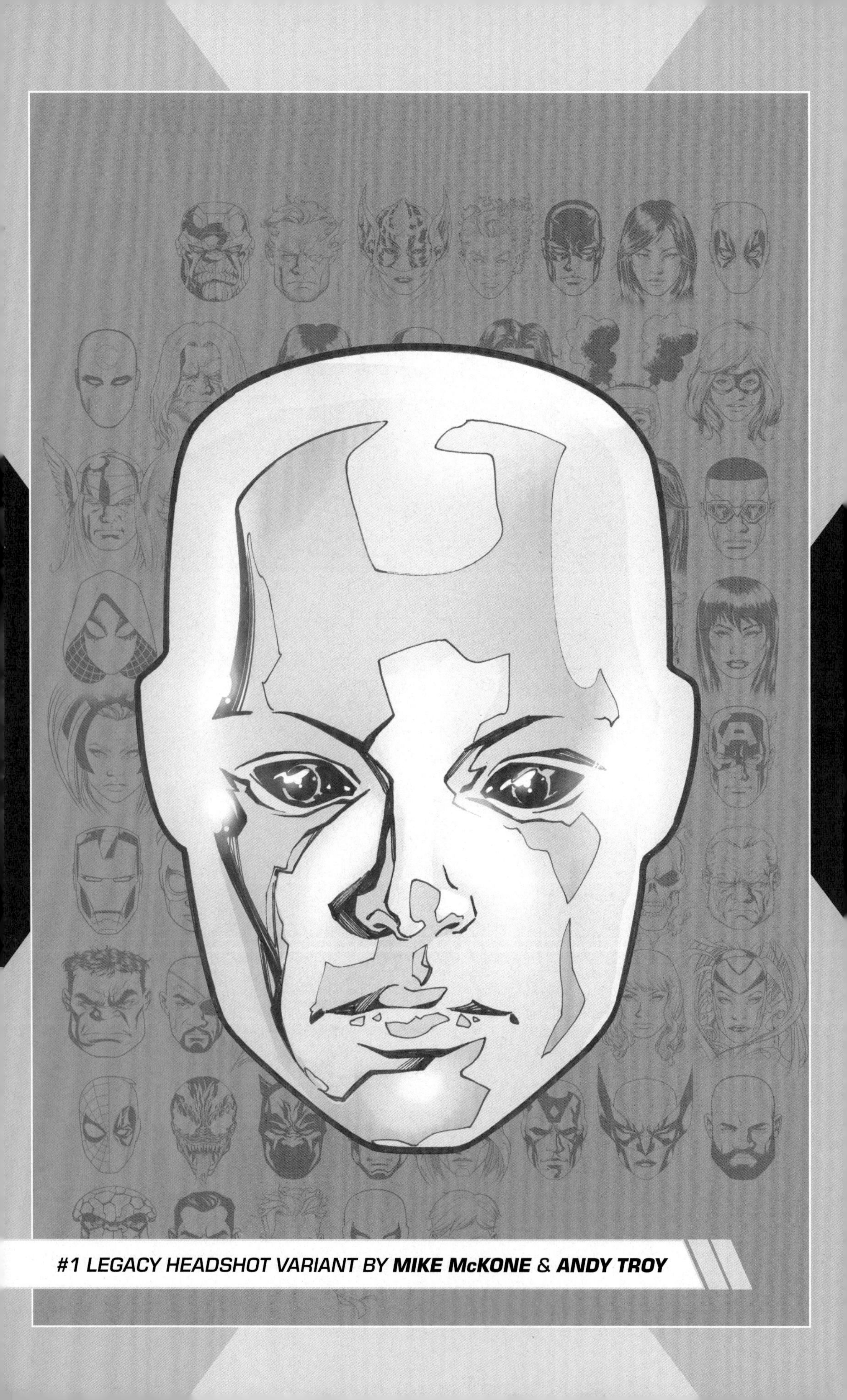

#1 LEGACY HEADSHOT VARIANT BY **MIKE McKONE** & **ANDY TROY**

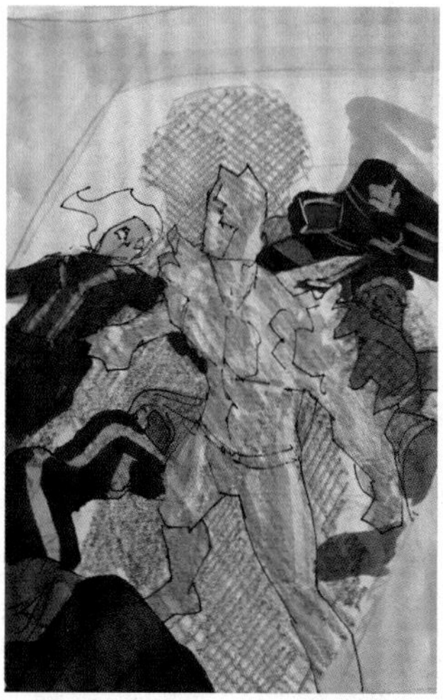
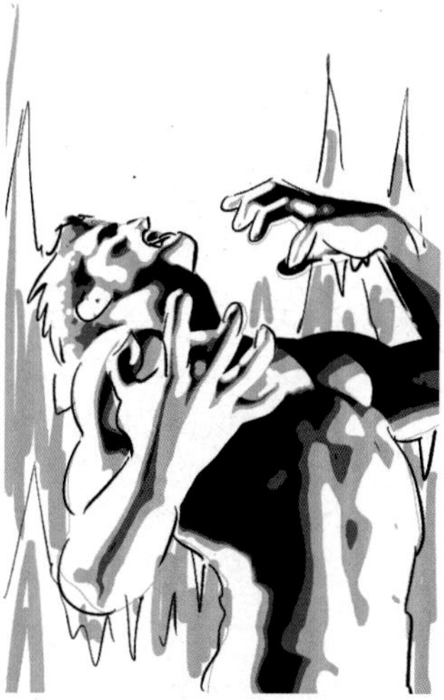
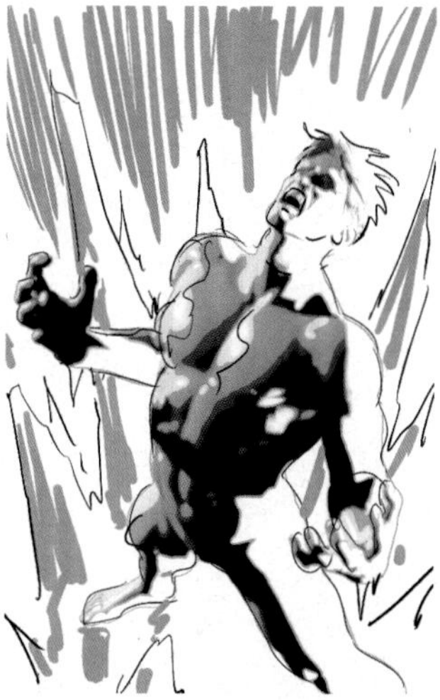
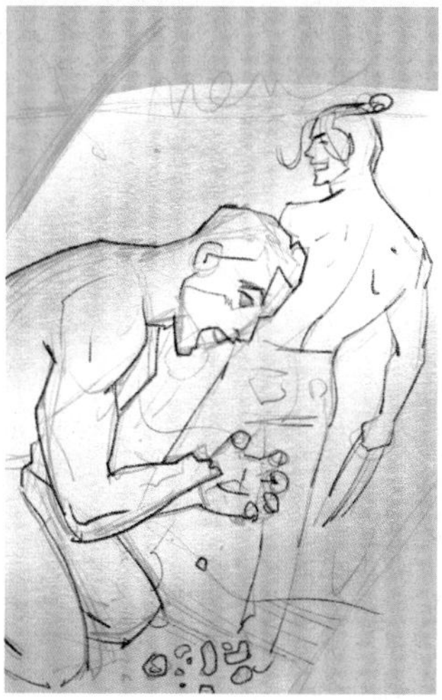
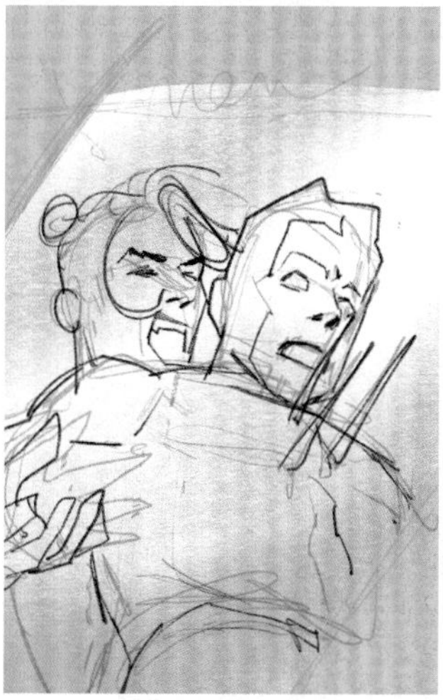
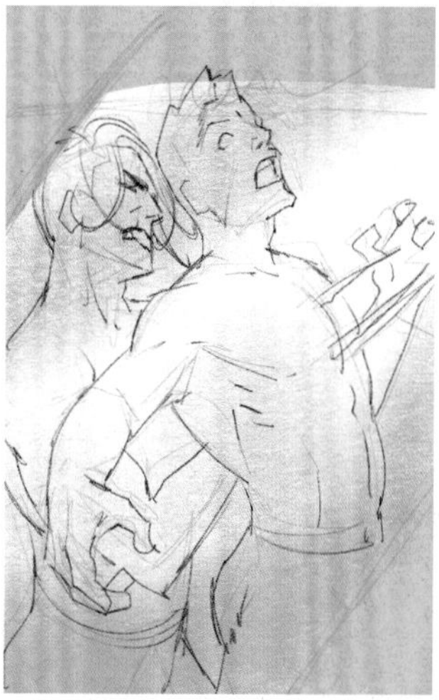
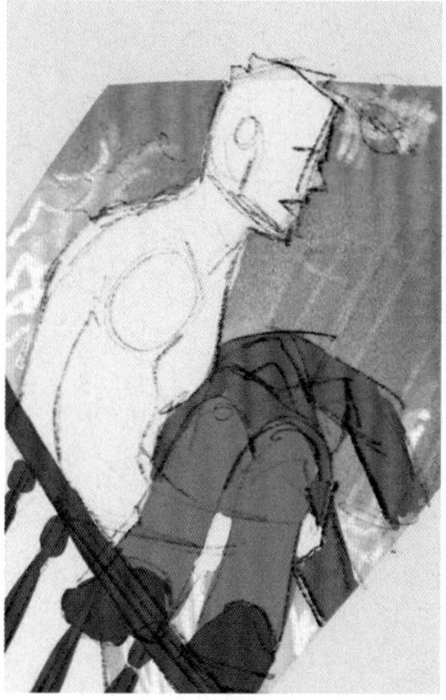
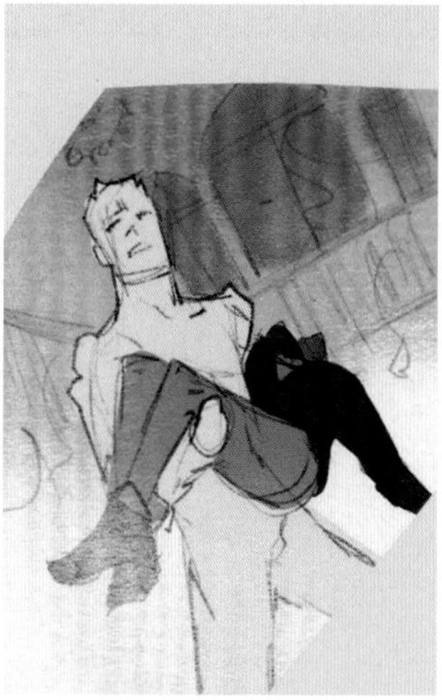

#7-10 COVER LAYOUTS BY **KEVIN WADA**

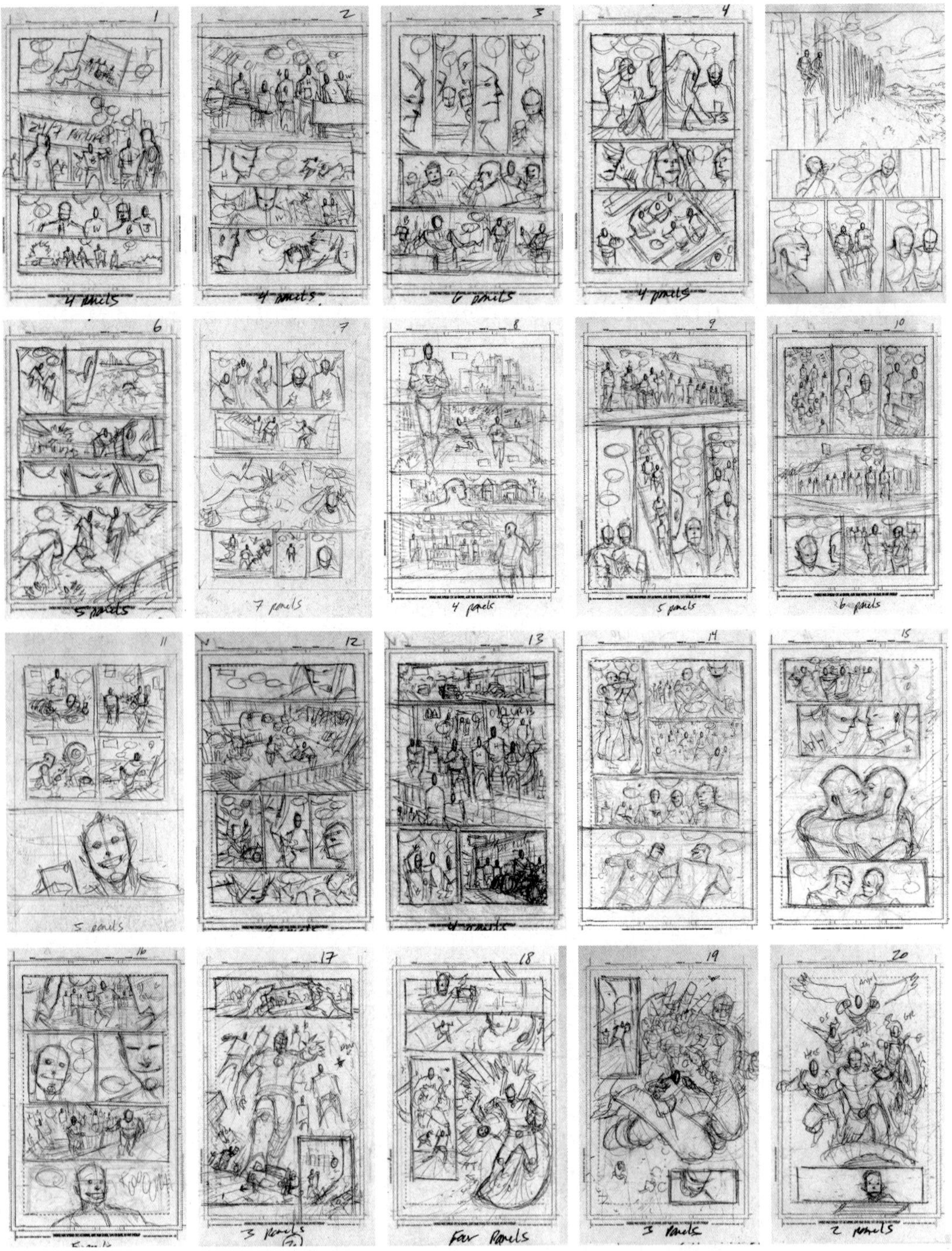

#6 LAYOUTS BY **ROBERT GILL**